ORGANIZING GOD'S WORK

Also by Margaret Harris

ORGANIZING VOLUNTARY AGENCIES: A Guide through the Literature (*with David Billis*)

VOLUNTARY AGENCIES: Challenges of Organisation and Management (*co-editor with David Billis*)

Organizing God's Work

Challenges for Churches and Synagogues

Margaret Harris
Acting Director
Centre for Voluntary Organisation
London School of Economics

First published in Great Britain 1998 by
MACMILLAN PRESS LTD
Houndmills, Basingstoke, Hampshire RG21 6XS and London
Companies and representatives throughout the world

A catalogue record for this book is available from the British Library.

ISBN 0–333–67221–6

 First published in the United States of America 1998 by
ST. MARTIN'S PRESS, INC.,
Scholarly and Reference Division,
175 Fifth Avenue, New York, N.Y. 10010

ISBN 0–312–21501–0

Library of Congress Cataloging-in-Publication Data
Harris, Margaret, 1945–
Organizing God's work : challenges for churches and synagogues /
by Margaret Harris.
p.   cm.
Includes bibliographical references and index.
ISBN 0–312–21501–0 (cloth)
1. Church polity.   2. Synagogues—Organization and administration.
3. Religious institutions—England—Case studies.   I. Title.
BV650.2.H36   1998
254—dc21   98–13513
                                                          CIP

This book is printed on paper suitable for recycling and made from fully managed and sustained forest sources.

10   9   8   7   6   5   4   3   2   1
07   06   05   04   03   02   01   00   99   98

Printed and bound in Great Britain by
Antony Rowe Ltd, Chippenham, Wiltshire

To the memory of my father, El Roer

Contents

Acknowledgements

The idea for this book was born more than ten years ago when I first realised that churches and synagogues, just like the rest of the voluntary sector, were battling with 'organizational' difficulties. During the time which has elapsed since then I have been supported in my research by numerous people, most of whom I can only mention here in general terms.

I am deeply grateful to those people working in and with congregations who so generously shared with me their time and their insights – the 55 people interviewed for the pilot and main studies, as well as those who allowed me the luxury of wide-ranging discussions at the pre-pilot stage. The perspectives of these many people have not only provided the very bones of this book, but have also greatly enriched my understanding of religious commitment and the work that goes on within English churches and synagogues.

At the London School of Economics, I have been surrounded by academic and administrative staff who have been unfailingly kind and helpful. Howard Glennerster supervised the doctoral research which began this project with tactful and timely interventions. Staff of the Centre for Voluntary Organisation, including Romayne Hutchison, David Lewis, Colin Rochester and Sue Roebuck have, each in his or her own way, encouraged me to present my material with precision and clarity. Special thanks are due to David Billis, the Director of the Centre, who has been my teacher and colleague since 1981. He has provided me with an enduring model of commitment to rigorous and 'usable' scholarship.

During the research process I was stimulated by collegiate criticism from Jay Demerath, Peter Dobkin Hall, Thom Jeavons, Jim Wood and other associates of the Project on Religious Institutions, sponsored by the Program on Non-Profit Organizations (PONPO) at Yale University and funded by the Lilly Endowment. And I was helped by discussions I had with Helen Cameron, Lena Fajerman, Barry Palmer and other members of the Partners in Leadership programme of the Leo Baeck College, London. More recently, Carl Milofsky and other colleagues in the Association for Research on Nonprofit Organizations and Voluntary Action (ARNOVA) have

ix

Acknowledgements

given their time generously in discussing with me the implications
of my findings. David Barker has provided support and advice for
my voluntary sector research for many years and for this project in
particular his guidance was invaluable.

I was proud and happy that my son and daughter, Keith and
Ruth, found time to act as my research assistants at crucial stages
and to ensure that I was kept abreast of the latest thinking in social
science as taught at Birmingham and Cambridge Universities and
Goldsmiths College, London. I would like to acknowledge too, the
wider circle of friends, colleagues and postgraduate students who
spurred me on with regular enquiries about my progress, contributed their own knowledge about work in congregations and
generally helped me to feel that this was a worthwhile project.

The last words of gratitude are reserved for my husband, Paul.
He has lovingly supported my interest in organized religion and
ensured that I had the time and space to write undisturbed.

Finally, I should draw attention to the fact that earlier versions of
parts of this book were published as research monographs and in
academic journals and that I have benefited from comments made
about those papers by colleagues and anonymous reviewers: *Care
by Congregation: Features and Issues of Organisation* Working Paper
15, Centre for Voluntary Organisation, LSE, 1994; *The Church is the
People: Lay Volunteers in Religious Congregations* Working Paper 16,
Centre for Voluntary Organisation, LSE, 1995; 'Quiet Care: Welfare
Work and Religious Congregations' *Journal of Social Policy* 24(1),
53–72, 1995; 'The Organization of Religious Congregations:
Tackling the Issues' *Nonprofit Management and Leadership* 5(3),
261–274, 1995; and 'An Inner Group of Willing People:
Volunteering in a Religious Context' *Social Policy and Administration*
30(1) 1996, 54–68.

MH
April 1997

Part I
Organizing Congregations

1
Local Churches and Synagogues

INTRODUCTION

The village church surrounded by cottages and an inn, its steeple visible across the countryside, its graveyard open to all, its priest an integral part of the local community – this is still a widely held image of 'the local church' in England. But for several hundred years, this image has only partly reflected the reality of local religious activity. Diversity of religious commitment has existed at least since Henry VIII's quarrel with the Church authorities in Rome in the sixteenth century. Today a variety of Christian groupings exist at the local level in England and other major religions, including Buddhism, Hinduism, Islam, Judaism and Sikhism are also well represented.

People who adhere to similar religious values tend to meet together regularly. It is with these *congregations* – local gatherings for religious purposes – that this book is concerned.[1] Congregations are referred to in various ways – as temples, mosques, churches, chapels and so on. This book looks particularly at the congregations of two religions – Christianity, whose congregations are usually called 'churches' in England, and Judaism, whose congregations are usually called 'synagogues'.

Much scholarly attention has been paid to the theology, history and architecture of local churches and synagogues. Some key sociological questions have also been addressed; for example, the role congregations play in helping immigrants to adapt to new societies and the question of whether ministers of religion[2] are 'professionals'. But little attention has been paid by social scientists to *organizational* aspects of congregations: matters such as the allocation of work, the extent and nature of non-worship activities, internal decision-making processes, the role of lay people relative to ministers of religion, the impact of religious values on day-to-day

3

working and the link with wider denominational structures.[3] Of those few social scientists who have ventured into the field, practically none have extended their interest beyond a single congregation or beyond congregations within a single denomination.

Thus it is the *work* and *organization* of *local congregations, churches* and *synagogues* specifically, which is the focus of this book. I hope it will meet the need of those who work in congregations – ministers of religion and lay people alike – for a non-judgemental, explanatory analysis of the organizational challenges they face. It will also fill a gap in the literature of at least four academic fields: social policy and administration; nonprofit and voluntary sector management; the sociology of religion; and organizational behaviour.

This opening chapter considers trends within English churches and synagogues and within their policy environment which make a study of this kind particularly timely. It then looks at the historical context within which contemporary churches and synagogues carry out their work. Finally, an organizational study which looks across traditional denominational and religious divides is outlined.

WHY AN ORGANIZATIONAL STUDY OF CONGREGATIONS?

This part of the chapter argues that there are at least three good reasons for embarking on a specialist study of the organization of English congregations: there are indications that those who run congregations face complex organizational problems; there are rising expectations on congregations to take a more prominent place within the 'mixed economy of welfare'; and congregations are a part of 'civil society'.

Organizational Problems at the Grass Roots

A key motive for studying organizations of any kind is to attempt to respond to the problems and issues experienced by those who work in them. This is a long-established tradition within academic fields such as social administration, public administration, management studies and organizational behaviour and it is the tradition within which this study too is set.

That problems *do* arise in congregations, as in other kinds of organizations, has not been systematically documented up to now but is strongly indicated by stories in the national, local and religious press, by reports of denominational working parties and by 'insider' reflections. These anecdotal accounts are generally confirmed by the limited evidence from more academic studies; studies which, although not focused on organizational issues, incidentally provide relevant information. Taken together, this material not only suggests that there *are* problems at the congregational 'grass roots', it also gives a preliminary indication of how those problems are experienced.

One universal concern within congregations seems to be the dilemma of how to reconcile religious teaching with practical, organizational considerations; to build institutions which are capable of responding to, and surviving in, contemporary society but which, nevertheless, remain a 'true' reflection of religious principles. Questions are raised, for example, about the community role of churches and synagogues and about whether they are regarded by their members as anything other than social clubs. Within the Roman Catholic Church debates about how to implement the decisions of the Second Vatican Council at the congregational level continue three decades later. And appropriate roles for women in congregations continue to be questioned within both synagogues and churches (Baker, 1993; Coate, 1989).

The problem of reconciling religious principles with organizational practicalities is in part a reflection of the fact that religion, at least as expressed institutionally in congregations, is a relatively marginalized activity in contemporary England. Although the *extent* to which England has become 'secularized' is a subject of ongoing debate (Gerard, 1985; Sacks, 1995), the impact of secularizing tendencies on congregations has been widely noted. Churches and synagogues can no longer make universal claims to authority and allegiance and the activities which they sponsor are generally not the centre of communal life. There are also pressures on them to conform to secular organizational structures and procedures.

Some churches and synagogues fight against secularization and marginalization; they attempt to preserve 'traditional' values, practices and structures. But this can threaten organizational survival by alienating potential members. Other congregations try to accommodate to the surrounding secularized society. This path may help to retain and attract members in the short term but, in the longer term, churches and synagogues which 'adapt' too much may lose the 'religious core' which attracts the remaining members (Jeavons,

1994; Warner, 1994). In the United States, this perverse consequence of adaptation is seen by academics as the explanation for the long-term growth in theologically conservative or 'strict' churches, and the decline in theologically 'liberal' churches (Iannacone, 1990).

In practice, local churches and synagogues have tended to seek compromise solutions which preserve traditional approaches whilst at the same time recognizing the imperatives of the secular society. Reported responses by congregations to the pulls of a secular environment have included ecumenical activities; welcoming couples in which one partner is not an adherent; increased involvement in social welfare and community development activities; combining of worship and social events; allowing women to take on roles from which they were formerly barred; drawing lay people into leadership roles; and the use of everyday language for prayer.

Some commentators regard compromises of this kind as acceptable and, indeed, in keeping with 'tradition'. Dulles (1978, p. 152) says, for example, that church ministry has adjusted in every age 'so as to operate more effectively in the social environment in which it finds itself'. On the other hand, many have expressed disquiet about erosion of the 'authentic core' of organized religion. Goldner et al. (1973, p. 125) for example, argue that in the Catholic Church, the shift from the use of Latin to the vernacular has reduced the distance between priest and people, but, at the same time it has decreased the 'majesty' and the 'mystery' embodied in the priestly role.

Particular concern has been expressed about the impact on congregations of management theories and organizational structures derived from the secular world which are seen as obscuring the 'nonrational' core of congregational life. In an analysis of Anglican parishes, for example, Hutton and Reed deprecated the way in which clergy 'capitulated' to the advice of management consultants with the effect of 'turning the church into a manufacturing company with plants scattered all over the country' (1975, p. 25).

A second major organizational issue apparently faced by contemporary congregations is deciding the appropriate role of ministers of religion – clergy, priests, vicars, rabbis and so on. Ministers themselves seem to be chronically discontented and lay people too appear to be generally unhappy about what ministers do, or do not do (Coate, 1989). The relationship *between* ministers and lay people can be fraught.

Since ministers of religion usually carry prime responsibility for implementation of church and synagogue policies and since they work at the interface between their congregations and the surrounding society, they are particularly affected by secularization trends. Questions are raised about the nature and boundaries of their role. Education and professionalization in the surrounding society have tended to diminish the importance and distinctiveness of some of their traditional functions, with 'the encroachment of non-religious specialists into areas that were previously the domain of religious expertise' (Beckford, 1985, p. 129). Healing and comfort, for example, are now often provided by doctors, counsellors and social workers; judgements about 'correct' action are offered by lawyers; and the specialist educational role of ministers has been eroded as lay people have acquired expertise which was formerly their preserve.

Ministers of religion may also, it seems, be subject to competing expectations; to perform their 'traditional' functions and, at the same time, to exhibit knowledge of the secular world and conform with its norms. Marcus and Peck (1985) talk of the expectations placed on contemporary rabbis to have secular learning and to be worldly-wise, *in addition* to having specialist Jewish knowledge. Lauer (1973, pp. 189 and 195) describes the 'continuing punitive experiences' of clergy faced with inherently irreconcilable demands: 'To compete, yet to love, to be a man of God, yet equally apt in organizing and administering, to be diligent in study and prayer, yet faithful in visiting, listening, planning – both the multiplicity and inconsistency of the demands are evident'.

A range of individual responses to this combination of loss of role, low status and competing expectations have been noted. There are high drop-out rates and recruitment difficulties. Some model themselves on other professionals. For those who remain in post, stress is common. Neusner (1972, p. 48) describes the 'bitterly disappointing' lives of rabbis who compare themselves unfavourably with the 'scholar-saint' rabbis of the past and then doubt 'the authenticity and authority' of their own work. Some denominations have attempted to respond to problems surrounding the role of their ministers by commissioning reports to examine their 'crises' (for example, Morley, 1996; RSGB, 1986; Turnbull, 1995).

In these circumstances, where it seems clear that there are major organizational issues facing both Jewish and Christian local congregations, the case for a specialist organizational study is a strong one. Such a study holds out the promise of elucidating and responding to the practical problems. And by encompassing the congregations of more than one denomination and more than one religion, it also raises the exciting prospect of transferring organizational knowledge and understanding *between* congregations; a new kind of ecumenism.

The Changing Role of Congregations in Welfare

Since at least the late 1970s, there has been a trend in UK public policy to place increasing emphasis on non-governmental institutions as a means of meeting human needs of all kinds. In the broad field of 'welfare' or 'human service' provision, both the commercial and the voluntary sectors have expanded their roles and there are expectations that they will continue to do so (Billis and Harris, 1992; Glennerster, 1995). These rising expectations extend to churches and synagogues as well. As in the United States (Cnaan, 1995; Wineburg, 1992), congregations are expected to become an integral part of a pluralist welfare-delivery system. The Welfare State era appears to be ending and local congregations are returning to their historical role in 'almsgiving', philanthropy, charitable activities and care-giving (Cameron, 1994; Pemberton, 1990).

In addition to meeting the 'spiritual' needs of their members through a variety of formal and informal activities, contemporary churches and synagogues often attend to other more practical needs. Mutual aid is given between members of congregations and their ministers provide 'pastoral care', which includes counselling and advice-giving as well as visiting people who are sick, isolated or bereaved. This welfare role of congregations often extends beyond meeting the needs of their own members, to meeting those of their surrounding local communities. In recent years, for example, churches have involved themselves in the development of 'community care' (Clark, 1989) and inner-city churches have embarked on community projects funded by the Church Urban Fund, which was set up in 1988 following the Church of England's report 'Faith in the City' (Bowpitt, 1989).

The claim that churches and synagogues are now an integral part of the social welfare system rests not only on accumulating evidence of their involvement in the provision of care services but also on their 'advocacy' activities. They may be involved in local social action and community development projects (Finneron, 1993) or they may join with other congregations in activities which are explicitly of a pressure group kind (Davie, 1990; Midgley, 1990).

In an era of welfare pluralism, in which the expectations on congregations and other nongovernmental organizations are rising rapidly, it is no longer sufficient for social policy analysts to concern themselves solely with policy implementation via *governmental* welfare agencies. The boundaries of the fields of 'social administration' and 'public sector management' need to be expanded to encompass the welfare-providing agencies of the voluntary and commercial sectors and to include studies of the impact on those sectors of changing public policies (Billis, 1993b; Lewis, 1993).[4]

So here is a second reason why an organizational study of congregations is timely. Congregations have been drawn back into the 'mainstream' of welfare provision and hence the question of how they organize their work and the organizational problems they face has become a matter of public interest.

Congregations, Civil Society and the Voluntary Sector

The trends in social policy which have refocused attention on congregations as providers of 'care', are themselves part of a broader shift in public policy and academic analysis which extends well beyond the UK – a renewed interest in the public space which is the sphere of neither the state and governments nor individuals and households.

Those interested in this public space are rooted in a variety of disciplinary, theoretical and philosophical perspectives and they employ a range of different terms and concepts. One strand of thinking is concerned with 'civil society' and has been given impetus in recent years by two global trends: disillusion with 'big government' and 'nation states' and the puzzle of how to build new societies in the countries of Eastern and Central Europe and places such as South Africa and Palestine (Hall, 1995; Osborne and Kaposvari, 1996; Seligman, 1992; Walzer, 1995). A second strand is concerned with what in the UK is generally referred to as 'the voluntary sector'; those organizations which are part of neither the governmental, for-profit (market) nor informal spheres of activity. This sphere is also referred to as the 'third sector', the 'nonprofit sector', the 'independent sector', the 'social economy', and nongovernmental organisations ('the nongovernmental sector'). Further strands in thinking about the non-state public space are provided by writers on 'associative democracy', 'communitarian-ism', 'trust' and 'social capital' (Etzioni, 1992; Fukuyama, 1995; Giddens, 1990; Hirst, 1994; Pinker, 1993; Putnam et al., 1993).

All of these concepts differ in important ways from each other but all have in common a focus on the way in which people can do things for themselves and for others through collective action which is not dominated by the state. Many writers assume lack of domina-tion by the market as well. Some emphasize the importance of soli-darity and cooperation between individuals and many are essentially concerned with the building and maintenance of democracy. But the varied intellectual roots of writers in this area means that the definition of terms such as 'civil society' and 'the voluntary sector' is the subject of fierce academic debate and the question of whether they are desirable or achievable ends is also hotly contested.

All the same, one of the few things that writers do agree on is that religious congregations are within the non-state public space – they are part of 'civil society' and part of the 'voluntary sector' – however those terms are defined (Harris, 1995; Kumar, 1993; Smith, 1983). And there are a lot of them. The number of Christian congre-gations in the UK is estimated to be nearly 50 000 with a total mem-bership of over 6 million people (Brierly and Wraight, 1995) and there are estimated to be 365 synagogues in the UK with which over 190 000 people are associated (Schmool and Cohen, 1997).

So, without engaging in the definitional and normative controver-sies, it can be said that the current interest in 'civil society' and the 'voluntary sector' provides a third reason for thinking that an organ-izational study of congregations is now timely. For if there is to be a meaningful debate about the non-state public space, we need to understand the nature of the activities, groupings and organizations which occupy that space. As Ahrne (1996, p. 110) argues, 'one cannot think about civil society without putting the discussion in terms of organizational forms'. In examining congregations as organizations this book will hope to make a contribution to knowl-edge about the nature and potential of 'civil societies' and 'third sectors'.

THE HISTORICAL BACKGROUND

It would be misleading to study the organization of any contemporary institution in isolation from its historical roots; all the more so institutions like churches and synagogues whose historical roots are so long and complex (Jeavons, 1992). In this part of Chapter 1, then, historical factors which can illuminate organizational features of today's congregations are outlined. Following the path of many other organizational analysts, special attention is paid to issues of authority, organizational structure and organizational environment (Perrow, 1970) as well as to the way in which historical interpretations can impact on current organizational debates. Similarities between institutions and denominations, as well as differences, are noted.

Authority and Leadership

The concepts of 'authority' and 'leadership' are of central importance to theologians. They are also useful social scientific tools for understanding the organizational development of churches and synagogues, especially the relationship between ministers and lay people (Bartholomew, 1981). This section, then, indicates some of the issues around authority and leadership which emerge from the historical literature.

The founding of 'The Church'[5] is attributed by many Christians to Jesus himself. He is the ultimate source of authority and legitimacy for church activities, although 'he did not draw up its precise constitution or method of government, its discipline or its exact orders of worship' (Davies, 1988, p. 37). The first Christian congregations were modelled on synagogues and there were no positions of special religious authority. However, specifically *Christian* organizational frameworks quickly emerged to facilitate the gathering together of followers, to spread Christian teachings and to ensure the exclusion of 'heretics'. These structures were generally hierarchical and authoritarian, with membership based on acceptance of doctrine rather than religious inspiration (Drane, 1986).

A distinction was made between the laity on the one hand, and bishops, priests and clergy on the other. These latter had special authority by virtue of having been called by God and their ability to interpret teachings, whilst the laity had to be officially 'recognized' before they could participate and were seen as auxiliaries and supporters to the work of clergy. Thus, the concept of 'charisma' ('the gift of grace') was central to authority and power relationships in early Christianity. It was 'primarily concerned with the way in which Christian organization was attached to this quality of spiritual endowment rather than any other principle of administration.' (Hill, 1973, p. 147)

Despite the challenges to clerical authority posed by the Reformation, this general approach to religious authority and leadership remained the dominant model for Christians throughout the ensuing centuries. The emergence and development of a separate group of 'professionals' was 'a potent force for organizational differentiation and elaboration' (Scherer, 1972, p. 82). However, alternative authority models based on different interpretations of early Christianity – for example 'collegial ministry', 'community ministry' and 'lay ministry' – from time to time provided inspiration for groups and denominations which, to varying degrees, dissented from the models adopted by the Anglican and Roman Catholic churches (Davies, 1982; Hill, 1988). Bonham-Carter (1952, p. 189), for example, explains how 'nonconformists' in the nineteenth century viewed the Anglican parson as ' a permanent official who controlled their destinies'; whereas their own minister 'was one of themselves; not permanent at all, for he held office by permission – their permission.'

Debates about authority and leadership have continued in to this century within and between different Christian denominations and they affect the work and procedures adopted by local churches. Roman Catholic churches, for example, are still struggling with the organizational and ritual implications of the idea of a 'lay-centred' church, inspired by deliberations and decisions of the Second Vatican Council, which closed in 1965 (Doohan, 1984). And the current popularity of less formalized and less institutionalized forms of Christian expression such as 'house churches' generally rests on theological interpretations which emphasise the importance of individual experience, self-development and local organization.

The organizational roots of synagogues are less obviously theological and more cultural and social. Synagogues are thought to have developed several centuries BC to provide local religious services for those Jews unable to worship at the Temple in Jerusalem (Lieberman, 1970). Later, in the diaspora, they were places where Jews gathered to study and pray. As Heilman (1976, p. 64) explains, the synagogue, 'unlike places of worship in other religions, was never the result of human implementation of a divine decree'. This had implications for the way in which leaders and leadership were viewed. Synagogues differed from most churches in several respects.

First, relationships and structures within synagogues tended to be influenced more by traditional Jewish ideas about 'partnership' and 'voluntary agreement' than by notions of hierarchy and obedience (Elazar, 1978). Second, leadership was vested in lay people, even for acts of worship. 'The synagogue has never been, and is not today, a place where religious sacraments are performed. It is not presided over by priests, nor are any mystical rites performed in it.' (Maccoby, 1989, p. 59)

Thus, issues of authority within synagogues did not arise in a manner analogous with churches. Leadership in matters of Jewish law and practice generally rested with 'rabbis'; that is, teachers or scholars who had authority not by virtue of 'a calling', personal magnetism or descent, but by virtue of their great learning. Rabbis were central figures in Jewish communities but were not necessarily associated, at least until recent times, with one particular synagogue (Sharot, 1975). Nor were they generally seen as prime leaders in synagogue organizational matters. There was a strong tradition of *lay* leadership. In fact, the idea of a synagogue 'employing' a rabbi, one of whose prime functions is to lead acts of worship, is a relatively recent innovation amongst Northern European Jews, one modelled on local churches in which one person 'combines the sacerdotal (priestly) and teaching roles' (Maccoby, 1989, p. 7). It has never sat comfortably with the tradition of rabbis as primarily scholars and teachers, nor with the tradition of strong lay leadership and democratic organization within synagogues.

Thus, questions about authority and leadership have, historically, been of central importance, although manifested differently, in both churches and synagogues. The next section looks at their histories with respect to organizational structures.

Organizational Structure

As mentioned above, the model for the development of 'The Church' has been generally hierarchical and authoritarian. This has had implications not only for the nature of the relationship between local clergy and laity, but also for the relationship between local churches and their 'parent' denominational structures. Generally, there was strong ecclesiastical control within denominations, especially within those with an episcopal (bishop) structure (Barnett, 1988). So local churches had limited opportunities for controlling or influencing matters such as appointment of clergy, forms of service, or even church architecture and furniture. Only the non-episcopal denominations, whose local churches and chapels were financially self-supporting, were able to retain a substantial degree of congregational autonomy (Gay, 1971).

Synagogues, by contrast, from the time of the resettlement of Jews in England in the seventeenth century, were self-governing, autonomous communities, independent of civil organizations and not part of any wider Jewish organizational framework (Freedman, 1955). During the nineteenth century, however, synagogues started to group together into wider associations. Drives towards centralized control were evident in the establishment in the late nineteenth and early twentieth centuries of the 'United Synagogue', the 'Federation of Synagogues', the 'Association of Synagogues in Great Britain' and the 'Jewish Religious Union' (Romain, 1985).

Thus, both churches and synagogues operate now within a historical context of strong pulls towards centralization and denominational control. The extent to which local institutions have been able to be autonomous in theological and ritual matters has tended to be related to the extent to which they have been financially self-supporting. It would be misleading, however, to analyse the development of organizational structures solely in terms of internal ecclesiastical and financial imperatives. The organizational history of local churches and synagogues also reflects environmental influences.

The Organizational Environment

As would be predicted by organizational theorists, the organizational environment emerges from the historical literature as having been a prime influence on the organization of synagogues and local churches. The functions which congregations have aimed to fulfil, and the organizational structures established to achieve them, have been guided not only by religious tradition but also by pragmatic, economic and social imperatives (Currie et al., 1977).

Anglican churches, for example, enjoyed a period from the Reformation to the end of the seventeenth century when it was assumed for official purposes that every member of the local population was a 'member' of the Established Church; all those within the parish served by a particular Anglican church had financial and ritual obligations to it (Gay, 1971). At the same time, that parish church took on major responsibilities in respect of the populace's religious, social, and moral welfare and local clergy and church wardens carried out a number of broad administrative functions.

This kind of link between 'sacred' and 'secular' functions is in the very nature of an 'established' church, but it has manifested itself historically in local churches of other denominations as well. Methodists and 'nonconformists', for example, attempted to provide responses to the spiritual *and social* needs of classes and groups neglected by the Church of England (Barnett, 1988). The relationship between sacred and secular aspects of church organization was also apparent in the impact on Christian clergy of changes in secular society in the nineteenth and twentieth centuries. The growth of literacy, the rise of other caring professions, organizational differentiation and complexity, and the development of ideologies competing with Christianity, have all been noted as having had important effects on the role and work of local clergy (Martin, 1978b; Russell, 1980).

The influence of contextual societal factors on organizational development and responses is also evident in the history of local synagogues in this country. The effect of the 'Emancipation' of Jews in Europe from the end of the eighteenth century, was to change the function of synagogues from being a central institution of a miniature Jewish homeland within the host country, to an institution with more limited educational and ritual responsibilities for a population in closer contact with non-Jewish society. As Hardon (1971, p. 45) describes, '… Judaism took on more and more the features of the rest of society, where organizations with specific functions replaced, in fact if not in theory, the role of the synagogue as the heart of the Jewish community.'

These changes had a commensurate impact on the role and status of rabbis. The impact on Jews of integration and secular learning was an erosion of the competence of lay people in specifically Jewish topics; and it raised expectations based on knowledge of the work of local churches and priests. So, on the one hand, rabbis were obliged to take on educational, pastoral and ritual functions formerly performed by laymen. On the other hand, they were no longer necessarily central figures in a fairly closed local Jewish community (Sigel et al., 1980).

By the middle of the nineteenth century, the efforts of Jews to assimilate to English society were evident in the organizational forms and business procedures adopted by the emergent movement of 'Jewish United Synagogues'; in the creation of the office of 'The Chief Rabbi' closely modelled on that of the Archbishop of Canterbury ; in the search for 'English gentlemen' as 'ministers of religion' (Goulston, 1968, p. 59); and in the establishment of the 'West London Synagogue of British Jews' from which the present-day 'Reform Synagogues' movement developed.

The waves of Jewish immigration from Eastern Europe at the end of the nineteenth and the beginning of the twentieth century not only caused changes in the aims and purposes of the United Synagogues organization, but also gave rise to yet another grouping of synagogues, 'The Federation of Synagogues', which aimed to meet the religious and welfare needs of the more pious, largely working-class, Jewish immigrants. Indeed, the themes of class, status and immigrant absorption permeated the history of Anglo-Jewry during the nineteenth and early twentieth centuries and left a legacy of organizational fragmentation (Romain, 1985). Martin (1978a, p. 28) notes such 'status divides' as being common in English religious organizations. The historical development of non-conformist churches, for example, was closely tied to class interests (Davies, 1988). And Roman Catholic churches have a long tradition of providing points of identity for immigrant groups (Currie et al., 1977).

In sum, the historical literature indicates that the societal context within which local churches and synagogues operated generally had an important impact on their work and organization and on the expectations placed on their religious functionaries.

The Quest for Authenticity

So far, this part of Chapter 1 has outlined issues of authority, organizational structure and organizational environment which provide a *background* to current organization of churches and synagogues. But historical factors can be more than merely contextual; in the case of church and synagogue organization they may also be an integral part of *current* organizational debates, particularly debates about goals and purposes. As will be outlined in this section, a number of commentators on churches and synagogues compare current purposes and structures with historical accounts. Often these comparisons cast unfavourable light on the current situation and they may also be precursors to pleas for a return to the historic 'authentic' core of a particular religious institution (Beckford, 1973).[6]

The contemporary role of religious functionaries is often discussed in terms which imply that there is a 'true', 'essential' or 'traditional' role which modern institutions have moved away from. Thus, Blizzard (1956, p. 509) regards 'preacher, priest and teacher' as the traditional role of the Protestant minister, with pastor as a 'neo-traditional role', and 'administrator and organizer' as a 'contemporary' role. And Jackson (1974, p. 191) deprecates the use of the concepts of role and job specification in relation to priests and favours a return to the 'traditional' concept of office which 'stands for that which one ought to do in the way of service, for the duty attaching to one's station, for a position of trust, authority or service under constituted authority.'

Similar debates about the 'authentic' rabbinical role are evident in the literature on synagogues which draws attention to the range of expectations currently placed on synagogue ministers and argues that the 'traditional' or 'essential' role of the rabbi as learned scholar and teacher 'is being relegated to an inferior position, and the roles of preacher, pastor, rector, and priest are coming to occupy the resulting void' (Sklare, 1955, p. 178). Writers urge a return to the traditional rabbinical role which has 'authenticity and authority' (Neusner, 1972, p. 48).

This kind of historically-based discussion about 'authenticity' extends beyond the roles of religious functionaries to congregations generally. In the case of churches, the search for an organizational 'essence' or 'core' may go hand in hand with a concern about the range of tasks to be encompassed. Carr (1985, p. 69 and p. 44), for example, argues that the prime task of a church in history and theology is 'apostolic' and that 'any attempt at organization that does not take as its first principle the church's task will prove suspect'. At the same time, he says, churches must learn 'to manage the institution's boundaries' and to avoid taking on boundary-less tasks of 'responding to all society's casualties'. In the case of local synagogues, the concern about tradition and authenticity tends to refer to their historically multi-purpose nature; as places of prayer, study and meeting (Heilman, 1976, p. 63). As with churches, it is argued that the impact of trends in modern society has been to increase the tasks and functions placed on synagogues, to the extent that their original purposes are obscured.

Wilson (1969) comments that this kind of reinterpretation which emphasizes traditional preoccupations and distinctive competence is characteristic of religious leaders who are conscious that they are losing social influence and privileges. However, the literature seems also to reflect a genuine desire to move to another stage of organizational development without losing valued organizational features or losing touch with the overarching 'mission'. Thus, recent debates within Roman Catholic churches following the Second Vatican Council have sought to develop an 'authentic' role for lay people while retaining the 'essence' of the priestly task (Bishops Conference, 1986, p. 24). And on synagogues, Sandmel (1973, p. 146) asks a series of probing questions and suggests a range of possible responses in order to try to clarify 'the nature of Rabbinic service' in an age when 'the bulk of Jews are so indifferent as to be outside the synagogue even when they pay their dues'.

The liveliness of these contemporary debates about 'authenticity' reinforces the overall impression given by the literature referred to in this part; that interpretation of historical experience should be regarded as an intrinsic part of the work and organization of contemporary churches and synagogues. Historical factors are explicitly included in contemporary organizational issues in congregations to an extent which does not normally apply in secular organizations (Miller, 1983).

CONCLUSIONS – STUDYING THE ORGANIZATION OF CHURCHES AND SYNAGOGUES

The Need for a Study

Why has there has been so little scholarly interest up to now in the work and organization of congregations? Organizational analysts and students of administration have tended, at least until recently, to be interested in commercial and governmental agencies, rather than the 'third sector'. And the marginalization of religion in contemporary society does not encourage academic enquiry about religious institutions or the application of organization theory to churches and synagogues (Mason and Harris, 1994; Warner, 1993). In addition, social scientists may have been discouraged from the topic by a tendency amongst those associated with religious institutions to be sceptical about the relevance of 'management' and 'organization' to their work (Laughlin, 1990; Nelson, 1996). Although a few sociologists in the United States *have* had an interest in the broad concept of 'religious organization' (for example,

Beckford, 1985; Demerath et al., forthcoming; Scherer, 1980) and despite the development in the US of a field known as 'congregational studies',[7] no single social science discipline has 'claimed' the organization of churches and synagogues.

This chapter has argued that an organizational study of English churches and synagogues is now timely. There is anecdotal evidence of organizational challenges facing those who carry out the work of congregations; the role played by local congregations in social welfare is expanding; and there is a rising interest in civil society – of which congregations are a part. The historical context within which contemporary churches and synagogues operate has also been examined and the way in which historical debates and dilemmas impact on today's institutions has been noted. This is a good moment to make an initial contribution to a literature of congregations, and to analyse their work and organization in particular.

Where to begin? Any study which tried to encompass all kinds of English congregations, or even a representative sample of them, would have to be pitched at the most general of levels. But a broad-brush approach of that kind would not sit comfortably with organizational analysis which generally demands a more detailed approach; one which examines environments, structures, processes, participants and goals of organizations and groups of organizations. A better approach, then, would be to conduct a series of focused, but interlinked, organizational studies whose accumulated findings would allow a picture to be built up of local congregations in England.

Thus, the empirical study described later in this book should be regarded both as exploratory and as constituting the first link in a chain of research projects of this kind. In line with this approach, the study is limited, as indicated earlier, to the congregations of two religions only – Christianity and Judaism. This allows boundaries to be placed around the study whilst at the same time ensuring that the project is not dominated by the perspectives of one religion only. By looking *across* congregations, denominations and two religions, this book will facilitate learning across the traditional institutional divides.

Social Science and Sacred Institutions

In choosing to study the organization of congregations within a social science framework, I am by implication rejecting the view of some theologians that congregations belong in a special category of 'sacred' organizations which are totally distinct from secular ones and which are therefore not proper objects of study by social scientists. There is much to be gained from empirical investigation of religious institutions by social scientists and such investigations neither detract from nor invalidate investigations of the same topic by theologians. There can be, as Brinkman (1988) suggests, two different 'registers' of thought about religious matters. Each has its own merits and the pursuit of one does not preclude the pursuit of the other.

Churches and synagogues can be perceived not only as divine creations, but also as 'human creations, amenable to analysis by empirical methods and to planned change efforts' (Carroll, 1985, p. 319). Dudley (1983, p. 212) goes further and argues that churches positively *need* the organizational insights of social science, in addition to theology, to ensure success. He says that: 'social sciences, along with theology and the personal spiritual disciplines of the pastor, are essential to the resources used by the Holy Spirit to shape and strengthen church leadership.'

Arguing an equivalent case for the social scientific study of Jewish organizations such as synagogues, Klausner (1981, p. 192) explains: 'Sociological concepts are intellectual tools of Western civilization – more particularly of European rationalism. The study of Jewry in a sociological frame of reference is a reconstruction, in a rationalistic scientific schema, of the reality constructed by the Jews living in it. The selectivity inherent in these concepts obscures the essentially Jewish. However, through these concepts, Jewish particularity may be understood and intellectually evaluated by comparison with the social life of other communities.'

All the same, the fact that the legitimacy of social scientific investigation of congregations has been questioned at all does signal some important lessons for the current project. For example, it leads to the conclusion that, while taking a social science approach, the researcher should also be sensitive to the distinctive features of religious institutions, even if the study of those features belongs partly within the realm of theology. Students of congregations must try to see them both 'as organizations among other organizations and thereby possessing the same structural attributes and processes as are common to all organizations; and also as unique and possessing distinctive attributes by virtue of their transcendent outlook and commitments' (Scherer, 1980, p. 4).

The aim in this book, then, is to positively acknowledge 'the transcendent dimensions of the church's life' (Carroll, 1985, p. 321); to acknowledge, for example, the idea of a partnership or 'covenant' with God that underlies Jewish organizational forms (Elazar, 1978), or the fact that Christian theological considerations 'frequently sanctify particular organizational forms or proscribe certain institutional arrangements' (Wilson, 1968, p. 436). At the same time, caution will be exercised about attempting to analyse such special religious features using inappropriate concepts. As Martin (1980, p. 2) says, '[when] we describe man's activity as a social being we cannot insert a separate mysterious X as a God variable. God is not a part of the ensemble of variables. Nor is he a residual factor left over when the rest of the variance has been satisfactorily accounted for.'

Neither will the research attempt to use the concepts of both social science *and* theology (cf Jeavons, 1994; McCann, 1993; Martin, 1996). Within a social science frame, the questions to be asked about the nature of congregational organization differ from those that might be asked by a theologian. (Mary Douglas (1990, p. 513) has pointed out that 'Theologians can ask "What is sin?" Anthropology can only ask "What ideas do people have about sin?".') The aim in this book is to conduct a study within an avowedly social science framework, whilst remaining sensitive to the impact of theology on congregations and those who participate and work in them.

Plan of the Book

Following this introductory chapter, the next chapter draws together material on 'congregational organization' from earlier studies and identifies some key issues that appear to face English churches and synagogues. This is followed by the final chapter of Part I which describes four English congregations in the 1990s; the congregations selected as cases for empirical organizational research. Their structures, goals, technologies, participants and organizational environments are all examined, taking a cross-congregational approach.

Part II focuses on the challenges which face the case congregations as they carry out their work. One chapter each is devoted to choosing and implementing goals (Chapter 4); the role of ministers of religion (Chapter 5); the position of lay volunteers and lay employees (Chapter 6); issues surrounding change, growth and organizational structures (Chapter 7); and dilemmas of caring in a congregational context (Chapter 8).

In Part III, congregations are reconsidered in the light of the starting purposes of this study. Chapter 9 brings together the main findings from the case studies and earlier literature and discusses the organizational similarities and differences between congregations. It also proposes models which provide explanations of the organizational issues congregations face and a basis for discussion and change within them. In Chapter 10, the final chapter of the book, congregations are examined in the context of the broader environment and the social and public policy expectations on them.

2

Cause for Concern:
Emerging Organizational Issues

INTRODUCTION

Up to now social scientists have paid little attention to organizational aspects of churches and synagogues. In this chapter initial
steps are taken towards building a specialist body of knowledge on
'congregational organization' by drawing together the disparate
material on the subject. First some preliminary comments about
existing writings are needed.

The Need for Boundary Markers

Those few scholars who *have* addressed organizational aspects of
local congregations have mostly done so incidentally. They have
been based in different disciplines and have used a variety of theoretical approaches. So any search for relevant material must range
widely. At the same time, some boundaries are needed. This
chapter uses three boundary markers.

First it borrows from the social administration tradition an
approach which is not only interdisciplinary but also primarily
focused on organizational insights. Second, it focuses on research-
based material supplemented by 'in-house' documents such as
handbooks and working party reports and by 'practitioner'
accounts by ministers of religion and involved lay people. The third
boundary marker is geographical; English and UK sources are used
supplemented by other English-language materials. However,
material from outside the UK is used with caution since religious
organizational activity is strongly influenced by its cultural and
societal context (Goulston, 1968; Hill, 1973). The need for caution
applies particularly to material from the United States where membership of religious congregations is high and a 'way of joining the
American mainstream' (Cohen, 1983 p. 44). This contrasts with the
English situation where the general trend has been to marginalize

religious activity and institutional forms of religious expression (Davie, 1990).

Towards a Collective Conceptualization

In addition to the need for boundaries, another feature of the knowledge-building task must be mentioned at this point. With one exception (a study of religious functionaries by Ranson and colleagues published in 1977), empirical studies in the UK which *have* addressed organizational aspects of religious institutions have been denominationally based; they have ignored the possibility that churches of different denominations, and even institutions of different religions, might share organizational features and problems; that findings and insights might have applicability *across* congregations of different denominations and religions.

Yet, there are a number of reasons why congregations of different denominations and religions might be expected to have common organizational features and to experience similar problems. In the first place, they have broadly similar purposes – what Berger (1967, p. 26) refers to as the 'human enterprise' of establishing 'a sacred cosmos'. Their work is characteristically centred on providing a framework for corporate acts of worship. Following the theoretical approach of the 'neo-institutional' school of organizational analysis, congregations might therefore be expected to adopt broadly similar organizational mechanisms for implementing their similar organizational purposes (Scott, 1987; di Maggio and Powell, 1991). Second, local congregations share a common, often uncertain, organizational environment (Benson and Dorsett, 1971; Scherer, 1980). Again following a 'neo-institutional' approach which emphasizes the way in which organizational environments shape structures and processes, churches and synagogues might be expected to be subject to isomorphic pressures, that is pressures to become more alike (di Maggio and Powell, 1983; Nelson, 1993).

Preliminary support for this hypothesis is provided by Takayama and Cannon (1979, p. 323) who suggest that, in the case of American Protestant churches, denominations have adopted similar organizational structures in order 'to solve adaptive and integrative needs and problems'. Similarly, Biddell (1992, p. 95), who studied the resources of American congregations, notes that: '... when it comes to matters of staffing, raising and handling money, or the day-to-day operations of the church, most congregations of similar size look surprisingly alike, regardless of denomination.' Luckman (1969, p. 147) extends the point, for the US at least, across *religions*: 'There can be little doubt ... that Catholicism, Protestantism and Judaism are jointly characterized by similar structural transformations – a bureaucratization along rational businesslike lines – and accommodation to the "secular" way of life.'

In the case of synagogues, they appear to be subject not only to the isomorphic pressures of the surrounding secular society, but also pressure to conform to *Christian* organizational norms which remain an influential feature of UK society. Newman (1977) for example, describes how the implementation of the role of 'Chief Rabbi' has been strongly influenced by the episcopal structure of the Church of England. And Glinert (1985, p. 27) argues that Jewish forms of public worship have been 're-modelled' in contemporary Britain 'to conform with Christian worship'.

So in spite of intellectual compartmentalization up to now, a collective conceptualization of congregations (specifically churches and synagogues) is in line with organizational theory and also opens up the possibility of transferring organizational insights from one denominational or religious setting to another. It is, as well, an approach which is in line with a general trend observed in British society. Discussing Jewish–Christian dialogue, Solomon (1991, p. 66) points out: 'The modern way of looking at things tends to place less emphasis on doctrinal matters, and to see rather that which religions have in common ... People seek that which they have in common, rather than that which divides them.'

Thus, the remainder of this chapter has two main purposes. First, since the relevant literature is disparate, it draws it together. Second, since the literature has been denominationally based, the chapter seeks out cross-denominational and cross-religion themes emerging from writings about organizational aspects of churches and synagogues.

THEORETICAL AND CONCEPTUAL FRAMEWORKS

Writers who have dealt in some way with organizational aspects of congregations have conceptualized them in a variety of ways. In this part of the chapter some of the more popular theories and concepts employed are highlighted.

Churches, Denominations and Sects

Much of the sociological writing about Christian institutions derives from, and builds on, the work of Niebuhr (1929), Troeltsch (1931), Yinger (1957) and others, who elaborated distinctions made originally by Weber (1964). These writers propose a typology which uses both organizational and social variables – basis for membership, role in society, relationship to the state, and degree of formal organization – to distinguish between 'ideal' types of religious organizations. The number of types distinguished varies, but most writers indicate at least three: 'churches', 'denominations' and 'sects'.[1]

A 'church' in this typology is a large, formal, autonomous organization with a paid hierarchy of officials and leaders. It is integrated into the social and economic order of society, as was the Catholic Church in medieval Europe. Its goal is to 'cover the whole life of humanity' (Jackson, 1974, p. 50) and local institutions are organized to this end. According to Wilson (1968, p. 434), 'churches' in this sense 'are found only in Christianity'. In contrast, a 'denomination' is detached from the state and tolerates other religious organizations. It does not seek to dominate the society of which it is a part and, even where it has a hierarchical structure, it usually offers opportunities for lay involvement in governance. 'Sects', on the other hand, are small groups with egalitarian relationships and no formal hierarchy and often little formal organization at all. They may have charismatic leaders. Membership is voluntary and tends to exclusiveness. In contrast with the universal goals of 'churches', sects 'aspire after personal inward perfection, and they aim at a direct personal fellowship between the members' (Jackson, 1974, p. 50).

Authors have used this typology to explain how religious organizations respond to the personal needs of adherents; the ways in which religious groupings relate to their surrounding communities; or the link between theological positions and organizational characteristics (McGuire, 1987). It is also used to describe growth and change in local congregations. Accounts are given of the way in which religious groups have moved from one category to another; for example, sects may evolve into denominations (Isichei, 1967) or disaffected groups may break away from churches to form sects (Yinger, 1957). The typology has also been used to throw light on 'the way in which different religious orientations may interpenetrate so that within a single institution there may exist distinct and sometimes competing definitions of its structure' (Hill, 1973, p. 77).

Community and Association

Another framework used to analyse growth and change in local religious institutions draws on, or resembles, the distinction articulated by Tonnies (1955) between *Gemeinschaft* (community) and *Gesellschaft*' (association) ideal types of relationship and organization. 'Community' in this framework corresponds roughly with traditional groupings based on personal and diffuse ties. 'Association' corresponds to rationally constructed organizations based on contractual relations.[2]

As with the 'church/sect' framework, recent writers have developed and refined the basic theory and have also used different terminologies. For example, 'associations' are often referred to as 'bureaucracies', while some writers follow Turner (1969) and draw a distinction between 'commmunitas' (signifying spontaneous relationships and intimate bonds without regard to status, wealth or property) and 'structure' (signifying groups which are pragmatic, goal-orientated and intentionally organized).

The association/community distinction has been applied to historical accounts of organizational change. Thompson (1970) for example, conceptualizes the development of the Church of England as a move from a communal form to one in which increasing scale and complexity of organization demands an associational form. Like the church/sect framework, the basic community/association distinction has also been used to throw light on the *mixtures* of relationships, purposes and pressures which can occur concurrently *within* local churches. Thus, in a specific application of the theoretical framework to one congregation – a US Baptist Church – Williams (1983, p. 59) suggests that 'the basic cleavage in the congregation appears between the majority who are satisfied with the structural "corporate" church and a minority who seek a more demanding "spiritual" communitas.'

Formal Organization, Power and Authority

In an exploratory discussion about the organizational structure of churches, Hinings and Foster (1973) note the pervasiveness of analyses of formal organizations rooted in Weber's theories of authority and bureaucracy – a point reflected in the two sections above. They argue that Weberian models are not totally applicable to churches as they are not essentially 'employer' organizations and they have relatively unspecific aims in which expression of 'values' is of great importance.

Despite this, Weberian models of bureaucracy – and related concepts such as 'hierarchy', 'formal structure' and 'rational-legal authority'- remain popular analytical tools for studies of religious organizations. After analysing the coordination and control mechanisms of the Church of England, for example, Thompson (1970, p. xv) describes Anglican churches as 'highly rationalised bureaucracies'. Similarly, Ranson and his colleagues who studied three Christian denominations in England, conclude: 'Churches are, by definition, hierarchically organised, with full-time professionals, developed procedures, articulated belief systems ... Essentially a Church has formalised and routinised the administration of the means of grace' (1977, p. 112).

The Weberian distinction between 'traditional', 'charismatic' and 'rational-legal' forms of authority has also been widely employed to analyse congregations. Harrison (1959) conducted his examination of the American Baptist Convention in terms of different kinds of authority and power manifested at different points within the organization. In examining the 'loss of authority' of modern rabbis in the United States, Carlin and Mendlovitz (1958, p. 377) refer to the undermining of 'traditional authority structures and the legitimations and value systems upon which they relied'.

Other writers have cited and applied Weber more explicitly. Thus, Bartholomew (1981) points out that 'authority' is a key concept in theology as well as in sociology and considers the ways in which 'theologically legitimated authority' and 'institutionally legitimated authority' are used in differently structured religious organizations in America (p. 124). Nelson (1993, p. 653) applies Weber's 'three pure types of legitimate authority' to his organizational analysis of three multinational denominations in Brazil and the United States and suggests that each denomination 'is controlled and legitimized by different types of authority' (p. 658).

'Legitimate authority' is a key idea in another conceptualization of religious organizations; one grounded in the formal ideologies or 'polities' of Christian churches. In brief, local churches can be regarded as being part of 'episcopal' (hierarchical), 'presbyterian' (collegial) or 'congregational' (autonomous) organizational structures (Scherer, 1980). The terms reflect different understandings of the appropriate authority relationships between religious functionaries and lay people, and between an individual local church and its broader denominational organization. Zald and McCarthy (1987, p. 81) regard the classification as '... essentially a measure of the centralization or dispersion of power and control in religious organizations ...'. However, Beckford (1973, p. 97) is critical of its use by social scientists since '... it introduces theological and ethical complications in to supposedly objective and ideally scientific studies of organizational structures and processes'.

Open Systems Theory

Some recent writers on congregations have favoured an 'open' or 'natural' systems framework which views an organization as 'a bounded group of individuals harnessed together by incentives and commitments to a relatively small set of goals (some of which may be conflicting), yet open to new pressures from the environment as it both obtains and gives back resources to that environment and, simultaneously, attempts to affect its internal constituent parts and its environment' (Zald and McCarthy, 1987, p. 80). Writers have argued that this approach has a number of features which make it particularly applicable to religious institutions. It emphasizes the impact and importance of organizational environment (Beckford, 1973), especially the local community with which churches and synagogues interact (Carr, 1985). It also recognizes the way in which organizations face dilemmas of 'conflict, strain, [and] imbalance' which require 'adjustments in goals and strategies' (Scherer, 1980, p. 3). Finally, there is a 'symbolically appropriate' (Thompson, 1973, p. 295) correspondence with Christian theology. Rudge (1968, p. 66), after reviewing a range of organizational theories, argues that the open systems perspective is the most appropriate for the study of 'ecclesiastical administration' because it 'has the greatest weight of biblical support and is nearest to the central stream of Christian thinking'.

Beckford (1973) employed an open systems framework for the analysis and presentation of his review of the sociological literature on 'religious organization'. Other writers have applied the perspective more specifically to the analysis of conflict and change in religious institutions. Benson and Dorsett (1971), for example, conceptualize local churches as open systems 'subject to a variety of pressures towards structural change' (p. 141) from their communities and their denominations, including 'bureaucratization, professionalization, integration, [and] secularization' (p. 138).

Other Approaches

The four sections above outline the theories and concepts most often used by writers who refer in some way to organizational aspects of churches and/or synagogues. These are essentially sociological concepts and theories. But sociologists do not have a monopoly of interest in the subject.

Theologians have analysed church structures too.[3] Some of them have argued that, since religious institutions are constructed by God, it is not appropriate to apply to them the 'secular' analytical tools of social science. Others have argued the need to *combine* a theological perspective with social scientific analysis. The organization of churches, they suggest, has an 'extra' or 'distinctive' dimension; the need to reflect Christian teachings and imperatives and to provide a framework within which they can be implemented (Hinings and Foster, 1973; Jeavons, 1992; McCann, 1993; Nelson, 1996). Yet other writers apply specific theological insights to specific organizational issues. Hill (1988), for example, proposes that the role of local Catholic churches should be defined in terms of a 'ministerial collegialist' theology of authority rather than the prevailing 'magisterial papalist' one. Similar attempts to apply theological insights to organizational issues are made by Doohan (1984) and by Greenwood (1988), who debate the role of lay people in Catholic and Anglican churches respectively.

Psychologists, as well as sociologists and theologians, have also commented on some aspects of congregations' work. Mostly they have been interested in the dilemmas and problems arising in the relationship between religious functionaries and their congregants. The concept of 'dependency', in particular, is frequently used in both the UK and the US literature. Brannon (1971, p. 30) for example, notes that a clergyman is 'psychologically dependent on the support of his congregation'; clergy are thus passive and insecure and this contributes to the 'organizational vulnerability' of local churches. Publications by Reed and his colleagues at the Grubb Institute, on the other hand, analyse clergy–lay relations in the Church of England in terms of the 'immature' dependency of *laity* (Reed, 1980, p. 14) and its implications for the organization of church life and the roles of church leaders. The underlying hypothesis is explained by Hutton and Reed (1975, p. 20): '... using psychological terms, we can say the people "project" their feelings on the church and its leaders, seeking to find someone whom they can depend on.'

Building on the concept of dependency, writers have sought to explain apparently irrational behaviour within local religious organizations as well as the difficulties faced by religious functionaries in implementing their roles. Freedman (1988, p. 4) for example, sees the role of rabbis and synagogues in the US as being 'to manage the dependency needs of the Jewish people'. He cites as an example of 'the culture of dependency' established in religious institutions, the fact that members of lay boards in synagogues 'typically seem to have left behind the competence and the initiative that they are accustomed to exercise in the outside world' (p. 7) and he goes on to suggest that rabbis should respond to problems of this kind by becoming 'familiar with the psychodynamics of groups and organizational life' (p. 8).

Thus, writers have drawn on the disciplines of theology, psychology and sociology and they have conceptualized religious institutions in a variety of ways.[4] No single theory or concept emerges as pre-eminent but two comments may be made. The first is that, with the exception of the church/sect theorists, scholars have generally not seen the analysis of congregations as requiring the development of specialist theory. For the most part, they have taken a generic approach; theories developed initially for other kinds of organizations have been applied to congregations. The second point is that with the exception of the psychological explanations about 'dependency', the writers referred to here have not been much concerned with responding to, or explaining, the kinds of practical issues of congregational organization outlined in Chapter 1.

ORGANIZATIONAL FEATURES AND CHALLENGES

This part of the chapter looks at the findings of the analyses referred to above. It continues to take an interdisciplinary, cross-denominational and cross-religion approach, attempting to identify common themes. Findings from earlier researchers are synthesized and analysed under four broad headings which emerge from the literature as areas in which major organizational issues arise in churches and synagogues: goals; religious functionaries; change; and denominational structures. Information is drawn out from the literature both about organizational *features* of churches and synagogues, and about the organizational *problems* they face.

Organizational Goals

As predicted by 'garbage can' theories of organization (Cohen and March, 1974), the goals[5] of churches and synagogues are often ambiguous and contested. Writers have drawn attention to the problems of clarifying the purposes of churches or synagogues, and to the negative organizational implications for those which fail in the task. Religious institutions face special challenges in developing and implementing organizational goals; they have to reconcile the desire to reflect their religious values with the practicalities of running an organization and ensuring its survival (Jeavons, 1992; Rudge, 1968).

Difficulties in clarifying purposes in churches and synagogues are sometimes traceable to unresolved debates and disagreements about overarching religious principles. Hornsby-Smith (1989) for example describes the 'struggles' within Catholic parishes trying to reflect post-Vatican II theology[6] in their activities and internal structures. And Card (1988, pp. 85 and 96), in a discussion of the future of Christian churches in the Western world, distinguishes 'two diametrically opposed views of life and faith' which are in conflict and which have different implications for organizational structure and purposes. 'Essentialist' values, he argues, go with churches which are 'institutional' and part of a centralized, hierarchical framework; whereas the 'existentialist' view would demand a diversity of local churches, loosely linked to their denominational framework and with a communal, local focus.

There can also be serious debates within congregations about the relative importance of what Blau and Scott (1963, p. 43) have referred to as 'mutual benefit' or 'commonweal' aims; that is, about whether to focus activities primarily on the needs of the immediate members, or whether to take a more outward-looking approach towards the needs of the community and be, in effect, a part of 'civil society' (Roozen et al, 1984). In the Church of England, this dilemma has been conceptualized as reflecting a theological question: a 'universal tension between two modes of engagement of Church and Society' (Ecclestone, 1988, p. 6). Two models are distinguished: the 'parish church' and the 'associational church'. The members of the parish church are orientated towards the needs of the 'community at large' and see themselves as having 'an account-ability to human beings because they are in need'; whereas associa-tional churches 'will be barely conscious of their local community, neither will the community take much notice of the church' (Ecclestone, 1988, p. 7).

The US literature suggests that an equivalent dilemma may arise in synagogues. Schwarz (1957) notes the resentment felt by subscribing members of synagogues when the facilities they sustain are treated as 'communal' facilities and used by non-members. Elazar (1983, p. 242), however, concludes his study of decision-making processes in the American Jewish community with the argument that '... it is absolutely vital that synagogues cease to be considered the private property of their members and be recog-nized for what they are – public institutions bearing significant communal responsibilities.'

There can also be differences of opinion within churches and syn-agogues about what are 'appropriate' goals in a religious organiz-ational context. There may be perceptions of incompatibility between 'authentic' (that is, religious) goals on the one hand, and 'inappropriate' goals concerning organizational maintenance and survival, on the other hand. Suggested manifestations of such 'inappropriate' concern with organizational survival include: an emphasis on 'efficiency' and management techniques (Carroll, 1985); a diminution of congregational autonomy (Luidens, 1982); and a tendency to place the immediate needs of church members before the needs of the wider community (Carr, 1985).

Even where religious values are not contentious, there may be practical difficulties in implementing them organizationally. Winter (1973, p. 21) for example, debates the structures needed to enable lay people to 'fulfil their vocation as Christians' and argues that the 'ideal size' for local churches is 20 to 30 people who should be based in homes rather than separate buildings; a recommendation likely to be found impractical by many lay people and clergy, however much they might agree with the underlying religious principle. The difficulties of matching theology with organizational realities is reflected in Martin's observation (1988, p. 49) that '... the liberalizing notions that got in to the Catholic Church after 1960, did a great deal of organizational damage ... You may say that they got closer to the theological truth *and* lost people.'

Underlying debates about religious values emerge, then, as a major contributor to problems surrounding goal definition and implementation in synagogues and churches. But others are also suggested. Several writers have noted, for example, that modern churches and synagogues have acquired a *wide range* of different kinds of goals; not only theological and spiritual, but also psychological and sociological ones. In addition to their wide range, the sheer *number* of goals in existence in churches and synagogues can be confusing. In a study of 'institutional' churches in the United States, Webb (1974, p. 669) generated a list of 28 goals 'from a variety of sources which included official presbytery goals, in-depth interviews with clergy and relevant literature.' In the case of synagogues, Neusner (1972) has suggested that the impact of trends in modern society has been to multiply their tasks and functions to such a degree that their original function as centres for local Jewish communities has been obscured.

The combination of multiple and wide-ranging goals with religious values about fellowship and neighbourly love can be particularly problematic. As Lauer (1973) points out, the 'multi-purpose' nature of the modern church means that conflict is inevitable. But, 'since solidary incentives are so important in maintaining member commitment ... there is a temptation for ministers in local congregations to avoid conflict if they believe there is dissensus on an important issue' (Zald and McCarthy, 1987, p. 82).

Thus, not only do churches and synagogues experience difficulties in clarifying their organizational purposes, they may also lack the means to debate and resolve differences of opinion when they do surface. As Scherer points out (1980, p. 21), the difficulties of maintaining unity of 'mission' make religious organizations 'structurally fragile'.

Roles of Ministers of Religion

The impact of unclear and multiple goals is felt especially by ministers of religion as they try to prioritise their work and implement their roles. At least eight possible functions[7] for ministers of religion can be derived from the accumulated literature on their roles: religious celebration, preaching or 'prophecy', education, pastoral care, community leadership, public representation, administration and managerial leadership. Not surprisingly, rabbis and clergy face numerous different expectations about how they will select priorities and implement their role – from their peers, from their denominational structure, from lay leaders of their church or synagogue, from active volunteer helpers, from potential members, and from the local community. The minister has not only to cope with the volume and breadth of the expectations, but also with conflicts between them and with the consequences of inevitable failure to meet every demand (Coate, 1989; Heilman, 1976).

In addition to the numerous expectations placed on them by their various 'constituencies', clergy and rabbis also face the day-to-day exigencies of institutional maintenance and survival (Crittenden et al., 1988; Goldner et al., 1973). They may be sole full-time paid employees in their congregations and there are rarely sufficient secretarial, book-keeping and caretaking staff. Thus, irrespective of official 'job descriptions', religious functionaries may be obliged to spend large proportions of time performing managerial and administrative functions; from representing the church's viewpoint to the press and ensuring its financial viability, to answering telephones, locking up premises, and dealing with mail.

The difficulties are compounded by the fact that ministers are also influenced in implementing their roles by their personal preferences and by norms derived from their training. They may feel that their personal abilities make them more competent to perform some tasks rather than others. Or their perception of their religious calling and their theological perspective may suggest 'ideal' or 'authentic' interpretations of their role. But whereas the self-perceptions of clergy and rabbis tend to be grounded in denominational, theological, and professional considerations, the expectations of laypeople are often more pragmatic or self-centred in origin (Scherer, 1972). They are grounded in their personal needs for security (Hutton and Reed, 1975); in their desire to be part of a group (Carroll, 1981); in their preferences for particular personal attributes (Sigel et al., 1980); and in consumerist expectations that they are 'buying' a service and that they should have some control over its quality and form (Katz and Schoen, 1963).

Blizzard (1956, p. 509) summarizes the problem: 'On the one hand, the church has a traditional set of norms by which he [the Protestant minister] is expected to be guided. On the other hand, the parishioner has a set of functional expectations by which the minister's professional service is judged. This is the minister's dilemma. He faces basic ambiguities in performing the practitioner roles.' And in lighter mood but with serious intent,

Schwarz (1957, p. 110) similarly contrasts the traditional attributes of the Jewish rabbi – 'a fine human being with knowledge and character that everybody can look up to' – with the expectations of modern American congregations: 'A Superman, that's what you want. He has to be everything, not only a hot marriage and funeral performer, but a fine preacher, grand teacher, colossal mixer, superb bridge player, liked by the Gentiles, hail fellow with the newspapers, a good heckler in the public schools, and a few more things I can't think of right away – except he ought to be handsome too.'

Moberg (1962 p. 509) emphasizes the resulting stress, describing clergy as, 'frustrated by an unfulfillable self-image of the minster as one ordained to a holy calling, filled with vocational guilt for spending major portions of time on pointless parish piddling, ... [and] embittered by the bureaucracy that makes them office managers, committee maneuverers, and publicity directors instead of scholars and preachers of God's Word'. Clergy and rabbis seem to find it especially difficult to acknowledge the stress they experience; it is thought 'not to be quite respectable' (Coate, 1989, p. 12).

Difficulties of role definition are not experienced just by clergy and rabbis. Lay people too may be unclear about what is expected of them and the relationship between lay people and their ministers may be especially fraught. Some of the problems seem to stem from the ambiguous employment situation of ministers. They are generally paid a salary for the work they do (either by the congregation itself or by the denominational organization) so they are, in a sense, 'employees' with all the usual legal and traditional responsibilities and accountabilities which attend that status. But at the same time, ministers carry within their congregations a degree of authority which is separate from, and independent of, their employee status; authority which is attached to their status as trained and qualified religious functionaries and professionals (Carroll, 1991; Falbo et al., 1987).

This authority may be experienced by ministers as incompatible with the employee status and its implications of the lay man's 'right to instruct the minister in his duties and responsibilities' (Dempsey, 1969, p. 59). Describing the authority of Church of England clergy, for example, Paul (1973, p. 131) says 'the status of its ministers can never be only that of the paid, professional, servants of a supreme body. They are who they are and where they are because they have been given authority over the Church.' Similarly, an American Reform rabbi (Glaser, 1986, p. 95) argues that congregational rabbis must be independent of their lay 'bosses', paying heed only to 'serving God'. He advises rabbis to follow the Jewish sage: 'Be not like slaves who minister to the master for the sake of receiving a bounty, and let the fear of Heaven be upon you.'

Thus, the problem of defining the ministerial role does not stand alone. The *relative* authority of lay people and religious functionaries can also be unclear. Dempsey (1969, p. 71) says of the Australian Methodist churches he studied, 'Neither the position of the minister, nor the authority necessary for the adequate fulfilment of his role is well-defined.' As Hornsby-Smith (1989, p. 196) says in his summary of lay/priest relationships in Catholic churches, 'there is always the potential for conflict'.

Organizational Change

The literature suggests that, in churches at least, religious values can be powerful both as inhibitors and facilitators of organizational change (Beckford, 1973, Wilson, 1968). On the one hand, religious values can drive forward organizational change; for example, a developing theology of the laity has been an important factor in encouraging mechanisms for lay involvement in churches, even where lay people and clergy remain reluctant participants (Hornsby-Smith et al., 1995; Hougland and Wood, 1982). Equally, religious values may inhibit changes which seem 'necessary' judging by secular organizational criteria. Thus, Isichei (1967, p. 201) describes how Quaker institutions are 'biased against change' because they regard their original organizational structures as 'established in accordance with the divine will'. And women and homosexual men continue to be barred from ministerial posts in many churches and synagogues, despite practical difficulties in filling posts with those traditionally qualified for them (Fletcher, 1990).

Ideas about authority are especially likely to inhibit organizational change in churches. Since authority structures 'are based (and/or justified) to a considerable extent on theological principles' (Cantrell et al., 1983, p. 277), they are difficult to change or ignore, even when they appear to be no longer requisite. Thus Harrison (1959, p. 7), who studied the bureaucratization of the Baptist Church in the United States, says: 'In recent years some Baptists have called for recognition and acceptance of the power of the denominational leaders. But it is extremely difficult to make a formal change in the polity system without altering the doctrine of the church.'

Religious values may also provide less specific barriers to change; a general atmosphere in which certain courses of action, responses to problems, organizational structures or styles of decision-making are implicitly viewed with disfavour as 'inappropriate' or 'not authentic'. The values which inhibit change may be traditional and cultural rather than theological. Yet, as Scherer (1972, p. 98) points out, they are no less powerful in their impact: the 'infusion of historically conditioned forms with ultimate value can be a barrier to change'.

For example, bureaucratic organizational structures are widely seen as inappropriate for religious organizations such as churches (Hinings and Foster, 1973; Ranson et al., 1977). Thompson (1973, p. 295) finds a tendency for 'sweeping condemnation of the symbolic inappropriateness of the [bureaucratic] organisational form as judged by particular theological ideals about organisation'. He mentions especially the theological concept of the church as a divinely inspired 'body', which can lead to a 'fascination' with organic, rather than bureaucratic, organizational models. Bureaucratic structures are also opposed in those local churches 'with strong theological dispositions to congregational polity and lay control' (Wilson, 1968, p. 436).

Opposition to 'bureaucratic' forms in churches can be linked with perceptions that there is an irreconcilable dichotomy between 'efficiency', 'effectiveness' 'rationality', planning and systematic procedures on the one hand, and religious or 'spiritual' values on the other hand. Thus, Carr (1985, p. 38) notes that 'the application of management to the church arouses instinctive opposition'. The impact of this dichotomous approach to church organization is described by Laughlin (1990, p. 106) who shows how the establishment of accountability mechanisms within the Church of England has been hindered by the 'relegation' of financial accountability to the realm of the secular. The Church, he says, would regard demanding more financial accountability from local churches as 'unspiritual'. It 'has never come to terms with seeing the parish as anything other than a sacred unit and has never operationally created a separate organisational unit to handle these issues.'

Links with Denominational Structures

The last three sections focused on cross-denomination themes concerning the internal organization of local churches and synagogues.
This final section looks at the broader organizational framework of
local congregations; and at the issues that arise in the relationship
between local churches and synagogues on the one hand, and the
denominational institutions to which they are affiliated on the other
hand.

Both Jewish and Christian denominations vary widely as to the
degree of autonomy officially granted to local affiliates by their
'formal polities'. At one extreme is the structure of the Watch
Tower movement described by Beckford (1975) in which there is
no form of 'regional or representative democracy' and in which
the central organization imposes 'direct control over all congregations'. Similarly, prior to Vatican II, local Catholic churches were
firmly controlled by bishops and the local laity were left to 'pay,
pray and obey' (Leege and Gremillon, 1985). At the other extreme
is the Reform Synagogues of Great Britain, in which affiliated synagogues are officially autonomous and free to make their own
decisions on all matters, including the hiring and firing of rabbis
(RSGB, 1986).

In practice, the literature suggests, the relationship between an
individual church or synagogue and its denomination may differ
substantially from official statements. Nominally autonomous congregations may be subject to important controls by their denominations. Conversely, congregations in nominally centralized
denominations can maintain a considerable degree of informal
independence. In a study of Protestant denominations in the US,
Ashbrook (1966, p. 398) notes 'a democratization of governing prac-
tises in the more authoritarian traditions and a centralization in the
more congregational traditions.' He concludes that 'a theological
examination of the church discloses little about the dynamics of its
organizational life'.

The very existence and recognition of such discrepancies
between theory and practice can be a source of problems in the
local/denomination relationship. For example, US studies have
indicated how tensions can arise when denominational structures
become centralized and there is a clear disjunction between formal,
theological statements supporting congregational autonomy, and
the reality of strong denominational control (Luidens, 1982).

Harrison (1959) argues that where denominational bureaucratization is 'unofficial', it is particularly difficult to question and denominational power is reinforced.

Irrespective of 'formal polities', the local/denomination relationship appears to be inherently one of tension (Beckford, 1973). Harris (1969, p. 178) found in a study of Welsh Anglican churches that they regarded the national organization as 'a parasitic superstructure'; and Newman's historical account (1977) of the development of the 'United Synagogue' in England provides several examples of difficulties, and even open conflicts, between individual synagogue affiliates and the central office. One such dispute – dubbed the 'Jacobs Affair' by the national press which reported it in depth – involved the 'headquarters' organization refusing to accept the wish of a prominent London synagogue to appoint as its rabbi Dr Louis Jacobs, an internationally respected scholar. The synagogue's board of management was required to resign and those who favoured Dr Jacobs founded their own independent synagogue.

Local churches and synagogues need independence and a degree of flexibility in order to fulfil spiritual, personal and community development goals. Yet, they also want the many advantages of resources and legitimacy that flow from being part of broader, formal structure (Warner, 1994). The price paid for belonging is some loss of autonomy and some degree of formalization (Benson and Dorsett, 1971; Hornsby-Smith et al., 1995). Coming to terms with this is a problem which cuts across denominations and religions. Harrison (1960, p. 236) summarizes the contradictions in the US Baptist convention which officially espouses congregational autonomy: 'On the one hand, they [local churches] require a bureaucracy to realize the mission of their organizations; on the other hand, their ideology is rooted in democratic traditions which are inimical to the tendency of technical bureaucracy to depersonalize the individual and to segregate roles on a functional and hierarchical basis.'

In relation to the Church of England, the conflict between local church autonomy and the traditional power of the Anglican hierarchy has been attributed to two conflicting theologies of authority (Thompson, 1970); one emphasizes the importance of the organizational totality, the other emphasizes grass-roots power. As Paul (1973, p. 145) says: 'The monarchical and hierarchical theory of the Church supposes the flowing down of the divine charisma through the agency of religiously superior persons, ordered in rank, until, diminished and diluted, we may suppose it reaches the laity [in local churches]. On the other hand, the theology which argues for the Church as the Body of Christ cannot possibly support this medieval notion.'

As with other organizational difficulties in local churches and synagogues, the impact of local/denomination tension is often felt most by rabbis and clergy. Their role places them in a boundary-spanning position between local and denominational levels and they find themselves caught between the conflicting demands of the two, or absorbing the resentment their congregants feel for 'ecclesiastical bureaucratization' (Dempsey 1969, p. 70).

CONCLUSIONS – EMERGING ORGANIZATIONAL ISSUES

This chapter has drawn together hitherto disparate material and is an initial attempt to build a body of social scientific knowledge about the specific topic of congregational organization. The chapter has looked broadly across writings by academics and 'practitioners' and across the literature of several denominations and two religions (Christianity and Judaism). The wide range of disciplinary and theoretical frameworks employed implicitly and explicitly to discuss organizational aspects of churches and synagogues has been noted.

Churches and synagogues have in common that they experience organizational challenges in at least four areas of their work; their goals; the roles of ministers; organizational change; and links with denominational structures. When drawn together in this way, the literature on organizational aspects of churches and synagogues provides initial support for the hypothesis set out at the beginning of this chapter; that there *are* organizational features and problems which are common to congregations of different religious persuasions and formal structures.

The synthesis of earlier literature also provides a starting point for the next stage in building a body of knowledge on congregational organization. To what extent are the findings about organizational features and issues assembled in this chapter borne out by focused empirical study of contemporary English congregations? In the next chapter, four case congregations are introduced.

3

Three Churches and a Synagogue:
Four Case Congregations

INTRODUCTION

This book aims to contribute to building a specialist body of knowledge on 'congregation organization'. An initial step was taken in the last chapter where hitherto disparate material was drawn together thematically. This chapter moves to the next stage in knowledge-building and describes an empirical study focused on congregational organization.

The purpose of the empirical study was to investigate the extent to which churches and synagogues have common organizational features and the extent to which they experience common organizational issues and problems. It was also hoped to generate 'usable' or 'explanatory' theory which could be of practical use to those working in churches and synagogues, and could provide a basis for further research (Billis, 1984; Silverman, 1993). The four broad organizational themes identified in the previous chapter provided an initial research agenda.

A Research Approach

Taking into account the research aims and constraints, it was decided that an appropriate method would be to conduct organizational case studies in churches and synagogues of different denominations, using a qualitative approach to data collection and analysis.[1]

The case study method has been widely used in the past by scholars of institutions (for example Perrow, 1970; Selznick, 1957), including those working in the social administration tradition (for example Donnison et al., 1975). It has several advantages. First, by conducting two or more case studies in different contexts, it is often possible to identify similarities and linkages between cases and variables which were not previously apparent. Second, case studies are a means of 'providing an understanding of areas of organizational functioning that are not well documented and which are not amenable to investigation through fleeting contact with organizations' (Bryman, 1989, p. 173). And finally, they can be a resource-efficient method of generating rich data which can contribute to building theoretical insights, but which can also be added to and reviewed by subsequent researchers.

It was also decided to combine the case study approach with a 'qualitative' methodology. The religious values underpinning churches and synagogues and their possible impact on the perceptions of key participants demanded a methodology sensitive to 'organizational culture' and one which gave weight to interviewees' own 'construction of reality' ((Berger and Luckmann, 1967). In qualitative research, priority is given to 'the perspectives of those being studied rather than the prior concerns of the researcher, along with a related emphasis on the interpretation of observations in accordance with subjects' own understandings' (Bryman, 1989, p. 135). In sum, the approach was likely to be acceptable to potential interviewees; to provide insights grounded in practical experience; and to allow new perspectives to emerge.

Selection of Cases

Four case congregations were selected for study using a staged selection process. As indicated in Chapter 1, the study was to be confined to the congregations of Judaism and Christianity but, within those boundaries, the cross-religion perspective suggested that at least one synagogue and one church should be included; while the cross-denomination perspective suggested including religious institutions of different denominational structures. Congregations were also varied with respect to other factors hypothesized to be correlated with organizational behaviour such as founding history, geographical location, funding sources, extent of 'strictness' in religious orientation, number of ministers, number and type of lay employees, and ethnicity of members. This process was not an attempt to provide a representative sample but to ensure that the four cases would differ as widely as possible *prima facie*. The more the cases differed in this way, the more interesting and significant would be generic organizational themes to emerge from the multiple cases (Yin, 1994).

The reasons for trying to select a range of organizational cases applied equally to the selection of interviewees within each case congregation. The aim was to obtain as wide a range of perceptions as possible so as to take account 'of the complexity of a situation by playing one interpretation against another' (Morgan, 1986, p. 331). The views of both religious functionaries and lay people were relevant and, amongst lay people, it was thought important not to confine investigations to office-holders, but to also include other kinds of 'actors' in the congregation. As Young (1977, p. 13) points out, 'Elite actors define the research situation differently from non-elites'. Those finally interviewed in each congregation were selected such that they represented a range of ages and positions, and such that the gender balance of interviewees reflected the pattern of congregational participation by males and females.

Data were collected through a combination of interviews, participation and examination of documents. Interviews were semi-structured in order to ensure that the topics and areas pre-identified from the literature (including factual information) were covered and covered consistently between the four different cases. At the same time, interviewees were given latitude over what they said and how they said it. Data generated from interviews was supplemented and complemented by information obtained through attending religious services, 'business' meetings and social events and from the study of 'in-house' documents such as magazines and reports.

This Chapter

In this chapter, descriptions are provided of the four case congregations. The focus here is on organizational *features* of the congregations, as organizational *issues* will be the focus of later chapters in Part II of the book. The chapter first outlines key features of each of the four selected case congregations. Then, since this study aims to provide an organizational perspective which looks *across* individual congregations, the remainder of the findings are presented synthetically rather than case by case. Data on the congregations are brought together to describe four key organizational 'elements': structure, goals, technology and participants. The organizational environment of the congregations is also described.

Following the 'institutional' and 'neo-institutional' approaches to organizational analysis which recognize the importance of 'the myriad subterranean processes of informal groups' within organizations (Perrow, 1986, p. 159), both the 'formal' and 'informal' aspects of congregation organization are examined. 'Formal' statements (also called 'normative' or 'manifest' statements in organizational literature) are concerned with what is officially the case. But there can be gaps in organizations between what is 'supposed' to happen and what happens in practice.

In keeping with the interpretivist approach which seeks to uncover the 'meaningful social world' (Silverman, 1993, p. 21) of research participants, and bearing in mind the need not to distort participants' beliefs 'by forcing them into the framework of a conceptual system which is alien to them' (Hamilton, 1995, p. 33), the presentation and analysis of data in this and subsequent chapters 'draw[s] heavily on the language of the persons studied' (Reinharz, 1983, p. 183).

THE CONGREGATIONS

Here, case by case descriptions are provided of the four congregations studied.[2] The selection and presentation of material is guided by the work of Pugh and his colleagues (1969) who identified 'primary' aspects of 'organizational context' including history, size, and location.

Congregation A

Congregation A is a Roman Catholic parish church in an inner city area. The area is ethnically mixed and this is reflected in the attendance and activities of the church. Up to about 25 years ago, the church was predominantly attended by Irish people. Today, the church still caters to a range of first-generation immigrants and to refugees, many of whom are only resident in the area for a short time.

The church was established at the end of the nineteenth century by a religious order which funded the building of the church and an associated school. In addition to the church, the congregation uses a presbytery for meetings and hires rooms as necessary in the school. At the time of the study, three members of the order were working in a priestly role in the parish and the congregation paid a modest sum to the order in recognition of this. In addition to the priests, the congregation had a full-time lay pastoral assistant, a half-time social welfare worker and three people employed for a few hours each week (on music, secretarial and cleaning duties).

The average total attendance for Sunday services was 1600. Elderly people and families with children were the most highly represented groups at services. People in the 16–25 age range were less well represented. About two thirds of regular attenders were men. The church had a list of 4000 people who lived in the area and associated themselves in some way with the parish. A priest estimated that there were a total of 7000 baptised Catholics living in the parish, 'people who might turn up'.

Day to day operating costs were met from weekly collections (about £1500 per week) and from rental income. The religious order gave extra financial help in the form of subsidies and occasional special grants. Thirty per cent of income was paid to the diocese.

Congregation B

Congregation B is a Pentecostal church which espouses a 'strict' or 'fundamentalist' Christianity. (As one lay interviewee said, 'You have to accept the whole bible as it is, as the truth'.) It is not subject to any denominational organizational structure; in fact, the congregation is itself looked to as a 'headquarters' by five 'branch' congregations. It is physically located in the centre of a medium-sized industrial county town, but it draws its membership from a wide area, including other towns in the county and beyond.

The church was started in the early 1960s 'because of the rejection of West Indian immigrants by established Christian churches in the town'.[3] Today it remains the case that, with one or two exceptions, the members are Afro-Caribbean people.

For many years the congregation did not have its own premises. It met in houses and huts and was dependent on the goodwill of short-term landlords. Eventually it was able to acquire a site in the town centre from the local authority and the first permanent building was completed in 1979. Since then, a large extension has been added. In total it now has three halls (holding 300, 200 and 100 people) and numerous small rooms used for offices, prayer and committee meetings. The congregation also owns three local houses, one of which is used for visitors, and the other two as temporary accommodation for homeless people.

There were no paid staff employed in Congregation B. However, the pastor worked full-time on church business and was financially supported by voluntary donations.

The official membership at the time of the study was 105, excluding children, and the average attendance at the main Sunday service was 80. At services, there are usually several visitors, often from abroad or from other black-led Pentecostal churches. Attendance at services ranges across the age groups but the middle-aged and elderly predominate, as do women. Numbers attending services and in membership have remained steady for several years. Members are lost through people returning to the Caribbean.

The activities of the church are wholly financed by donations and fund-raising by members themselves. Members meet all their own expenses in connection with work they do for the church, including travel, training, educational materials and provision of flowers.

Congregation C

Congregation C is an Anglican church and one of three churches in an ancient parish whose boundaries are roughly coterminous with a market town. The church was started in 1968; a 'daughter' to the parish church in the town centre and one intended to serve the needs of a post-war local authority housing estate at the edge of the town. As the congregation grew, three extensions were made to the building. In addition to the main church which holds 120 people, there is now a church hall, one office and one committee room. 'In spite of the eight pillars and three floor levels which do cause some headaches, the church itself has retained an informal and homely character which many continue to value very highly.'[4]

At the time of the study, Congregation C had its own vicar but he worked as one of a parish team of clergy. There were no other paid staff except a part-time cleaner. A member of the congregation was paid on an occasional basis to keep the church gardens tidy. The work of secretary, sacristan and organist was done by congregants working on a part-time voluntary basis. The congregation also benefitted from paid secretarial and administrative work provided for the parish as a whole (for example, the production of a monthly parish magazine).

There were about 130 people on the electoral roll (that is, official members). The average attendance at the main Sunday service was 65, excluding children. It was thought that the number attending services was starting to increase after having fallen for a few years. Most of those who attended the church lived within easy walking distance. There were two distinct age groupings amongst members and adherents: those over 55 years old (predominantly women) and young mothers with their children. The vicar estimated that about 10 per cent of service attenders were men. Some of the congregation's social activities attracted high proportions of people who were not members and who did not attend religious services.

The majority of normal church expenditure is covered by weekly giving by church adherents (about £250 per week) supplemented with a few fundraising events each year. Help is available from the parish and the diocese to cover exceptional needs. In general the congregation finds it difficult to keep within its budget. A percentage of congregational income, calculated according to a standard formula, is paid to the diocese.

Congregation D

Congregation D is a Reform synagogue located in a suburb with a high proportion of Jewish residents. It is affiliated to the 'Reform Synagogues of Great Britain' (RSGB) but this leaves it autonomous with respect to major matters including funding and finance, and employment of rabbinic and lay staff.

It was established in the early 1960s. The present main synagogue building dates from the early 1970s and seats 400. There is also a smaller hall which holds 100 people and some offices. The children's Religion School (which meets on Sunday mornings) cannot be accommodated on the premises and the congregation hires a local school. The building is now considered inadequate but plans for development have been delayed.

At the time of the study, there was one full-time rabbi and two assistant rabbis who were employed for a few hours each week. An administrator, a youth leader and a caretaker were employed full-time and there were several part-time lay employees including two secretaries, Religion School teachers and head teachers, and kindergarten teachers. Some regular teaching and administration was done by congregants on a voluntary basis.

The congregation had just under a thousand adult members and was growing steadily. Average attendance at a Sabbath service was 100 adults plus children. The full age range was represented and there were roughly equal numbers of males and females at most services. Many of the synagogue's members do not live in the immediate vicinity of the synagogue and travel from other adjoining suburbs; several of which have Reform synagogues located in them which they choose not to join.

Except for kindergarten fees, all expenditure is covered by member subscriptions, tax recovered from covenants, donations and income from fundraising events. At the time of the study, the congregation was experiencing financial difficulties; as a result of the recession and employment difficulties amongst members, an increasing proportion of members were paying reduced subscriptions. The congregation paid 20 per cent of its income to the Reform Synagogues of Great Britain.

ORGANIZATIONAL ELEMENTS

In this part, descriptive data on individual congregations is brought together and a framework suggested by Scott (1987) is used to describe four key organizational 'elements': structure, goals, technology (how work gets done) and participants.

Structure

With regard to their formal polities – the official link with their denominational structures – the four congregations spanned a range of degrees of centralization; with Congregation A (Roman Catholic) being the most centralized, followed by Congregation C (Anglican), and then D (Reform Jewish). Congregation B (Pentecostal) was at the other end of the spectrum, being unaffiliated to any denominational structure.

In practice, the case studies suggested that Congregation C was more subject to denominational control than Congregation A. In the latter, the religious order was apparently a key factor in mitigating the influence which would normally be exerted on the congregation by the diocese and the wider Roman Catholic structure. The order contributed crucial human, financial and physical resources to the congregation and had been doing so for the preceding

100 years. The congregation was thus able to act relatively independently and it took 'liberal' stances on matters such as participation by women in liturgy and involvement of divorcees.

In contrast, Congregation C appeared in practice to be *more* subject to denominational control than might be expected from formal statements of Anglican polity. This was largely attributable to the fact that the congregation was part of a parish team structure. Its vicar was placed in a junior position relative to the parish Team Rector, part of whose role was to ensure the implementation of diocesan policies. Thus, the congregation had been obliged to change the format of some services because the Rector felt they did not conform with Anglican guidelines. And the congregation was under pressure to develop its 'outreach' to the local community and to Anglican communities abroad; despite a feeling within the congregation itself that this was beyond their current capacity.

With respect to their internal organizational structures, the four congregations varied as to the relative authority officially attributed to clergy and laity and to the power they enjoyed in practice. Congregation A, reflecting the theology of the Roman Catholic church structure, gave the least official authority to lay people. It had a 'Parish Council' but this was described by a priest as 'consultative ... it doesn't strictly have any power ... it makes suggestions.' Key decisions on both policies and activities were taken at the weekly meetings of the 'Parish Team' of clergy and paid staff. In so far as the power of priests and their rights to make decisions were questioned at all, this mainly happened through informal lobbying of individual members of the Team. The role of the full-time lay pastoral assistant was especially important in this respect. As a theologically educated lay person, she straddled the boundary between the ordained priests and the congregants and was able to act as a channel of communication between the two groups and to encourage the Team to take account of parishioner views expressed to her informally.

Congregation C officially allocated more relative authority to lay people. In line with Church of England practice, it had its own Church Council to which lay people were elected annually and it was also part of a complicated web of elected councils which brought together the three congregations within the parish. In interviews, historical accounts of clashes with previous vicars indicated that lay people, if they so wished, could use the Church Council as a forum for challenging the wishes of their vicar.

However, the normal expectation was, as in Congregation A, that there would be a striving for consensus and that, in case of conflict, the clerical view would prevail; an expectation reflected in the fact that the vicar chaired meetings and set the agenda.

According to official statements, Congregations B and D had structures which gave more authority to lay people. Both had annual meetings of members at which a council of lay people was elected and both had ministers who were financially dependent on their congregants. This official situation appeared to be largely reflected in the day to day structure of Congregation D. The chairperson of the council was potentially extremely powerful and a number of examples were cited of clashes in which the rabbi's views on important issues had not prevailed. The power enjoyed by rabbis was contingent on the relationship with lay leaders; and as the maximum term of service for a lay chairperson was three years, the relative power of rabbis and lay leaders was constantly being renegotiated.

The situation in Congregation B was different. Despite a manifestly democratic organizational structure, the lay members of the congregation appeared to have voluntarily ceded total power to their pastor and a group of deacons and deaconesses.[5] There were various fora, including the group of charity trustees, in which decisions were made about key policy and developmental matters. But interviews suggested that in practice these functioned very much as in Congregation A; that is, it was understood that lay people were to act as consultants and to affirm and implement the decisions of clergy. This was reflected in the fact that, in practice, most people described themselves as having been appointed to posts of responsibility by the pastor. Those 'elected' had been approached and approved by him and saw themselves as responsible to him and the deacons.

Goals

Looking across the four case congregations, five broad goals[6] emerged as important in all of them: liturgical expression of religious commitment; education; welfare provision; organizational continuity; and social integration.

Liturgical expression of religion (primarily worship on congregation premises but also including events and ceremonies in the community) was the prime 'output' goal in all the congregations.

Not only was this officially the case, it was also reflected in the way in which human and financial resources were allocated in practice. The only dissent from the view about priority of liturgical expression was found in Congregation D where there were a substantial proportion of members for whom attending services was not a *personal* priority; their priority was to give expression to their Judaism in other ways such as social and community service and learning about their religion. All the same, there was no dissent from the view that the synagogue *as an organization* should give priority to liturgy.

A second priority in all four congregations was the provision of religious education; in the first place for children and converts and then for existing adult members. There was a link between the liturgy goal and the education goal since much of the education in the congregations was aimed at enabling people to participate in religious worship. However, in Congregations A, B and D, education was also intended to provide a broader perspective on religious practice and to enable members to live a 'religious life' beyond attendance at services and other congregational activities. For example, Congregation A ran courses for personal spiritual development and Congregation B ran a weekly bible study group, whilst adult education in Congregation D included instruction on Jewish approaches to various aspects of every day life.

A third goal which was agreed upon and a source of pride in all four congregations concerned social care or 'ministry'. This goal was implemented in a range of ways; not only through pastoral visiting and informal help between members but also through more formal mutual aid groups and through welfare projects delivering services outside the congregation on a regular basis (for example, a prison visiting scheme run by Congregation B and lunches for homeless people provided on synagogue premises by Congregation D). The range of welfare provision found in the four congregations confirmed the suggestion made in Chapter 1 that churches and synagogues are an integral part of the current social welfare system.

All four of the congregations were also giving explicit attention to securing their own organizational continuity. However, the way in which this was expressed varied between the congregations and appeared to be related to a number of factors including their stage of organizational growth, their theology, and their cultural environment. Thus, Congregation A was situated in the midst of a large

Catholic population and knew that it was already in touch with a high proportion of them. It was also not totally dependent on its congregants for financial viability. It was, therefore, less concerned about congregational survival than about meeting the religious and social needs of existing adherents and about coming into closer contact with those at the margins; for example, parents of children at the school who did not attend services, or 'lapsed' but identifying Catholics. A similar situation existed in Congregation D which had grown rapidly in recent years and was having difficulty meeting the religious and educational needs of existing members within available resources. Maintaining the quality and range of their response to needs was their main concern. This was seen as a route to retaining members and to attracting new ones in the future.

Although Congregations B and C were of similar age to Congregation D, their future survival was not taken for granted in the same way and the congregational continuity goal was more explicitly concerned with ensuring survival. In both these congregations, their 'myths, sagas, and legitimating accounts' (Meyer, 1984, p. 187) seemed especially important. The story of their founding and early years was repeatedly recounted in their publications and in interviews; a reflection, perhaps, of anxieties about the future of the congregations and feelings of not yet being firmly rooted. Thus, thirty years after the founding of the church, a respected 'elder' of Congregation B wrote:

> I was there when the rain was falling and the water would come through the roof of the old building. I was there when both male and female had to queue outside in all sorts of weather to use the old run-down WC. I was there that Saturday night when the Lord spoke to [the Pastor] to tell the people that they must march around the church and claim the land by faith.[7]

And a founding member of Congregation C said in interview:

> There really is something there ... People there have actually built it ... Everybody laughed at the building originally and called it a hen house and a cattle shed. But the smallness and the newness threw us together in that small space.

As an evangelical congregation, Congregation B was explicit about its goal of 'bringing new people to Jesus'. The congregation had a number of activities geared to conversion such as open air preaching and prison visiting. But underlying the official, biblically based, justifications for evangelical activity, were more practical, cultural concerns; that the first generation children of Afro-Caribbean immigrants were not as motivated to join and devote themselves to a religious congregation as their parents had been. There was thus a danger of the congregation dying as the founder generation died.

Congregation C, in keeping with its Anglican theology, was less explicit about wanting to convert people. However, interviewees were similarly concerned about the impact on the congregation of long term demographic change; the generation which had set up the church originally was ageing and the younger generation seemed less able to take on major responsibilities.

> There is a group of older people who have been doing things for the church for a long time. Many of them are now in their 70s. They have nobody to hand over to ... There is a leadership gap. (Lay Leader, Congregation C)

The vicar and senior lay people were seeking to increase the number of congregational adherents in a low key manner by, for example, encouraging local residents to attend social and other non-religious activities on church premises and by conducting services for groups outside the church.

> The more people we get over the threshold the happier I feel... . Once we get people in, we speak for ourselves. People will see God and our mission. (Vicar, Congregation C)

Finally, the fifth goal, and again one shared by all four congregations, related to social integration and reflected the 'civil society' theme discussed in Chapter 1. The social integration goal was most explicitly expressed in Congregation D where, in interviews and in congregational publications, the function of a synagogue as a meeting place for Jews appeared to have a 'taken for granted' status. For the three Christian congregations, social integration was less a 'manifest' than a 'latent' goal yet its importance in practice emerged clearly from interviews. People spoke about 'caring' and 'fellowship' and emphasized the importance of bringing people together. In Congregation B Afro-Caribbeans were brought together; in Congregation A, people of disparate nationality and race who were often transient residents of the inner city; and in Congregation C, the residents of a housing estate geographically separated from the main town.

> We have people from different countries and they can all feel a bond for the church. (Social Welfare Worker, Congregation A)

> ... there is a feeling of neighbourliness ... People started saying hello to me in the street within a few weeks of starting going to church ... Because of the church, I feel I belong. (Lay Leader, Congregation C)

Sometimes the social integration goal was implemented in the congregations through explicit befriending of people regarded as lonely or in need of care, or through drawing them in to practical and social activities within the congregation. The goal was also implemented through overtly social activities organized under congregational auspices (such as barbecues, dances and outings); fostering of 'common interest' groups such as evening classes, Brownies, choirs and senior citizen circles; and through informal socializing surrounding meetings for worship. In all four of the congregations, this socializing had been institutionalized through the practice of providing light refreshments following services.

Technology

Following the description of the organizational structures and goals of the four congregations, this section describes the way in which the congregations carried out their 'work' and 'activities', concentrating, as in previous sections, on the commonalities between them.

In Congregations B and D, the main means of carrying out the work of the congregation was through a network of committees of lay people with interlocking memberships. In Congregation B, the committees and their respective chairs were appointed in practice by the pastor and a board of elders. In Congregation D, they were nominally sub-committees of the elected lay council; although, in practice, several of them appeared to be only 'loosely coupled' (Meyer and Rowan, 1977) to the council. In some cases they could be described as 'fiefdoms' of individual lay leaders, who often remained in post for several years and carried the major responsibility for the relevant area of work.

Some of these committees are headed by very powerful people ... Theoretically, each of the groups are sub-committees of the Council. In practice they tend to act autonomously. (Lay Leader, Congregation D)

In both congregations B and D there were also *ad hoc* working groups, often convened by ministers, whose status and accountability most interviewees were unclear about. Methods of working in Congregation D appeared to be heavily influenced by the rabbi's personal interest in group work; whereas in Congregation B, the major influences seemed to be cultural (Afro-Caribbean) and religious (Pentecostal).

The committees were generally effective means of getting work done. Congregation D had committees to direct and manage, for example, the work of child education, youth activities, the kindergarten, charitable fundraising and social events. Congregation B had committees, headed by active 'officers', who ensured the running of social welfare activities, the Sunday School, evangelical activities, music, missionary work, and the prison visiting. They worked to guidelines laid down by the pastor, but had some autonomy. This 'bounded autonomy' was described by one interviewee as follows:

I take responsibility for finding music and teaching new songs to the choir. I buy music ... and decide what is nice and what is suitable to use in the church ... you do what you know is the expected job ... [Pastor] will tell you if there are to be any changes. (Congregation B)

The other two congregations – A and C – had different technologies. Congregation C's work was mainly carried out through rotas of lay individuals. There was a general reluctance amongst lay people to take *responsibility* for particular areas of activity but large numbers of people were happy to take their turn on a rota if they did not feel they had a long-term commitment. Even the teaching at the Sunday School was carried out on a rota basis to ensure that no voluntary teacher had to teach every week. And the job of verger was shared between six people in rotation. In this way, definable, bounded tasks were generally carried out conscientiously in the congregation. However, it was left to the vicar and a handful of lay leaders to monitor and coordinate work and take initiatives.

The work of Congregation A was carried out mainly through a group of paid staff (three priests, and two lay people who constituted the 'Parish Team' and were described by one of the priests as 'the dynamo of the parish'). They met weekly to take key decisions and to plan and monitor the work of the congregation. Most congregational activities were given oversight or support by one of the Parish Team. The only recognizable 'committee' was a Finance Committee which was said by one of the priests to be 'required by Canon Law'. Its main job was to prepare budgets but a priest retained responsibility for financial management and for making decisions about large items of expenditure. He also 'hand-picked' the members of the committee.

Lay involvement in services of worship in Congregation A (by altar servers, readers, choristers and eucharist ministers) was under the direct supervision of one of the priests. Three other essential jobs – organization of sacred music, church cleaning and office work – were done by people who received a small payment. They too were supervised by a priest. Beyond this, smaller tasks such as flower arranging and answering the door to casual callers were done on an informal basis.

In all four congregations, the key role of religious functionaries in a range of congregational activities, not just those which were specifically 'religious', was apparent. This seemed to be not only because of the special authority they carry (referred to in Chapter 2) but also for the practical reason that they move between different activities and aspects of the congregation and therefore have an overview of congregational happenings. They are also frequently on the spot when emergencies occur; anything from news of a sudden death or the arrival of a congregant in distress, to the leaking of the roof or the discovery of lost property after a service. They therefore tend to get drawn in to a wide range of activities.

Ministers in Congregations A and D did regularly delegate tasks to the lay people who were paid employees of the congregation. And the pastor of Congregation B was also able to divest himself of some routine tasks; but in his case, this was more a reflection of the culture of the congregation in which it was considered to be an honour to provide support for the pastor and to contribute to the congregation in any way possible. Congregants were positively looking for ways of being helpful and volunteered to take on tasks. One interviewee in Congregation B explained that there was an expectation that newcomers to the congregation would volunteer for the most menial tasks such as cleaning the toilets or tidying books. If these were performed well, the member could hope for promotion to more responsible tasks, often on the recommendation of the pastor.

In fact, in all four of the congregations, there was an identifiable cadre of highly committed lay people whose work on a voluntary basis was crucial to the work output of the organization; a point discussed further in Chapter 6.

With regard to decision-making within congregations, interviewees in Congregations A and B emphasized the role of religious principles.

> ... we listen to each other and solutions emerge ... [the root is] listening with respect to the views of others, grounded in prayer ... you do not seek ego trips in team meetings. We are here to serve the people. (Team Member, Congregation A)

In Congregation B, it was explained that when difficult decisions had to be made,

> we seek an answer through prayer ... we give God a chance to speak ... Everyone is always in agreement because everything we decide and suggest is for spiritual development, not for ourselves ... we don't leave until everybody is satisfied. (Lay Leader, Congregation B)

On major issues, God's voice was, in practice, most usually heard in Congregation B via the pastor, often following a period of fasting with congregational leaders:

> God reveals his will to [the pastor], like when God kept telling him to 'put on a bigger coat'. For a long time, he did not understand what God was telling him. Then he realised that God was saying we should build an extension to the church. So we did. (Lay leader, Congregation B)

Lay Leaders in Congregation B also described their own inspirational decision-making:

> We believe in the Holy Ghost so we get inspiration through prayer and fasting. The spirit suggests things to you ... The Lord leads

me spiritually in who to choose to do things and which topics to address. The nitty gritty, I discuss with the [other leaders] and it's a down to earth discussion. (Lay Leader, Congregation B)

In Congregations C and D, integration of religious principles into decision-making was less explicit. In both, committee meetings began with a prayer or scriptural reading, but further explicit reference to religious guidance was not usual. Indeed, in the case of Congregation D, several interviewees recounted with disapproval the way in which the rabbi had justified a proposal he was making by suggesting that it was God's will.

He [the rabbi] said the situation was a God-given opportunity to do something new. Most people saw this as manipulation. They were stunned. They are not used to this. (Congregation D)

A lay interviewee in Congregation C spoke in similarly cynical terms about appeals to God:

[A previous vicar] used to pray for things that he wanted for the church. He prayed for an answering machine and got one from somewhere. (Congregation C)

Participants

Many of the characteristics of the participants in the congregations have now been mentioned. This section focuses on characteristics common to the participants in all four congregations.

In all the congregations, the importance for members[8] of the social integration functions performed by their congregations was apparent. People were drawn to congregational participation because it could respond not only to their spiritual needs but also to their social ones. Interviewees valued highly the capacity of congregations to care for people who were lonely, experiencing a life crisis, or otherwise searching for comfort through human interaction. In Congregations A, B and D, members were additionally drawn in by the opportunities provided to mix with people of similar background; not only religious but also ethnic, cultural or national.

The key thing is getting people together but at the same time you encourage them to keep their culture ... the church keeps going because of the groups ... Masses are not enough. (Lay Member from an ethnic minority, Congregation A)

Even in Congregation B, where membership was said to be contingent upon 'accepting the Lord as your personal saviour' and where visible signs of a conversion experience were expected, the motivation of congregation members appeared to be not solely religious. Interviewees emphasized the importance of being accepted and of being swept up into a range of activities which became a way of life:

> Every night there is some way of worship organized. There is always something happening. There is no time for the devil to get in and we keep people on their toes. (Lay Leader, Congregation B)

Many interviewees in Congregation B described the feelings of isolation and despair they had experienced prior to their conversion when they felt marooned within a largely white, alien society. The following is typical:

> [When I came to the town] I started going to the Methodist church. I went there for 7 years but I have never felt so lonely in my life. I don't think a single person there knew my name. Nobody would sit in the same pew as me ... I felt empty and alone ... I visited [Congregation B] a few times ... I was well accepted ... Since then, there has been a dramatic change in my life. (Lay Leader, Congregation B)

Interviews suggested that members of all the congregations valued not only the care and support that they received from their congregation, but also the opportunities provided for self-development and self expression.

> I enjoy it [evangelizing outside the congregation] immensely. ... I feel I am doing something when I go outside. (Lay Member, Congregation B)

> I was overwhelmed when I was first asked to do it [offer the chalice during communion]. My first reaction was 'Am I worthy?' ... I got used to doing it. I love to see the children from this side of the altar ... a great honour. (Lay Member, Congregation C)

I enjoy being recognized for being me in the community ... My husband keeps saying, 'everyone knows you and I'm just known as your husband'. (Lay Leader, Congregation D)

Participants also valued the opportunity to be part of a 'worth-while' collective enterprise:

It's a very friendly church ... People talk to each other and to strangers ... not like [the neighbouring church] which is very cold ... It's a caring church. (Lay member, Congregation C)

In short, participants value their congregations as places in which people care for each other and the world beyond the congregation and in which opportunities for self expression are plentiful; again the link with the theme of 'civil society' is evident.

Relationship between Elements

Scott (1987, p. 20) says of the four 'elements' of organization, that 'no one element is so dominant as to be safely considered in isolation from the others'. Indeed the linkages between the different elements emerged clearly from the case studies.

Although the four congregations had similar goals, their ways of approaching their congregational work (their technologies) were markedly different. This was the case, even where there were similarities between congregations with respect to other organizational features; for example, Congregations A and D both had several paid staff in addition to their clergy, yet they had not adopted similar technologies. Choice of technologies within congregations appeared to be less influenced by considerations about desired ends or outputs, than by denominational organizational traditions (structure element), by the preferences of powerful individuals, especially clergy, and by the culture and needs of members (participants element).

Thus, the rotas in Congregation C were regarded as suitable for a membership which was reluctant to take on major individual responsibilities; and the clergy-controlled committees in Congregation B were unquestioned by a predominantly female congregation which traditionally gave respect to male leaders. The fact that mechanisms for lay participation were being only slowly introduced into Congregation A was seen as an acceptable approach where congregants had been brought up within a paternalistic and authoritarian religious tradition. Again, the committee structures in Congregations B and D, and the proliferation of social groups in Congregation A had the function not only of carrying out tasks, but also of providing frameworks for social interaction between people who, outside of their congregations, were generally in an ethnic or racial minority.

The influence of ministers' views on ways of working was evident, for example, in Congregation D. The rabbi had expertise in psychology and difficult decisions and debates were generally dealt with in small *ad hoc* informal groups in which 'brain storming' and other group work methods were employed. In Congregation A, the influence of the priests' training was differently reflected in the technology. The priests' order emphasized consensus in decision-making and this was reflected in the manner of discussion in both the weekly Team meetings and the Parish Council meetings.

These points about the relationship between organizational elements reflect the view of institutional theorists that 'many of the most fateful forces [in organizations] are the result not of rational pressures for more effective performance but of social and cultural pressures' (Scott, 1987, p. 115).

THE ORGANIZATIONAL ENVIRONMENT

Having looked at four key organizational elements of the case congregations – structures, goals, technology and participants – this part of the chapter looks at their organizational environments since 'No organization is self-sufficient; all depend for survival on the types of relations they establish with the large systems of which they are a part' (Scott, 1987, p. 19).

At the broadest level, as they were all studied at roughly the same time and were all in England, the four congregations shared a common environment. They were all subject to similar economic and social trends including the recession and major changes in public policy, as well as the long term secularizing tendencies discussed in Chapter 1. Case congregations were also affected by, and tried to respond to, their particular location and cultural environment. For example, Congregation A ran an advice service for refugees and Congregation B ran a day centre for elderly Afro-Caribbean people.

This part of the chapter describes *organizational* entities within the environments of the four congregations, including denominational institutions, other religious organizations, voluntary agencies, and statutory organizations.

Denominational Institutions

As explained earlier, the four case congregations varied as to their formal polities; that is, as to their official position in relation to a broader denomination. Yet, for all of them, other organizations within the same religious tradition were key features of their environment.

For Congregation A, neither other Catholic congregations, nor the diocesan structure were of major organizational significance to them in practice. Because of their size and relative financial independence, the diocese did not have much to offer the congregation; it was too remote. Priests and lay people did go to diocesan and national events and they occasionally used members of diocesan staff in a consultancy capacity (for example in developing educational programmes or gaining musical expertise). But more important for them were a Catholic college which was described as giving 'support and guidance' to the parish on difficult pastoral issues; Catholic special interest groups; and the local Catholic schools. Of these latter, a primary school which was located next to the church and shared its name, was especially important. Many adults and children were brought in to active participation in the congregation because of the school. The school, in its turn, welcomed the use of church resources including the participation of its priests and the advice of its pastoral assistant.

Congregation C was also relatively distant from its diocesan structure and other Anglican congregations outside its parish. In this case, distance was attributable to the fact that the Parish Team of clergy and the related committees acted as a buffer between the congregation and the extra-parish denominational structure; and to the fact that congregants were mostly interested in their own immediate needs. They were generally not much interested in the possibilities offered and encouraged by the diocese for broadening the scope of their activities. So, as in Congregation A, it was the element in the denominational structure which was organizationally closest to the congregation, which was the key feature in the denominational environment of Congregation C; in this case the Parish Team of clergy and congregations.

Congregation D offered the best example of a congregation for which the denominational 'headquarters' *was* a significant environmental factor. The congregation is geographically located sufficiently near to the headquarters to be able to participate with ease in denominational committees and to take advantage of the social activities and support services available. All the same, several interviewees expressed strong reservations about the denominational structure and queried whether the congregation was getting value for the denominational dues. As in Congregation A, there was a thread of opinion that the congregation could be largely self sufficient and that the denominational structure was, on balance, a drain on resources.

> We do use the facilities offered by [denomination] ... But they get a lot from us too. For example, they are now using our bar/bat mitzvah programme ... When I think of [denomination], I think of ... the amount we have to pay them each year and I think of what the synagogue could do with all that money. (Lay Leader, Congregation D)

Congregation B, itself a 'headquarters', was in a different formal position from the other three congregations. This may explain why it was the only one of the four congregations studied which described close and frequent contact with other congregations of the same denomination. Congregation C was linked with the other two churches of the parish through the parish team structure; the three congregations occasionally 'visited' each other and shared major projects. And Congregations A and D were both officially members of networks of neighbouring congregations of their respective denominations. But only Congregation B interviewees expressed any enthusiasm for their contacts with other congregations within their denomination.

Other Religious Organizations

Although all four of the case congregations reported links with other religious-based organizations which were not within their own denomination – of varying degrees of formality and cordiality – it was, again, interviewees in Congregation B who attached most importance to such links. That congregation regularly held joint services with other local Christian congregations, sent choirs to participate in meetings and invited representatives of other religions (Christian and non-Christian) to their premises. They also participated in an annual national meeting of Afro-Caribbean churches and maintained loose links with a black-led Pentecostal denomination in the United States whose educational and evangelical material they displayed and used.

The three churches studied all reported being linked with local church groupings but none of the interviewees were enthusiastic about the links or felt them to be a significant contributor to their own congregation's work. The vicar of Congregation C, for example, described the local 'Churches Together' group as 'struggling' and as riven by conflict between 'established churches and house churches over evangelism.' And a priest in Congregation A described local ecumenical relationships as 'polite rather than warm'.

Congregation D had a one-to-one link with a local Catholic seminary which facilitated visits to the synagogue and Jewish homes by seminarians. They were also represented on the local Council of Christians and Jews and the Board of Deputies of British Jews. But, as in the Christian congregations, most interviewees in Congregation D seemed to regard their congregational links with other religious organizations as a necessary, but rather tiresome, chore. The benefits of the links for the congregations were largely seen as being public relations ones; participation was recognized as contributing to the legitimacy of the congregation in the local community.

Although physical meetings between congregational representatives were generally not talked of with enthusiasm, all of the congregations in practice seemed to keep in touch with activities of neighbouring religious organizations and to be stimulated by them. Thus, a lunch for the homeless project in Congregation D was modelled on a scheme running in a local Methodist church; the warden of Congregation C had adopted a number of ideas from other local churches for the internal lay-out of the church; and Congregation A's work in the housing field was initiated by somebody who admired the work being done by another local church.

Voluntary Agencies

In all the congregations, the obligation to support charitable activity seemed to be taken for granted. All gave financial contributions as a matter of course to both local and national charities; only some of which were religiously based. In addition, Congregation A permitted local groups (for example, Marriage Guidance/Relate and Alcoholics Anonymous) the use of its premises, and the other three congregations (B, C, and D) actively encouraged members to give volunteer time to local charities; as members of management committees, or as direct providers of services. In some cases, individual congregants were regarded as official representatives of their congregations but mostly the question of the status of a congregational volunteer was not regarded as important by congregational interviewees; what was important was the idea that the congregation was contributing in some way to its local community.

Congregations also had links with local voluntary organizations for more instrumental reasons. Thus, the welfare officer of Congregation A maintained links with local voluntary agencies which could provide information and other resources. Congregations B and D both participated in their local race equality councils. Congregation C's playgroup was affiliated to the Pre-School Playgroups Association and benefitted from the expertise the organization provided.

Governmental Agencies

Links between congregations and statutory sector organizations were not sought after specifically but, as occupiers of buildings, all the congregations had the usual range of 'citizen' links with public services. Difficulties about planning permission at various stages of growth were cited by three of the congregations (A, B and D). In the case of congregations A and D, these were a cause of bitterness as they had not been resolved after many years. In the case of Congregation B, the local authority had been its landlord when it was in temporary accommodation, and the difficulties it had had in getting a long-term lease and then in obtaining permission to erect a permanent building, had become part of the frequently retold story of the congregation's struggle to establish itself.

In addition to citizen links, congregations had contacts with statutory organizations primarily in the course of their welfare work. Thus, Congregation B was an active participant in the chaplaincy for three prisons and Congregation C provided visitors for local schools and residential homes. At the time of the study, members of congregations B and D were involved in discussions with their respective Social Services departments who were taking over responsibility for welfare projects (the day centre for the elderly run by Congregation B and the lunches for the homeless run by Congregation D). Congregation D was also in receipt of a two-year local authority grant which subsidized its employment of a youth worker.

CONCLUSIONS – FOUR CASE CONGREGATIONS

This chapter has introduced four congregations which were investigated using a case study approach. Case by case descriptions have been given of contextual features of each of the congregations including their history, size and location. Then material on individual congregations was brought together to describe four key organizational 'elements': structure, goals, technology and participants. The final part of the chapter looked at their organizational environment.

Considering the data presented here in the light of the aims of this study given at the start of the chapter, two points are notable. First, it is confirmed that the selection of cases was such that they together vary widely as to religion, denomination, location, staffing, membership profile, history, funding, and the range and nature of activities. In fact, the congregations also vary with respect to other characteristics which were not specifically targeted in the case selection process. For example, they differ as to the proportion of members regularly attending sabbath services; the extent to which members live in the immediate vicinity; the nature and extent of work done by lay volunteers; the internal structures for carrying out work; the extent to which religious principles are explicit guides to organizational behaviour; the nature and extent of their links with other organizations; and the relative authority officially, and in practice, attributed to ministers and lay people.

Despite these wide variations between the congregations, a number of organizational similarities between the congregations also emerge. This is the second noteworthy point; that this chapter provides confirmation of the hypothesis that congregations have organizational features in common. All four of the congregations, for example, have similar broad purposes and they use similar means to implement them. As was expected, religious functionaries play a key role in all the congregations; in participating in activities, in providing leadership, and in influencing operating styles. Less expected was that they play a key role in such a wide range of activities, including those which are not normally seen as 'religious'. There are also similarities between congregations in members' motivations for participation; people are drawn to congregations by the opportunities they offer for social integration, for personal self-expression and for the opportunity to be part of something 'worthwhile'.

Congregations also share a similar approach to their environments. In general they are highly responsive to their geographical, cultural and organizational environments; adapting activities and setting priorities in order to maximize the human and other resources brought to the congregation. Finally, all four of the congregations appear to share with other organizations a tendency for there to be a gap between day to day practice and 'official' statements. Thus, 'formal polities' did not necessarily reflect the day-to-day relationship between congregations and their respective denominational institutions. Nor did formal statements about the relative power of lay people and ministers necessarily reflect practice.

In Part II, the presentation of data about the case congregations continues but the focus shifts from descriptions of their organizational features to analysis of the organisational *issues and problems* they faced.

Part II
Challenges for Congregations

4

Mission Impossible?
Choosing Goals and Implementing Them

INTRODUCTION

In Part II of this book the focus is on organizational issues and problems faced by the four case congregations. This is in keeping with the study aim of responding to 'grass roots' problems in congregations. It is also an essential part of understanding congregations as organizations. As Demerath and Hammond (1969, p. 167) argued when they studied religious organizations in the United States, 'organizations cannot be realistically understood merely in times of harmony and in terms of their public face. Instead they are best revealed at moments of crisis and conflict.'

The dual presentation of empirical material in this book – describing both features *and* issues – reflects the approach of those scholars who attempt to encompass two approaches to the study of organizations: the approach which is aimed at 'describing existing features and relations of organizations in order … to better understand their nature and operation'; as well as the approach which is focused on organizational problems and the search for their solution (Scott, 1987, pp. 11–12).

This chapter begins the analysis of organizational issues faced by congregations by looking at the problems surrounding the setting and implementation of goals. As in Part I, the emphasis in this and subsequent chapters is on looking *across* congregations.

The difficulties of defining and analysing 'goals' have been widely noted in organizational literature. Scott (1987, p. 19) suggests that the 'concept of organizational goals is among the most important – and the most controversial – concepts to be confronted in the study of organizations'. And Perrow (1970) draws attention to the multiplicity of types of goals which coexist within organizations and

71

can conflict with each other: societal goals, output goals, system goals, product characteristic goals and derived goals.[1] (The special difficulties thought to arise in relation to goals in *religious* organizations were discussed in Chapter 2.)

In this chapter, as in Part I, the term 'goals' is used in a general sense to refer to 'purposes' or 'ends'; both those provided by official statements and ideologies and those which motivate congregational participants. A distinction is made as necessary between 'broad purposes', 'banner' or 'mission' goals and 'lower level' or 'operational' goals. Since the study was focused on participants' own perceptions and responses to issues and problems, a range of views was sought about congregational purposes and there was no attempt to pre-classify types of goals. Nor was it assumed that issues raised in earlier literature (as presented in Chapter 2) were necessarily those that would be of most concern to interviewees.

SETTING GOALS

Agreeing Broad Purposes

Broad purposes ('banner' or 'mission' goals) were rarely the subject of major debate in the case congregations. There was an assumption that those who retained their membership accepted the congregation's broad purposes – including not only basic religious values but also congregational customs. Those who disagreed either never became really involved in the congregation, or chose to leave – generally without open argument. The assumption that everybody shared a commitment to broad purposes and practices was reflected by a lay leader in Congregation B:

> We believe in worshipping every day. This comes from way back. We all know this and this is how the church is organized. (Lay Leader, Congregation B)

Moreover, it seemed that a latent function of the education activities in congregations was to maintain and reinforce shared purposes.

> The sacramental programmes are ... not just a talk from the priest. It makes you think seriously and gives better relationships and better understanding. (Lay Member, Congregation A)

The improbability of dissenters from broad purposes remaining within a congregation is probably reinforced, in churches at least, by theologically justified cultural norms which discourage overt conflict as 'inappropriate' (Lauer, 1973).[2]

> Being confrontational is very difficult in a Christian context. If you challenge people in any way, they accuse you of not being Christian. (Priest, Congregation A)

> A Christian should be able to sort things out and leave without animosity because the Holy Spirit brings us together. (Lay Member, Congregation B)

Interviews did indicate, however, that, at least in Congregations A and D, there *were* individuals – including some in leadership positions – who had doubts about key manifest purposes of the congregation. For example, three interviewees in Congregation A were critical of recent papal pronouncements on birth control, abortion and divorce and described how they sought the most liberal interpretations of them possible. And in Congregation D a lay leader said that she had only social motivations for synagogue involvement and was disinterested in religion. Yet these people had never made their views explicit within their congregations and did not intend to do so. The appearance of consensus was maintained. The choice was seen as being between 'exit' and 'loyalty'; 'voice' in relation to broad mission goals, was not seen as an option in any of the congregations.[3]

Within this general consensus about broad purposes, issues arose as choices had to be made about 'operational' goals; the means through which broad purposes were to be achieved. Some of these issues were essentially about roles and role relationships – the relative authority of clergy and lay leaders, for example – and they are described in later chapters. But many of the issues were about the goals themselves and they are examined in this part of this chapter.

Mutual Benefit and Commonweal Aims

As indicated in Chapter 2, earlier researchers suggested that congregations may feel pulled between focusing on the needs of their own members and taking a more outward approach towards the wider community; between what Blau and Scott (1963) refer to as 'mutual benefit' and 'commonweal' purposes. The case data confirmed this to some extent. One of the Officers of Congregation B, for example, perceived the lack of money for space and transport for her 'department' as attributable to the efforts that had been put into fundraising for a new branch of their church. And in Congregation A there were disagreements about who should be given priority in allocation of places in the adjoining Catholic primary school which was heavily oversubscribed. A decision to allow applications from local children who were not regular church attenders was resented:

> A lot of people feel very bitter that they are genuine Catholics and they cannot get their kids in … People are far more upset about this than the priests realise. (Lay Member, Congregation A)

But in general this kind of dichotomous thinking, in which one direction was seen as *precluding* another, was not usual in the case congregations. The situation was more complex. For one thing, congregations were seen as having a finite store of resources; thus doing a good job *within* the congregation simply inhibited work further afield, however much they wanted to do it in principle.

> We haven't developed strong relationships with local institutions … our energies go in to Catholic activities. (Priest, Congregation A)

> I had a vision to go back to Jamaica and make a Christian Centre. The Church Board is supporting this but we have just finished raising money for the extension to the church … (Lay Leader, Congregation B)

> There is a lot of unobtrusive caring and support and keeping the building going. There is no energy for less parochial activities. (Vicar, Congregation C)

The fact that they could not do as much external work as they thought appropriate was a widely shared concern in all of the congregations.

> A greater effort is needed not to think of the church as a place for a holy huddle. (Pastoral Assistant, Congregation A)

We need to respond to elderly West Indian people in [town] (Lay Leader, Congregation B)

We should have something for young mothers on the estate. (Lay Leader, Congregation C)

We are weak ... as regards Israel and Soviet Jewry ... We cannot seem to sustain our efforts. (Lay Leader, Congregation D)

Thus the issue was not so much that mutual aid and commonweal goals were seen as being alternatives but that commonweal ones were seen to be generally squeezed out by responding to the immediate needs of members. The general assumption was that it was incumbent upon congregations to face outwards *as well as* inwards; to be what Lohmann (1992, p. 57) has described as 'mixed benefactories' which 'engage in both intrinsic and extrinsic benefactions'. In fact, several interviewees were uncomfortable with the distinction between 'inward' and 'outward' facing goals.

People stretch their hands out to others ... not just to church members. If people come to us, we always try to help. (Lay Leader, Congregation B)

There is no way that I could draw a distinction between who has need – members of the synagogue, Jews, non-Jews, homeless etc... . We are not interested in Jews/non-Jews; need/not in need. This is just not an issue. (Lay Leader, Congregation D)

Maintaining Longer Term Perspectives

At the time of the study, Congregations A, C and D had recently made attempts to assess their overall balance of activities and to make strategic plans. The Parish Council of Congregation A was discussing a strategic planning document initiated by one of the priests. Congregation C was involved in a parish consultation exercise which had pinpointed areas for special attention by the three parish congregations. In Congregation D, a working party had recently completed four years of deliberations and had presented to the Annual General Meeting proposals for a refurbishment and development of the congregation's buildings, predicated on assumptions about future growth. There had also been a special half-day meeting of the Council to debate the implications of membership growth.

Despite these conscious attempts at rational decision-making and goal-setting, interviewees suggested that it was difficult to maintain long-term visions and overall perspectives for their congregations. First, the immediate needs of members and local communities could drive out considered attempts to allocate scarce resources or to maintain 'spirituality'. Congregation B, for example, had found themselves using as temporary accommodation for homeless people, two neighbouring houses they had originally purchased for congregational use. A priest in Congregation A explained the dilemmas posed by immediate pressures:

> You should distinguish between 'things you should do' and 'things you have to do'. There are two kinds of things you *have* to do. First there are the immediate pressures to respond to individual problems ... Second, there are things which are regular commitments and they just have to be done ... It means that you often have to leave the longer term things.

Similarly a lay leader of Congregation D said:

> In Council, we get so bogged down with day to day running that we lose sight of this as a place of spirituality.

A second obstacle to maintaining long-range vision was the tendency of individuals to fight their own cause rather than think about congregational needs as a whole.

> One of the problems with the Parish Council is that it comprises representatives [of groups and activities] ... We need people on the PCC who are there to comment generally on the issues affecting the church. (Priest, Congregation A)

> The pressure is to respond to those who are already heavily involved and who want ... to reinforce their own interests. (Priest, Congregation A)

> Nobody looks at things as a whole ... it's hard to get people to do things together in this area. People are very individualistic ...

People want to get brownie points where they're blowing the trumpets and flapping the wings. (Lay Leader, Congregation C)

Congregations face a major dilemma here. On the one hand, they want to retain 'vision', reflect their guiding religious principles, and plan ahead for growth and change in a constantly changing environment. Yet on the other hand they cannot neglect the immediate demands made on them by their members; individuals whose needs are not met will 'vote with their feet' and so cannot be ignored. Likewise, legitimacy within the immediate surrounding locality is often essential to congregational survival. As anticipated by the 'civil society' discussion, congregations are closely linked in to other institutions in society and cannot operate without paying attention to them.

Difficulties in Setting Priorities

Earlier literature drew attention to the multiplicity of goals in congregations and the strong norms against open conflict. This was reflected in the case congregations which experienced difficulties in choosing between goals and setting priorities. Some interviewees drew attention to the way in which meeting one goal (for example, caring or organizational survival) could mean other equally important goals were neglected; either because of competition for resources or because fulfilling one goal could preclude simultaneously fulfilling another and thus upset a particular interest group.

The emphasis on families marginalizes those who are single or who do not want to be married or whose marriages have failed. (Lay Leader, Congregation A)

The people who can do things are overburdened with the routine running of the church ... so we don't have time for the things that the church should be all about such as organizing clubs and groups; visiting people; studying and discussing. (Lay Leader, Congregation C)

A prime example of apparently irreconcilable goals was found in all four of the case congregations and concerned the conflicting demands and needs of different generations in relation to worship. All the congregations wanted to educate children and young families and integrate them into worship and yet this aim was in constant conflict with the wish of many for 'prayerful' meetings.

Congregation B had attempted to resolve the dilemma by making clear its expectations that children should conform to adult norms of behaviour in their church participation; that is, they had in practice given priority to the wishes of older members.

> The whole purpose of the youth activities is to integrate the young people in to the mainstream of the church. (Lay Leader, Congregation B)

Congregations A, C and D, on the other hand, had all given high priority to the needs of young children and families in worship. In all of them this had become a matter for continuous complaint and resentment.

> The idea of a children's Mass is wonderful ... it shows real commitment to the next generation ... But the old guard don't like the informality and lack of discipline. (Congregation A)

> [Vicar] has changed things so that now the young children are inside the church during the service. People are upset because the children make a noise and run about. There was a big row recently. One long-time member of the church ... suddenly shouted out during the service to one of the mothers, 'Will you stop that child from running about'. The mother started crying. Now that couple [the older ones] have left the church. (Lay Leader, Congregation C)

> We have not found a way of handling the children on the High Holydays. It was just a shambles ... They couldn't cope. It was all geared to the younger children. The children were running around. We got nothing out of the service. (Lay Member, Congregation D)

Some interviewees argued that it was inappropriate to weight or choose between different goals in congregations since there are so many possible ways of fulfilling religious purposes.

> From the natural feeling of enjoying the company of people comes a sense of goodness and serving God ... This can come from a range of activities. (Priest, Congregation A)

Everything is part of the worship. (Lay Leader, Congregation B)

Everything is religious to a certain extent. (Lay Leader, Congregation D)

But there were also several interviewees who attributed the failure to make unequivocal choices about priorities, to amateurishness and incompetence and who were concerned about the organizational implications. Reluctance to set priorities explicitly could result in constant disharmony and internal lobbying.

Too many different opinions can lead to delays in getting things done. (Lay Leader, Congregation A)

It's a ship with an admiral and a lot of skippers on the bridge. And sometimes the boat just goes round and round. (Lay Leader, Congregation C)

There's an inability to make decisions on major issues like the new building. (Lay Member, Congregation D)

Against this argument for competent decision-making and rational priority setting, which seems to reflect notions about organization borrowed from the secular business world, other interviewees emphasized the importance of developing self-confidence in lay people and building consensus behind key decisions, rather than being 'businesslike'. This reflects earlier literature which suggests that some goals and actions can be perceived as 'inappropriate' in religious organizations. However, the objections to being businesslike in the case congregations seemed to be based on quite pragmatic organizational considerations rather than on religious principles.

In this type of area ... you have to build people up. (Lay Leader, Congregation A)

You have to try to get a good team. You've not to be too powered. You can destroy a team like that. You must not be abrasive. (Lay Leader, Congregation B)

You can soon clear your congregation if you try to change things too quickly. (Lay Leader, Congregation C)

A lot of people in the synagogue run their own businesses. They are not used to consultation, long time periods for reaching decisions, and their ... ideas being challenged and changed. (Lay Leader, Congregation D)

The conjunction of reluctance to be explicit about priorities, with the limitations on resources, tended to result in scarce resources being allocated mainly according to historical accident, rather than according to consciously set priorities. Once a group or activity had established its claim to resources, it was rarely openly questioned or withdrawn. Problems about claims to room space, for example, figured in all four of the case congregations and were depicted as running sores, causing ill-feeling between lay congregants.

... a group felt they had been ousted from rooms that they had been using in the presbytery. (Lay Leader, Congregation A)

We do not use the new extension for teaching – it's kept for prayer and meetings. If we had more space [for use by the Sunday School], we could split up the existing classes in to smaller groups which would be much more satisfactory. (Lay Leader, Congregation B)

There have been lots of problems ... over the use of the hall, especially with the Ladies Group ... There was a tremendous amount of friction [with the under-fives Group leaders] ... The issues were petty but it created a very bad atmosphere. (Lay Leader, Congregation C)

The building is overcrowded and so there are always problems about which activities are to have the use of them. There cannot be all the activities that people want. (Lay Leader, Congregation D)

A priest in Congregation A summarized the issues surrounding priority setting in congregations:

The only way you can ever do something fresh is by stopping doing something you are already doing – something that serves the already committed and that has been done before. (Priest, Congregation A)

IMPLEMENTATION OF GOALS

This part of the chapter moves beyond problems which face congregations in *setting* goals to the issues surrounding the *implementation* of goals. The case studies indicated that, irrespective of the
degree of clarity of goals and the degree of consensus in congregations, numerous problems and issues arose as congregations
attempted to implement them.

Dependence on Individual Enthusiasms and Skills

Since membership of a congregation in contemporary England is
voluntary, there are limits on the extent to which members can be
directed. Some goals or tasks may be widely agreed to be important
but if nobody can be found to implement them there is little that
can be done. In all four of the case congregations, activities which
were agreed to be very important were left undone for this reason.
For example, interviewees in Congregation A were concerned
that they had no youth activities and emphasized the need for
them in the inner city; but the congregation had been unable to
find anybody who was willing to take on the responsibility.
Congregation C had no choir for similar reasons. Congregation D
had virtually no activities to support Eastern European Jews or
Israel. Several interviewees emphasized that this was an important
part of any synagogue's endeavour but nobody was willing to take
a leadership role in that area.

This dependence on individual enthusiasm and voluntary commitment had another side to it. Not only could some goals not be
accomplished because nobody was interested in implementing them,
there was little possibility of balancing activities in any planned
manner. What took place in congregations was largely a function of
what lay people and ministers at the time wanted to pursue. So some
goals could be amply implemented whilst others never got to the
starting gate. And, since social integration is itself a widely espoused
goal of congregations as indicated in Chapter 3, congregations
could not easily curtail activities driven by individual commitment
and enthusiasm. On the contrary, they positively encouraged them.

> People arrange things themselves and then ask [priest] if it's
> alright ... the initiatives tend to come from the people and then
> the Team provides support. (Pastoral Assistant, Congregation A)

The idea 'for the day centre] developed gradually. We suggested
it to [pastor] and he accepted it and then we prayed for it.
(Welfare Officer, Congregation B)

This is a very creative place ... the community is not rigid. You
can start things if you want to. (Lay Leader, Congregation D)

The result was that, provided certain minimum liturgical needs
were met, the rest of a congregation's activities were largely ones
developed on an *ad hoc* basis by individuals with particular preferences. For example:

I started to look at what was needed in the area in the way of
accommodation ... The work slowly built up ... I explained the
problem to the priest who ... went to a special fund and got three
years' funding for me to do 20 hours a week ... This way I'm doing
what I love doing. (Social Welfare Worker, Congregation A)

In June 1968, the Lord revealed to me to start a meeting for
prayer every Tuesday night ... I lead the group ... There has been
a meeting every Tuesday since I started it. (Prayer Band Leader,
Congregation B)

I started the Prayer Link ... It grew out of my other caring
activities for the church ... It's a major commitment. (Prayer Link
Coordinator, Congregation C)

On Tuesday nights, I run a forum to explore new age ideas ...
I love new ideas ... It's supposed to be under the wing of the
synagogue but they leave me alone. It's my little thing. (Forum
Coordinator, Congregation D)

While this kind of *ad hoc* development of activities was functional
in meeting individual self-development needs, encouraging innovation and ensuring a wide range of activities in congregations,
it often flew in the face of secular norms of rational planning as
well as instructions from denominational structures. As in the
Norwegian churches studied by Hernes (1996) which consistently
failed to undertake the post-baptismal education their denomination required, case congregations only conformed with instructions from their denominations if they had people who were

willing to take responsibility for ensuring the instructions were carried out.

Even where people did take on responsibilities, the essentially voluntary nature of congregations meant that there were limitations on the degree of monitoring that could be done. If people failed to do things they had promised, or did them incompetently, there was little that could be done.

> It's very arbitrary as to how things get done. It depends on who happens to chair a group as to whether items for action are in fact followed up and acted on ... Some of the committee chairmen are just not up to leadership roles. (Congregation D)

Of the four congregations studied, only in Congregation B was there any overt attempt at monitoring; this was done by the pastor and was facilitated by the small size of the congregation and its fundamentalist underpinning religious principles which gave him great authority. Lay people in Congregation B were given responsibilities on the recommendation of the pastor and only when their ability to carry them out had been tested and established and when they could be trusted to work in accordance with congregational norms. The Pastor explained his viewpoint:

> Every person who is a Head of Department should know the Word enough to be able to know what to do ... People are responsible to God, not to me ... if they don't do it properly, they have to answer to God. (Pastor, Congregation B)

Practical Constraints

The literature on secularization (referred to in Chapter 1) juxtaposes religious principles with 'rational', 'secular' ones and conveys a picture of religious people and organizations under seige from secularizing tendencies. Other writers have talked about the difficulty of reconciling 'authentic' religious goals with the practicalities of organizational survival. To some extent both of these earlier findings were confirmed in the case studies. Ministers and lay leaders in all four of the congregations described how the exigencies of modern, secular society placed constraints on the extent to which religious goals could be wholeheartedly implemented.

In Congregation B, which is a manifestly evangelizing congregation always hoping for new converts, an interviewee explained how cautious they were, in practice, when dealing with potential members who were not Afro-Caribbean.

> We witness to everybody [tell people about Christianity and pentecostal religion] but we are careful if they are not black ... there are two women who were brought up as Catholics and they have been coming to the church and they have been born again. But their husbands are against what they are doing and we would not encourage the splitting of a family. We told the women to pray and witness away from the church. (Congregation B)

At the time of the study, Congregation C was also making a pragmatic adaptation of goals to meet 'realities'. The vicar and Church Council were aiming to increase the membership of the church by getting more people 'over the threshold' because:

> ... you can get people to come to services by making other activities welcoming. (Lay Leader, Congregation C)

However, the congregation's social activities were seen as a competition by the neighbouring community centre and there was growing ill feeling. Thus, Congregation C leaders were facing the possibility of curtailing their own evangelizing efforts in order to retain an amicable relationship with the community centre. This mirrored the experience of Congregation A when it proposed to provide meals for homeless people on its own premises; it was obliged to institute a soup run instead:

> It [feeding the homeless] was difficult to get it off the ground ... it was not very welcome here ... The residents would be worried about the effect on their property values of having down and outs and drug addicts around. (Congregation C)

These examples illustrate the point that, as part of 'civil society' congregations are obliged to take into account the wishes and needs of their geographical and organizational environment. Some lay interviewees were frustrated by this pressure to take a pragmatic approach to the implementation of congregational goals.

[There] should be more attempt to explain things, even if it means upsetting people ... People lack basic religious knowledge. (Congregation A)

Also, to the extent that they saw 'imperfect' behaviour apparently condoned, individual congregants were discontented.

You used to have to come to church to have your child baptized. Now ... things have become very lax. (Congregation C)

Quite a few get converted just for the marriage ... This upsets me ... I think people should be vetted more appropriately. I'd make the selection tougher. They make it too easy. (Congregation D)

... religious ignorance ... The lay leadership compound the difficulties because they themselves do not go to synagogue and they only pay lip service to education. They are not giving *religious* leadership. (Congregation D)

Thus, in the face of secular pressures, all four of the congregations had moved to some extent towards compromise, even Congregation B which was the 'strictest' of the four case congregations. Congregants and ministers differed as to the extent to which they felt this went beyond acceptable limits.

Financial Constraints

Although goal implementation in the four congregations was limited by resource availability, the main issues as seen by interviewees were more complex than just *lack* of resources.

At the time of the study, Congregation D was engaged in a major internal debate about how to make plans in the light of the adverse effect of the recession on members' ability to maintain their subscription payments on which the synagogue was totally dependent. The membership was growing at the same time as an increasing proportion of members were asking to pay reduced subscriptions. This raised questions not only about the feasibility of redeveloping the building, but also about the ability of the congregation to maintain its existing level of activities and staffing. In Congregations A and C, too, one of the key issues perceived by lay leaders was about raising awareness of the cost of running a congregation and about increasing voluntary contributions.

> You cannot get through to parishioners that they should pay for the use of rooms in the presbytery. We ask for donations but they only ever give small amounts on a one-off basis. (Lay Leader, Congregation A)

> They think they can just put 10p in the plate each week. People have to learn to make realistic contributions. (Lay Leader, Congregation C)

Raising awareness about costs of supporting a congregation was less of an issue in Congregation B, which, although it was a very small congregation serving people of modest income, had secured, and continued to secure, large contributions from its members.

> We started the building of the church in faith ... [Pastor] told people that they should lend their savings to the church. ... All the buildings were bought without mortgages through the gifts and loans of members ... Everything collected is used for running costs or outside work. Some people tithe one tenth of their income. But nobody puts pressure ... Everyone knows what is required. (Lay Leader, Congregation B)

Members of Congregation B covered their own costs for participation in church activities; those who arranged flowers bought the flowers themselves, the Music Director bought her own music, and a Sunday School Teacher said that she paid to attend training courses. Even missionary trips abroad to found new congregations were generally self-funded; in exceptional circumstances, a special church collection would be made to help.

> You pay for yourself [to go on missionary trips] if you can. It's not the church's responsibility ... If it's your will to preach, you should do what you can for the Lord. (Lay Member, Congregation B)

Even in Congregation B, however, there were concerns that some members – young adults in particular – were not sufficiently aware of the real costs of sustaining the activities which they enjoyed participating in.

The younger people have everything on a plate ... They are saved but they will not put the Lord's work first. They have the spiritual experience but they are more materialistic ... They will not limit their spending to give money to the church (Lay Leader, Congregation B)

In short, lack of financial resources was generally seen as being a result of lack of realism and lack of commitment by the bulk of congregation members. Those who knew the true costs of running a congregation emphasized the need for all members of congregations to have a sense of responsibility and ownership.

Dissent and Uncooperativeness

As discussed earlier, dissenters from broad congregational purposes do not usually remain within a congregation. On the other hand, it is not uncommon for both lay and ministerial members of congregations to have strong reservations about lower-level, 'operational' goals and, especially where they occupy key positions in a congregation, such people may constitute obstacles to goal implementation. Perhaps because of religious-based norms about consensus, dissenters often do not make their opposition explicit. Instead they impede goal implementation by failing to cooperate, to support colleagues, or to give necessary time and attention. Thus, a priest in Congregation A explained the difficulty of getting cooperation in some activities from other priests:

We are used to one person reaching the decision and the rest have a bargain to absolute obedience. But they moan about the decision and won't take responsibility for it. (Priest, Congregation A)

Opting out of this kind by a figure crucial to goal implementation was also described by lay people in Congregation D:

[The Rabbi] cannot fight everything. He walks away from things. (Congregation D)

Lay people can also actively impede implementation of goals with which they disagree. Thus, interviewees in Congregation C described how older members of the congregation were indicating their disapproval of some activities sponsored by younger people, by withdrawing from activities and voluntary commitments which they had hitherto undertaken willingly, such as tending the church gardens and cleaning the hall. The younger people were then forced to take on these duties themselves – at the expense of fulfilling their own priority goals. And in both Congregations A and D, the goal of child education was being sabotaged by parents:

> Gone are the days when the nuns and the priests taught the children ... now you have to pass the faith on yourself. It's difficult for parents to accept this. They feel it cuts back on their Sunday ... they try to fool her [the Head Teacher] by not coming and having excuses. (Congregation A)

> Parents give priority to other things. They say 'I didn't contract to send my child to synagogue on Saturday when I joined'... Parents seem to think they have to give their children religion in the same way as they used to give cod liver oil. They think it's good for the kids but it's not for them. (Congregation D)

It seems that, between 'voice' and 'loyalty' there can be in congregations an intermediate position in which no dissent is expressed but in which full loyalty is withheld.

Coping with Failure

Interviewees in all four of the case congregations referred to the distress they experienced in recognizing areas in which cherished goals had not been achieved, or only partially achieved. It seems that the nature of a religious congregation is that there are a number of goals that are 'givens'; it is not open to a group of leaders to change them, even when they do not have the means to achieve them. For example, if a congregation declares itself to be 'pentecostal', it is committed to evangelization and, in so far as it does not achieve converts, it is 'failing'.

> We have to get more souls in. The most important thing is to get people to repent, for the Kingdom of Heaven is at hand, because if they are not saved they will go to hell. (Lay Member, Congregation B)

Similarly, since great emphasis is placed in both Christianity and Judaism on passing on religious knowledge and tradition to the next generation, churches and synagogues experience as 'a failure' youth or education activities which are not successful.

> You always feel guilty in a church when you have to drop some activity. We used to have a 'Fish Club' for the older children and they kept trying to keep it going but they couldn't ... You feel you've failed. (Lay Leader, Congregation C)

Several further examples of feelings of anxiety or demoralization surrounding the *non*-implementation of goals were cited by interviewees.

> We don't actively welcome people; there should be a positive affirmation that we want them ... it's difficult to rationalize the gospel message if you don't do that. (Lay Leader, Congregation A)

> I hope for growth through youth and adults coming to know Jesus ... but I am not hopeful ... people love pleasure more than God. (Lay Leader, Congregation B)

> The young teenagers drop out and we can't get them back ... We should spend time thinking about this. We've got nothing for them ... the young people are the future. (Lay Leader, Congregation C)

> I've become closer to my own religious roots and I feel strongly about the fact that we are not a learning community ... we don't do enough about adult education. We are not integrating the religious side of our life. (Lay Leader, Congregation D)

More optimistically, an interviewee in Congregation D thought that disappointment was a necessary part of running a vibrant congregation which takes risks and tries new activities:

> We gaze at our navels a great deal ... We are always seeking to push out our horizons and blaming ourselves for our failures. (Lay Leader, Congregation D)

In fact, as the vicar of Congregation C pointed out, the very nature of some congregational goals is that although you are obliged to strive to achieve them, they are in practice unattainable:

This is one of the paradoxes of ministry – you know the goals are unobtainable but you are obliged to strive towards them. ... a favourite occupation for people who leave the ministry is the building trade – people are so desperate to see the fruit of their labours, which you can never do when you are a vicar. (Vicar, Congregation C)

CONCLUSIONS – SETTING AND IMPLEMENTING CONGREGATIONAL GOALS

It was noted in Chapter 3 that all four of the case congregations were committed to five broad goals – liturgical expression of religious commitment; education; welfare provision; organizational continuity; and social integration. This chapter has moved beyond descriptions of goals and analysed the problems and issues confronting the congregations in setting and implementing goals. Problems arose in trying to reconcile mutual aid and commonweal goals; in maintaining longer term perspectives and in choosing between goals and setting priorities. As regards implementation of goals, interviewees identified issues arising from congregations' dependence on individual enthusiasms; the practicalities of organizational survival; financial constraints and individual uncooperativeness.

In broad terms, these data confirm the suggestion made by earlier researchers that difficulties arise as congregations attempt to set and implement goals and that the sheer range and number of goals open to congregations can be problematic. Also as anticipated by the literature, religious norms about consensus – at least in Christian congregations – can militate against open discussion and conflict resolution.

The data also amplify and elucidate earlier findings. For example, there were rarely overt disputes over broader 'banner' or 'mission' goals but numerous problems did arise in relation to 'lower level' or 'operational' goals. It was also apparent that the roots of difficulties in goal setting and implementation often lay not so much in debates about religious principles as in practical considerations, such as the wish to keep to long-term plans in the face of day to day pressures, the necessity of encouraging individual enthusiasms and the need to avoid alienating internal and external interest groups. There was, for example, concern about meeting 'mutual benefit' and 'commonweal' aims as anticipated by earlier writers, but this was not posed as alternative courses or as a religious debate; rather the concern in congregations was how to achieve *both* goals in the face of limited financial and human resources.

At the same time, it seems that religious principles do play an important part in the issues surrounding congregational goals. Mostly, however, they appear to constitute a factor which can *exacerbate* a practical problem and make its solution more intractable, rather than a factor which is an underlying cause. Thus, religious injunctions about caring and neighbourly behaviour aggravate the difficulties of choosing between competing priorities, since choice inevitably involves upsetting somebody. Resisting pressures to respond to short term and immediate demands is harder if the demands are backed up by a religious argument; and not supporting an individual enthusiasm is more difficult if the proposer cites religious motivations. Failures to meet goals – however unachievable they may be in practice – can be especially demoralizing if there are religious principles prescribing those goals.

The material presented in this chapter also provides confirmation of the hypothesis that congregations experience organizational issues which cut across denominational and religious divides. For example, all four of the congregations served as routes to individual self-development for members and all four of them were trying to reconcile this function with the practicalities of congregational goal setting and goal implementation.[4] All four of them faced issues arising from their dependence on volunteers for goal implementation and their need to make pragmatic adaptations to their environments. All four of the congregations were also obliged, in practice, to give organizational maintenance goals priority over longer term goals. Finally, the problem of inherently unachievable religiously based purposes was a matter of concern in all the congregations.

At the same time, the findings provide some pointers to organizational *differences* between congregations. For example, the strict religious values espoused by Congregation B, and the related authoritarian culture, apparently enabled it to avoid some of the organizational issues confronted by the other three congregations; including competition between internal interest groups, difficulties in securing financial and human resources and problems of monitoring. Interviewees in Congregation B stressed congregants' shared understandings of both ends and means.

5

King Pin or Facilitator?
The Ambiguous Role of Ministers of Religion

INTRODUCTION

This chapter continues the examination of organizational issues which arise in congregations by looking at the difficulties faced by religious functionaries ('ministers') in defining and implementing their roles.[1] Issues are analysed under three broad headings: role boundaries; controlling or empowering laity; and struggles for power. A distinction is made throughout between the perceptions of lay people and those of ministers themselves.

The chapter relies heavily on interviews conducted in Congregations A, C and D. Interviewees in Congregation B did talk about the work of the pastor but, for the most part, they did not refer to *issues* or difficulties surrounding the pastor's role. Since interviewees in Congregation B talked openly about other issues they faced, it seems unlikely that this was just a matter of not wanting to open up to an outside researcher. A more plausible explanation is that the role of the pastor was so well understood in Congregation B and that respect for the decisions of the pastor was so great, that it was indeed rare for people to perceive the definition and implementation of the role as 'problematic'.

ROLE BOUNDARIES

Numerous issues were raised in Congregations A, C and D about the definition of ministerial roles; both by ministers themselves and by lay people. As foreshadowed by earlier literature discussed in Chapter 2, many of the concerns focused on the unbounded nature of ministers' roles. Ministers felt that they just did not have sufficient time to encompass all the possible functions that were expected of them and which they wanted to perform. (This perspective was shared by the pastor of Congregation B who spoke about sometimes working a 24-hour day.) Feelings of overload were attributable not just to the multiple and competing demands identified by earlier researchers, but also to ministers' own feelings of obligation to congregants and others.

> Many people see themselves as the only pebble on the beach – they have no idea of the workload being carried. (Priest, Congregation A)

> All the church groups would like me to pop in more ... it affirms their value. (Vicar, Congregation C)

> People expect immediate responses to their personal problems from the rabbi. (Lay Leader, Congregation D)

In the pressure to meet differing expectations, ministers' own priorities could be squeezed out:

> You end up not being able to find any space in your life. At times I feel I cannot take another external demand. (Priest, Congregation A)

> The Rabbi ... does not want the organizational burdens. He feels the weight of people's spiritual needs. He needs a full-time executive. Then he would have more time for religious things. (Lay member, Congregation D)

Inevitably, ministers were constantly overwhelmed by feelings of failure. They knew they could not achieve all the goals that they and their congregations had set for them, yet they could not desist from continuing to strive to meet them.

> You know the goals are unobtainable but you are obliged to strive towards them. (Vicar, Congregation C)

> At first [when I worked in the inner city] I hit the ground running ... They said I was too activist. I had to wake up to the fact that there was no hope of improvement and that survival was the greatest achievement. (Priest, Congregation A)

Some lay people interviewed were sympathetic to the problems faced by clergy in implementing their roles. For example, a lay person in Congregation A described her distress when, by chance, she found the senior priest had had to miss an important diocesan meeting because nobody else could be found on a Saturday afternoon to cook meals for a church event. She felt the answer to this was to have more priests. Similarly, an interviewee in Congregation D said that they needed 'more rabbis doing more hours'. This 'obvious' solution – to have more ministers rather than to think of other possible routes – was congruent with descriptions by ministers themselves of how they coped; they sought collegiate support.

> I have [members of the order] and a spiritual director who I turn to if I feel I am moving to burn-out. (Priest, Congregation A)

> Having colleagues [in the parish team] is very comforting ... the team brings in wider expertise. (Vicar, Congregation C)

They also tried to get lay people to share the burden of their key responsibilities such as pastoral visiting, teaching, preaching and public relations work. However, they rarely tried to divest themselves altogether of routine tasks.

Although there was general empathy amongst lay people for the strains of the ministerial role, many interviewees pointed out that there were some core requisite qualities and tasks for ministers and without them the very organizational survival of their congregations were in jeopardy:

> People do or do not want to go to church because of the personality of the priest ... [Under a previous vicar] we were averaging 100 communicants on a Sunday – purely because you could talk to him. Then ... the church population drifted down until we were under half the numbers. Now we have the new young man. There is an older, female, element in the church who are alienated. (Congregation C)

CONTROLLING OR EMPOWERING LAY PEOPLE?

Interviews indicated that it makes little sense to examine the role of ministers separately from the congregational context. Both the definition and implementation of ministers' roles are affected by, and affect, the roles of lay people. And the difficulties of working out role relationships which arise in most organizations can be intensified in religious congregations where, as suggested in Chapter 2, there can be contested views about the authority of ministers in relation to lay people.

Ministers as Bosses

Irrespective of changing theologies of laity in churches and the fact that rabbis officially carry no 'priestly' authority in synagogues, many lay people retain the view – one universally held by Congregation B interviewees – that their minister should be the congregational 'boss'.

> The laity are used to the paternalistic structure ... so people want the priest to be there patting them on the back and making it respectable ... they feel insecure ... they are not used to taking responsibility. (Lay Leader, Congregation A)

> I'm not used to the modern methods of vicars. Vicars used to be the king pin in a church. (Lay Leader, Congregation C)

> People look to the vicar as the decision-maker ... People don't want to take responsibility. The older generation have known only that way of relating to an authority figure and they could not take the power. (Vicar, Congregation C)

> He [the Rabbi] has the power and the respect. It's important for the synagogue that he's ... a key mover. (Employee, Congregation D)

In some cases these views about the final and superior authority of ministers were rooted in personal interpretations of religious principles; a perspective noted by Gilkey (1994) in which the 'holy' core of the congregation is seen as residing in ministers alone rather than all congregational participants. An interviewee in Congregation D, for example, suggested that congregants tended to see the rabbi as their 'surrogate Jew'; somebody with special authority to carry out religious obligations on their behalf. Similarly, an interviewee in Congregation A referred to the view of some lay people that priests have 'special zapping powers'. A priest in Congregation A talked in similar terms:

> ... the priest as Superman. This is partly a theological problem of people seeing priests as their substitute in all religious matters. Often people want the priest to do things even when they are things they could do themselves – everything from saying prayers to changing a light bulb. (Priest, Congregation A)

For others, the idea of ministers as 'bosses' seemed to be based in more pragmatic considerations; the need for a final point of decision-making within the congregation and the desirability of consensus on key decisions.

> Often I was pushed between [lay employee] and the priests... . As I see it, the priest should say how things are to be done. (Lay Leader, Congregation A)

> We are very dependent on having [Rabbi]'s seal of approval on all we do ... We have to feel we are all going together. We have to have his blessing on major decisions and his commitment. (Lay Leader, Congregation D)

Lay Empowerment

In contrast with those who wanted ministers to be unequivocally 'in charge', there were also those who thought more should be done to empower lay people relative to ministers. This was underpinned by both theological arguments and more secular, egalitarian, arguments.

> We should use the energy of the laity. The idea that Christ is in you through baptism is my particular central thing ... That's why it shouldn't be left to the priests; they don't have a monopoly. (Lay Leader, Congregation A)

> It is important for the priest to consult key people in the congregation when decisions are being taken involving financial expenditure or worship or the organization of the church ... The priest must see himself as part of it, rather than the boss. It is not a matter of the priest administering to the people ... the church *is* the people. (Lay Leader, Congregation C)

People think that because [Rabbi] says x, then x is right. We have to learn that he is not always right. (Lay Leader, Congregation D)

The Chair of the Parish Council in Congregation A emphasized the importance of providing organizational structures which facilitate lay empowerment. For example, having priests chair meetings inhibits laity:

> If a priest is in the chair, people will just accept everything he says and decides. When you have a lay person, you get far more arguments to the chair. (Lay Leader, Congregation A)

In the case of the synagogue, which had an elected lay council which employed the rabbi, the ambivalence of lay people about the relative authority of the rabbi was a constant theme in interviews. On the one hand, there was respect for the rabbinical role. At the same time, lay people were aware of the rabbi's position as their employee.

> I don't know who the Rabbi reports to. Nobody assesses him. My fees pay his salary ... There should be an appraisal scheme for him. (Lay Member, Congregation D)

Ministers' Confusion

Ministers themselves seemed confused about their authority relative to lay people. They generally espoused both democratic ideals and liberal theologies about lay people.

> We have to learn to empower people. This is an important theological point ... The more active the laity the better. (Priest, Congregation A)

> The Rabbi interprets his role such that there is more sharing of tasks than would be considered rabbinic elsewhere ... He sees the rabbi as a facilitator and empowerer. (Employee, Congregation D)

Yet they found it difficult to work out the practical implications. Thus, a Lay Leader in Congregation A pointed out that the priests consistently made decisions about matters such as the physical fabric of the church and long-term planning without consulting the Parish Council. He concluded that:

The priests have to learn that sanction and discussion are necessary. Priests come and go – the PC provides continuity ... changes
must meet parishioners' needs. (Lay Leader, Congregation A)

This can be contrasted with the viewpoint of a priest in Congregation
A who, after emphasizing the importance of lay empowerment,
regretted that lay people 'make themselves dependent'. He felt that
his attempts to empower lay people were limited by lay passivity and
that this was a matter of class and education; that the less educated
people were, the more likely they were to hold priests in awe:

People around here do not think of themselves as having abilities;
they discount their own competence. (Priest, Congregation A)

Similarly, an observer of Congregation C, who was also committed
to ideals of lay involvement, argued that Congregation C needed a
'strong, pro-active clergyman' because it did not have 'many
people who can take initiatives on their own'. He recognized this as
a dilemma in the context of a drive to lay empowerment and
described it as follows:

How do you sustain an organization in a way which enables
people to do things themselves? The Church has not been good
at this outside of the middle classes ... You must not be patroniz-
ing. (Congregation C)

In Congregation C, the new vicar had, in fact, taken *back* from the
laity a task which they had done themselves up to then: visiting
families who wanted their children baptized. At a Church Council
meeting, a lay member of the council suggested that he might like
some lay help with the visiting. The vicar declined the offer saying,
'It's something I enjoy.'
      The ambivalence of ministers about lay roles was reflected in
aspects of their working styles. Several lay interviewees noted that
the basic expectation in their congregations was that lay people
would adapt to ministers' working methods rather than the other
way round.

Nothing is ever planned very far ahead unless I raise it ... Often
the priest will tell me 15 minutes before the service that there
are going to be baptisms. I can cope but other people might

not be able to work in this casual fashion. (Music Director, Congregation A)

We've had to adapt ... [Present Vicar] is a business person; he likes it all done well. [Previous Vicar] got things done after he dealt with other priorities ... You have to work at it. It's easier when there's a pleasant working relationship. (Lay Leader, Congregation C)

The main difference between me and the rabbi is that he's process-driven whereas I am task-driven. I think I've moved towards his approach ... but he has not moved towards me. (Lay Leader, Congregation D)

The need for congregants to adapt to ministers, is symbolized perhaps in the following observation:

He [the Vicar] has some bad habits, like walking away from people while he is talking to them so that they have to follow him around. (Lay Leader, Congregation C)

Lay people were sometimes left with the impression that, insofar as they were given more power, it was because of necessity rather than conviction on the part of ministers:

Laity are demanding more participation and are doing more. At the same time, the number of priests is dwindling. So they are forced to let the laity do more. (Lay Leader, Congregation A)

A Time of Transition?

Although this pull between empowerment and control of laity was framed as a class issue in Congregations A and C, the finding of a similar tension in Congregation D, which had a predominantly middle class membership, suggests that there are factors intrinsic to modern congregations which make it especially difficult to resolve the dilemma. This may be a transitional period in which old certainties about the authority of clergy and rabbis have been eroded by democratic ideologies, new theological interpretations, shortage of ministers and secularization trends. However, neither ministers nor lay people have yet been able to wholeheartedly embrace the

full practical implications of the changes. At the point of implementation, it seems, ministers may have reservations about sharing
power with lay people. As an observer of Congregation D pointed
out, control is an easier option, at least in the short term:

> It's easy for a rabbi to draw firm task boundaries. This gives him
> control and something to show for the salary he's paid. (Employee,
> Congregation D)

And, as one of the priests in Congregation A admitted, not everybody is comfortable with the practice of democracy:

> ... most people who go in to the religious life are introverted ...
> they may think democracy is a good idea but they find it difficult
> in practice. Their instincts tell them to go it alone, to be a prophet.
> (Priest, Congregation A)

Equally, many lay people are ambivalent about acquiring responsibilities and power from clergy:

> Attitudes to the priesthood are complicated. Most people are
> friendly and respectful, but there can be tensions. There are
> people who like the priest to be on a pedestal – provided that
> they can kick the pedestal. (Priest, Congregation A)

This ambivalence of lay people could make clergy even more
uncertain about the nature and boundaries of their own roles. The
vicar of Congregation C felt:

> You are always eking out a role for yourself and pushing yourself
> in to situations where people are uncertain as to whether they
> really want you there or not ... You know you have the right to be
> there and you are seen as 'the vicar' but there is also concern
> about your role and your identity. (Vicar, Congregation C)

STRUGGLES FOR POWER

The Christian Congregations

As earlier writers have pointed out, Christian congregations may
have theologically-based norms which emphasize the importance

of consensus and discourage explicit protest. Thus, despite the existence in Congregations A and C of concerns about the nature of the clerical role and the relative authority of clergy and laity, these were not generally reported as being expressed in overt struggles or public arguments. However, interviewees indicated that significant struggles *had* taken place between clergy and laity and that those struggles were ongoing and concerned a range of issues including liturgical and other directly religious matters. An interviewee in Congregation C contrasted the power balance under the current vicar with the situation when the church was led by a curate:

> Twenty years ago they [lay leaders] thought they could dominate the curates – they would suggest how things should be done. (Lay Leader, Congregation C)

Another interviewee in the same congregation confirmed that the balance of power was now on the side of the vicar. She recalled recent 'discussions' about the organization of the Sunday School:

> He [the Vicar] chose the new syllabus. He presented it diplomatically, but we knew we would have to do it. Vicars always get their own way ... If there is an argument, the clergy view usually dominates. (Congregation C)

There had also been differences of opinion between clergy and laity in Congregation C over the form of healing services. Again, the Vicar's wishes had prevailed but several lay interviewees talked nostalgically about how 'beautiful' the services had been when they were informal and under lay direction.

A member of the Parish Council in Congregation A described himself as engaged in a long-standing, albeit quiet, battle with the priests over lay power:

> They [priests] don't realise that laity want to participate. ... I have chiselled away at them to get them to give more power to lay people. (Lay Leader, Congregation A)

This same interviewee also described being 'incensed' when the Parish Council were faced with a *fait accompli* on an important issue:

I thought it smacked of paternalism and I told [Priest] so. (Lay Leader, Congregation A)

The Synagogue

In Congregation D, the struggle for power between the rabbi and lay people was openly and extensively discussed. There are a number of possible reasons for this. Perhaps it was due to the culture of the synagogue which was not tied in to Christian theological norms; or perhaps it was because the researcher, being Jewish herself, was seen as less of an 'outsider' there than in the other three case congregations. Another possibility, which emerged from the interviews, was that the issue – by chance – was so much alive in the congregation at the time of the study that interviewees felt unable to consider organizational aspects of the congregation without referring to the power struggles taking place.

It seemed that the organizational structure of Congregation D was such that struggles between lay people and the rabbi were more likely to arise there than in Congregations A and C. In the latter two cases, the *official* structure gave unequivocal final authority to clergy; a point of reference in cases of major dispute. In the case of Congregation D, this was not the case. Control of all resources rested with the elected lay leaders and they also had responsibility for the hiring and firing of staff, including the rabbi. Juxtaposed with this 'rational legal' authority of the lay leaders was the 'traditional' and 'charismatic' authority of the rabbi.[2] Both parties were potentially powerful and there was no official point of final decision-making. An interviewee summarized a long-standing confusion:

> There is a big question about who is the leader – the rabbi or the chairman. I've never worked out what are the respective roles of the rabbi and the chairman … if I had been chairman, I would have disagreed a lot with [Rabbi] but I would have been unsure about whether I had the right to assert my view. (Congregation D)

As in the other case congregations, the working assumption seemed to be that key decisions would be made by consensus. But interviewees suggested that, historically, the degree to which this had been the case had varied according to the personality and work style of lay leaders. One interviewee described how a period of the rabbi and the chair being in accord and 'doing whatever they liked', was followed by a period in which a new chair had 'continuous rows' with the rabbi. The new chair used his power of veto over resources to control the rabbi during his period of office, although he refrained from *public* dispute with him:

> The rows mostly took place in private – you cannot defeat or control the rabbi in public ... He has a special status. (Congregation D)

As to the power struggle taking place in Congregation D at the time of the study, interviewees offered several explanations. One interviewee gave an analysis which was a reverse image of the situation described by Congregation A and C interviewees, suggesting that the struggles in Congregation D were due to the 'autocratic' work style of the *lay* leadership; a style which did not fit with the 'demand for openness and sharing' coming from the rabbi. Like several others, this interviewee thought that the autocratic style was borrowed from the world of small professional businesses from which most of the lay leaders were drawn.

> There are a lot of solicitors and accountants ... If they do manage staff they tend to be very autocratic ... They don't understand about motivating people and thanking them. (Congregation D)

In interview, the rabbi explained why 'autocratic' lay leadership was a problem; he referred to the interdependent nature of the rabbi's and chair's roles which, in his view, necessitated 'team work' and 'a shared sense of responsibility' between lay leaders and rabbi:

> The metaphor of the relationship between a rabbi and his community as a marriage is a strong one ... I don't have strong boundaries as a rabbi. At the same time, I need to be responsive to the community and so I need to build a partnership with the Chairman and the Council. They represent the needs of the community. (Rabbi, Congregation D)

The rabbi saw the prime goal of the synagogue, as well as the core of his own role, as ultimately about the implementation of *Judaism*.

As he was the expert on that subject, he felt that he should be able to have the final say in all matters to do with the synagogue. He had, he said, 'a closed conception' about 'the centre' of his role. Since many of the lay leaders at the time of the study were not very 'religious', they frequently differed from him in their assessment of priorities and, since they held key resources, they could override the rabbi as they wished. This was not something he could accept without protest.

In short, the rabbi's explanation reflected the debate about religious 'authenticity' which was referred to in Chapters 1 and 2. His view that there was a link between the core of the religious functionary's role and the broad purposes of the congregation, was one that was not contentious in the other three congregations studied. Indeed, the idea of the clergyman's role as the authentic expression of congregational goals was explicitly voiced by interviewees in Congregation B who frequently referred the researcher to the pastor for a definitive answer to her questions. In the other two congregations, A and C, the idea was rarely expressed in this way, but the tenor of interviewees' comments implied that this was taken for granted; even amongst those who were chafing against clerical control over laity.

Thus in terms of overt struggles for power between ministers and lay people, Congregation B was at one extreme with the pastor unequivocally dominant and no apparent signs of dissent from lay people, and Congregation D was at the other extreme with the rabbi's power in practice contingent on lay leaders' wishes. This was despite the fact that both congregations had similar organizational structures; they were autonomous units financially dependent on their members. Congregations A and C were between these two extremes with relative power changing according to issues and incumbents.

CONCLUSIONS – AN AMBIGUOUS ROLE?

This chapter has analysed the perceptions of interviewees about the issues that arise in congregations around the implementation of the roles of religious functionaries, under three broad themes: role boundaries; controlling or empowering laity; and struggles for power. As in earlier studies, role overload was widely seen as a key problem by both ministers and lay people. Ministers found it difficult to balance the numerous demands placed on them by their congregants and by their own professional and religious ideals. Difficulties in the relationship between lay people and ministers were also widespread in three of the congregations.

The fact that similar problems were *not* apparently experienced in Congregation B was also instructive. Thus, in addition to confirming earlier findings, the data from the case congregations provide some new insights into the problems surrounding the roles of congregational ministers.

New Insights

First, because they include the views of lay people as well as ministers, and because they set the problems within a congregational context, the data give a more rounded perspective. Whereas earlier literature generally painted a picture of misunderstood and isolated ministers, the data here indicate that lay people in congregations often have a fairly clear understanding of the problems ministers face and even empathize with them. At the same time, they see that congregational organizational needs are not easily reconciled with the personal and professional needs of ministers.

The data here also point to a link between congregational goals and the role of ministers. Embodying and representing the broad religious purposes of the congregation may be seen by lay people and ministers alike as a key function for ministers. A consequence of this is that ministers may feel tied to goals which are inherently unachievable but which they are powerless to change or abandon. Another is that debates between ministers and lay people can be seen as 'bottom line' struggles over the right to direct, or interpret the 'mission' of the congregation. In this way, feelings of failure and tension may be built into the ministerial role.

A third contribution of the case study data is to explicate the causes, nature and dynamics of those struggles for power between ministers and lay people which have been noted in the earlier literature but not explained. The findings indicate, for example, the wide range of views about the relative authority of ministers and lay people which can exist within the same congregation; views which may be rooted not only in religious perspectives but also in opinions about organizational appropriateness or in fear of change. The findings also suggest that both ministers and lay people may face confusion about implementing approaches to lay empowerment to which they have committed themselves in principle. This appears to be a period of transition in which traditional models of ministerial power have been eroded but in which implementation of new approaches is proving problematic.

A related finding from the case studies is that lay leaders are generally keen to reach consensus with their ministers on important issues; and, equally, ministers need the support and approval of lay leaders and other congregants to implement their roles effectively. Many of the issues raised by interviewees were about the negotiation of what appeared, in practice, to be an essentially *interdependent* relationship.

Common Issues?

To what extent, then, does the material presented in this chapter confirm the hypothesis about organizational commonality between congregations? The issues perceived to surround the implementation of the minister's role were similar in Congregations A, C and D. On the other hand, interviewees in Congregation B mostly perceived few issues in this area. One possible explanation for this difference is that the strict religious principles which underpinned Congregation B had an important impact on the definition and implementation of its minister's role; they discouraged lay people from questioning or debating. This explanation is consistent with data presented in the previous chapter on goal setting and implementation. If organizational decisions and procedures are regarded as expressions of God's will and if the minister is seen as an interpreter of God's will, this is not conducive to debate, and certainly not to open dispute.

The idea that underlying religious values impact on the way in which roles and role relationships are perceived in congregations is given further support by the differences which emerged in this chapter between Congregation D, on the one hand, and Congregations A and C, on the other hand. These were mostly differences of degree rather than substance, but they were noticeable all the same. Thus it appeared that Congregations A and C, in which the official, theologically based, stance was that clergy were the final point of authority and that conflict should not be necessary, were able to avoid some of the more acrimonious disputes about the ministerial/lay relationship which arose in Congregation D. In the latter case, official statements, grounded in traditional religious ideas of the rabbi as a teacher rather than a priest, were equivocal about the relative authority of lay people and could not, therefore, provide a basis for conflict resolution or consensus building.

Cultural factors might also help to explain some of the differences. For instance, with respect to Congregation D, the tradition of disputation amongst Jews dates back to biblical narratives in which even God is not immune to being questioned as to purpose and policy. The recent history of Anglo-Jewry provides numerous examples of disputes between rabbis and lay leaders over who should control whom (Goulston, 1968; Newman, 1977). In the case of Congregation B, on the other hand, the fact that the pastor was male whereas the overwhelming majority of the congregants were women, and the fact that practically the whole congregation was Afro-Caribbean, might have been factors particularly conducive to a strong role for the pastor.

In sum, the findings presented in this chapter have gone beyond confirmation of the earlier literature on clergy roles and added new perspectives and possible explanations. The findings have also provided further evidence that congregations of different religions and denominations can experience very similar organizational problems. At the same time, they also indicate that differences in underlying religious principles and cultural differences can be reflected in *differences* in organizational experiences between congregations, irrespective of formal polities.

6

Willing Spirits?
The Position of Lay Staff and Volunteers

INTRODUCTION

In the previous chapter it was suggested that the roles of religious functionaries are in practice interdependent with the roles of lay people in a congregational context. The ability of ministers to deal with multiple and competing expectations, and the power that they are able to exercise, are contingent to a large extent on the attitudes and actions of lay people in the congregation and the negotiations that take place between them. Yet the role of lay people in a congregational context has barely been mentioned by earlier researchers, in sharp contrast with the interest shown by both social scientists and theologians in the role of religious functionaries.[1] This chapter, then, looks at issues surrounding the roles of lay people in the case congregations. It examines both those lay people who are paid employees and those who are involved on a voluntary basis.

As in the previous chapter, there is heavy reliance on data gathered in Congregations A, C and D. Congregation B had no lay employees. More importantly, interviewees in Congregation B generally did not see the implementation of lay roles as problematic. There seemed to be a number of reasons for this. One was the power exercised by the pastor and a few senior lay people ('deacons' and 'deaconesses'). Once roles were defined by the pastor and people were allocated to those roles, there was little likelihood of questioning or dispute.

Everybody knows their job ... It's a strict mental thing.

The leaders tell us what to do. We can't do anything on our own.

The power of the pastor and the respect he enjoyed was rooted in a fundamentalist religious outlook which emphasized both the need to work in accordance with God's will and the key role of the pastor in interpreting that will.

> God has given us a vision of progress for all mankind. We have to cooperate with him with a willing spirit to get order, harmony and right.

> We wait for [Pastor] to tell us what is God's will.

Congregation B also had a well understood system of lay 'apprenticeship' which enabled people to slowly work upwards from simple tasks to more complex responsible ones. This, combined with the fact that membership of the congregation was for many people a way of life which accounted for most of their non-working hours, ensured that problems of recruitment and monitoring were minimized or prevented from arising. One interviewee described how she eventually became the congregation's Treasurer:

> I was growing in the spirit and people noticed the gift in me. I asked if I could help to clean the church ... this was the only time that I ever asked if I could do something. Since then, I have always waited to *be asked* to do things ... [She was asked to do more and more responsible tasks in the Sunday School] Everything my hand could touch, I did ... [She was asked to be Church Treasurer] By this time, I was filled with the spirit. I thought I was not able to do it, but they said, 'yes, you can' ... I had never even used a bank paying-in book.

LAY VOLUNTEERS[2]

Different Kinds of Commitment

In each of Congregations A, C and D interviewees distinguished between two different kinds of volunteers. On the one hand, there was a group of lay people who were seen to take on major responsibilities and do the majority of the time-consuming unpaid work.

> The people who volunteer [for onerous positions] are the key factor in how the parish works; they are the intermediary between the priests and the less involved laity. (Priest, Congregation A)

> There's an inner group of willing people ... the burdens fall on a small group of people. (Lay Leader, Congregation C)

> A lot of people do a huge amount behind the scenes in their committee roles ... the synagogue's lucky to have them. (Lay Member, Congregation D)

Some of these volunteers were essentially in 'governance' roles, for example as members of boards, committees or councils, and were often referred to as 'lay leaders'. Others were primarily concerned with 'operational' work, such as providing care services of various kinds, teaching, organizing social activities, or providing musical accompaniment for religious services. Still others took on 'support' functions such as fundraising, secretarial assistance, editing the congregation newsletter, maintaining the physical fabric of buildings, or assisting ministers during acts of worship.

In addition to this identifiable group of 'senior' volunteers, there was also in each congregation a large number of other members who were committed to voluntary work of some kind but who generally worked fewer, less regular, hours and were not regarded as part of the 'inner circle' of highly active members.

> There are little groups that do things like cleaning, flowers and collections. Everything is very informal. (Congregation A)

> There are separate rotas for cleaning, flowers and doing the coffee after the service and a rota of people who unlock the church and set up the altar. (Congregation C)

> The total number of people involved is high. A lot of people do little jobs ... (Congregation D)

Although interviewees drew a distinction between these two kinds of volunteering, they also tended to distinguish between volunteers as a group on the one hand, and the less involved congregation members on the other hand; those who did not, or could not, make any kind of time contribution.

> Many people in the parish do not realize how much has to be done ... for many people the parish is a railway station – they

come and they go and they don't ask to help ... they don't see it as 'my church and I must keep it going'. (Priest, Congregation A)

We have nurses, secretaries, financial consultants and book keepers amongst our young people who have the talent which could be put to the use of the church. But many are not converted. They come when they feel like it. (Lay Leader, Congregation B)

There are a lot of people who are content to sit back and let others do things. They say 'Why don't *they* do this or that?' (Lay Leader, Congregation C)

In Congregation C, it was felt that there were just insufficient people willing or able to make a contribution. Involving men was a particular problem:

I don't know why it has become an Anglican tradition to have women mostly active ... The men are unwilling to get drawn in. It's a vicious circle. As soon as an able bodied man appears, he is pounced on to do everything ... they feel threatened. (Lay Leader, Congregation C)

Thus, problems of volunteer recruitment emerged as a central issue in the congregations.

Recruitment and Retention of Volunteers

The need for continuous support and encouragement for lay volunteers was emphasized, both to recruit them in the first place and then to retain them:

... those who are not bold get lost ... people need a specific invitation to be involved in something. (Congregation A)

Lots of things cannot happen ... without nurturing ... But if you do that, many people ... can do wonderfully well. (Congregation C)

People don't come forward. They have to be identified and encouraged. (Lay Leader, Congregation D)

This required a great deal of tact and sensitivity on the part of existing senior volunteers, ministers and lay paid staff. Interviewees described the skill of discovering potential and fitting people to appropriate tasks and roles:

> ... drawing people in is an important part of the priest's role ... shy people want a specific task rather than to be invited to join in a group ... for religious tasks I look for people with a long term commitment who are acceptable to the congregation. (Priest, Congregation A)

> [Vicar] encourages people to do things ... He identifies their gifts and what they can contribute ... Each person has their own gift and role. There are many forms of ministry. (Lay Leader, Congregation C)

> Everybody has a unique talent; we have to help people make a splash ... We have to recognize different motivations. Some people are looking for individual rewards and others want to be a cog in a wheel. (Lay Leader, Congregation D)

Congregation C had responded to the difficulties of recruiting and retaining lay volunteers by setting up rotas for a wide range of tasks including Sunday School teaching and being the Verger. They had found that people who would otherwise refuse to do any voluntary work were willing to take on small parts of a role, or to take their turn in the performance of that role.

The fact that the approach to a potential volunteer was for a religious purpose was also often helpful in recruiting people:

> I approach them [potential teachers] and ask them to share their love of God and Jesus. I put them with another teacher at first and then gradually encourage them to take small groups aside. (Head Teacher, Congregation A)

> I don't like speaking out in public but you have to do it because it's a commitment. (Lay preacher, Congregation B)

> The church can get people to do things which they would not do for themselves ... You get a spiritual reward when you do things for the church. (Senior Volunteer, Congregation C)

And often volunteers could be recruited at points in their life when they were particularly appreciative of the benefits of congregational membership:

> Some people actively want to put something back into the community because they are grateful for help they've received. (Lay Leader, Congregation C)

> When something happens in peoples' lives – say a death or a barmitzvah – the synagogue touches them and they want to put something back. (Lay Leader, Congregation D)

Despite these special advantages which congregations enjoy in identifying and securing volunteer commitment, the case congregations still had difficulties in recruitment and retention, especially in relation to the more onerous voluntary posts. At the time of the study, Congregations C and D were both experiencing major problems. In Congregation C the problems were thought to be a reflection of the characteristics of congregants. The area had a high proportion of younger households and newcomers to the area:

> There are a lot of deep anxieties there and people are already carrying too much. So they have chronic problems in filling leadership positions. (Congregation C)

In Congregation D the difficulties were attributed mainly to the rapid growth of the congregation which placed particularly heavy responsibilities on members of the lay governing council.

> There is also the increasing size. The reality is you need paid staff to do the jobs. (Employee, Congregation D)

The difficult economic climate was also blamed:

> The recession has a lot to do with it. People have to pay more attention to making a living; or keeping their heads down to keep their jobs. (Senior Volunteer, Congregation D)

These explanations for recruitment problems can be set within the context of other information provided in interviews about the roles of the most senior volunteers.

The Roles of Senior Volunteers

Lay leaders and other 'senior' volunteers in the congregations often found themselves carrying major responsibilities, alone or with little support. For example, they might have responsibility for the continuity of a welfare project, for the supervision of building work, for meeting legal requirements, or for the care of large numbers of children. They could also be placed in the position of having to stand in for other volunteers at short notice. Thus a project in Congregation D to provide weekly lunches and other services for homeless people had thrown up a range of practical problems for the two voluntary coordinators, such as doing large weekly shopping trips and dealing with petty theft and occasional violence on synagogue premises. Many such volunteers felt themselves overwhelmed and overloaded by their congregational commitments.

> I don't think I can take on anything more … I would like to find a place for myself where I can do something without being sucked into the vortex of overload. (Lay Leader, Congregation D)

In Congregations C and D, interviewees expressed resentment at the way in which they had been 'lumbered', 'manipulated' or 'sucked in' to a major voluntary role with no way of leaving without letting down the congregation.

> I got pushed on to the Council and then I got shanghaied into becoming a Warden because [previous Warden] was leaving … It's the hardest job in the world to find somebody to be Warden. (Lay Leader, Congregation C)

> One of the reasons why lay people won't come forward is that they get manipulated into doing more than they intend and then they get burnt out. (Employee, Congregation D)

In addition to feeling burdened by the extent and depth of their voluntary responsibilities, senior volunteers can find themselves torn between their congregational commitment on the one hand, and loyalty to their families, friends and paid work, on the other hand.

> My work for the church takes up the whole of Sunday and some evenings. Sunday is difficult. Saturday is a big night out and I stay

up to 8.00 am and then I'm at [Congregation A] all day. Monday
is bad. (Young, single, Senior Volunteer, Congregation A)

If I was not single, I could not do this. My whole life is work and
church ... I talked to the Lord about it about ten years ago
because I was trying to do so much and the Lord opened a door
for me ... now I do temporal work only on three days a week.
This gives me enough to live on but I have time for the church.
(Lay Leader, Congregation B)

When I was chairman, there was nothing in my life except
[Congregation D] and work ... my [now adult] children still
resent the time my wife and I put into the synagogue when they
were young. (Former Lay Leader, Congregation D)

Examples were given of what was perceived as *over*-commitment to
the congregation.

There are a number of people who put all their waking hours
into the church. Often this goes beyond what I think is right.
People neglect their families ... out of loyalty to the church.
(Volunteer, Congregation A)

There is a relatively small number of committed people doing
everything – even to the point of making themselves ill ... You
sometimes have to make a choice between caring for the community and caring for yourself as an individual. (Senior Volunteer,
Congregation D)

Management, Control and Support of Volunteers

To what extent can voluntary work be 'managed'? This was a
sensitive issue in the congregations. Many volunteers were motivated by the opportunities for self-fulfilment and autonomous work
provided by their congregations. The corollary was that they did not
expect to be 'managed', 'controlled' or 'monitored'. Yet, not every
volunteer met role expectations and the consequences for congregation organization could not be ignored. Effective performance of a
voluntary role could be crucial to the continuity of a congregation.

If you are the Treasurer and you do not have enough commitment to make sure the subscriptions come in on time, you

[the congregation] get into a bigger and bigger overdraft. (Congregation D)

So could ministers and paid lay staff monitor or give instructions to volunteers? A lay leader in Congregation A criticized what he saw as the 'autocratic' behaviour of lay staff and suggested that some volunteers had left the church after arguments with them. Volunteers could also be resentful about receiving conflicting instructions from ministers and paid lay staff. In fact, as indicated in Chapter 5, lay people varied as to whether they thought it appropriate for ministers to control and supervise work done by lay people in a voluntary capacity. Some lay people seemed to expect close supervision, whilst others found it quite unacceptable to be given instructions by anybody. Nor did they want any kind of 'interference' in what they felt were their areas of competence.

> I have to be careful to ensure that I am in charge of the people on my rota. I don't want the Vicar to give instructions to them about changing things. (Senior Volunteer, Congregation C)

To the extent, then, that they saw themselves as being directed, controlled, or overridden, the loyalty of volunteers could be jeopardized. But interviews suggested that the issue was not only one of how to 'control' volunteers without destroying their commitment. Many expected positive reinforcement and thanks for their efforts and some interviewees were angry that there was insufficient recognition of their work:

> Everybody just assumes that the service sheets will be there when they come to church ... nobody ever inquires about how it gets done. (Senior Volunteer, Congregation C)

> Opportunities to show care and appreciation for voluntary commitment are often lost. (Former Lay Leader, Congregation D)

However much their contribution was recognized, congregational volunteers could suddenly drop out – for personal reasons or because they had taken offence. Volunteers may not feel obliged to 'give notice' and key roles can unexpectedly be left unfilled:

The person who took on Editor of the Newsletter just suddenly dropped it. (Congregation D)

Volunteers who fill key positions or who have scarce expertise may have to be handled with special sensitivity. As has been pointed out in earlier chapters, membership of a congregation is a voluntary status so those who are discontented can choose to 'vote with their feet' if their wishes are not attended to. Thus, in Congregation D a Council discussion about organizational structure was abruptly curtailed when the Secretary-elect said he would not feel able to take up the post unless the debate was resolved in a particular way. As nobody else was available for the post:

That did it. There was no way out. We had to do what he wanted. (Congregation D)

Similarly, Congregation C had had to give priority to buying a new organ when the only available organist refused to play the existing small one any longer.

... he put in an ultimatum for a new organ. At that time, we were trying to raise £50 000 for a church hall. But he said, 'Unless you agree that an organ is the next priority, I will not play.' (Lay Leader, Congregation C)

In short, then, there were strong pressures in congregations *against* controlling volunteers in any overt way. In fact, volunteers generally expected positive reinforcement for what they were doing and could easily be upset by what they perceived as lack of recognition of their contribution.

LAY EMPLOYEES

The focus in this part of the chapter moves from those lay people who did work in their congregations without pay, to those who did receive payment for their work. All those who received payment were, strictly speaking, 'employees' but the extent to which they were regarded and treated as such, and the extent to which they felt themselves to be employees, was itself an issue in the congregations.

The employment situation in each of the four congregations was described in Chapter 3. At the time of the study, Congregation B had no paid lay employees; although the pastor was hoping that it would be possible to make an appointment in the near future to relieve his 'burdens'. In Congregation C, the only widely recognized employee was a part-time cleaner. However, a member of the congregation was also being paid, on an occasional hourly basis, to do gardening and odd jobs – although interviewees were mostly not aware that he was not a volunteer. Conversely, several interviewees were under the impression that the part-time Secretary of Congregation C – who in fact received no payment at all – *was* an employee.

In addition to having several lay people who were 'semi-volunteers' or 'semi-employees' in this same way, Congregations A and D both had several lay people who were unambiguously employees on a full-time or part-time basis. For both of these congregations, having employees was a relatively new experience (within the previous five years); lay people and ministers were still in the process of adapting to their presence. Thus, the issues raised may be seen not only as issues about the roles of lay employees, but also as ones about organizational change in congregations, a topic which will be addressed again in the next chapter. This part of the chapter, then, draws largely on data gathered in Congregations A and D where there were several lay employees. It focuses on issues common to both.

Paying for Work

The appropriateness of paying lay people to do work was a debated issue in Congregations A and D. There was particular concern about the impact of paid staff on the commitment of lay volunteers:

> Volunteers chuck things at the office ... Now that there are staff, the volunteers think that they don't have to do things. (Lay Leader, Congregation D)

An interviewee in Congregation A suggested that employing paid staff had the effect of disempowering lay people and discouraging them from trying to tackle needs and problems on a voluntary basis. He described the impact of the appointment of the Social Welfare Worker:

> The Housing Advice was a group of volunteers but now he's taken it over and it's all dependent on him ... He should be training volunteers to do the work. But he thinks he's the only one who can do it. (Congregation A)

The retreat of volunteers was thought to apply not only to specific tasks but also to policy decisions:

> There are conflicts over room bookings. There is no strategic overview of how the building is used. [Administrator] is left to sort it out. (Lay Member, Congregation D)

Once work previously done by volunteers was paid for, confusion could arise about where the boundary lay between paid and volunteer roles:

> The Administrator feels that she is often asked to do things which should be done by volunteers. (Lay Leader, Congregation D)

In contrast with these views about the negative implications of paying lay people to work, some interviewees saw paying people as an important means of raising the quality of work done, ensuring that responsibilities were accepted, and generally responding to the problems of voluntarism described in the previous part of this chapter.

In both Congregations C and A, discussions about paying people to do work on a part-time basis had taken place prior to the study. In Congregation C the discussions had resulted in appointing a paid cleaner and quietly paying a congregant to 'keep the garden tidy'. Not only had volunteers proved increasingly unreliable for such essential tasks, but also the volunteers had become increasingly resentful about the work they were doing. This had led to acrimony within the congregation and payment was seen as the way of lowering tension. In Congregation A, similar discussions within the Parish Team had led to several part-time paid appointments including a sacristan, a secretary and an organist.

The Senior Priest explained that he saw the transfer of money as a signal that somebody was regarded as responsible for carrying out a particular function and that a high quality of performance was expected:

> It says in effect that we are trusting you to get things done in your own way and in your own time. It makes it clear that the person is officially that ... You can't say to a volunteer 'You're in charge' because all volunteers are equal. (Priest, Congregation A)

He thought that the results of giving payments for work in this way were excellent:

> [The Sacristan) has done well. In eight months she has transformed the church from a dirty and uncared for place ... This is the first time that things have been done properly. (Priest, Congregation A)

A lay interviewee in congregation D made similar points about the symbolic significance of payment for work and he also thought that the congregation's experience in recent years substantiated his viewpoint. Thus, by paying Religion School Teachers, the congregation had secured conformity with its rules and expectations; whereas refusal to pay members of the choir had resulted in a failure to achieve an acceptable standard of music.

> I have always felt it important to value voluntary contributions [but] ... I recognize that there are some things you can only expect if people are paid ... People complain about the quality and attendance of the choir. I say you can only expect reliable attendance and high quality if people are paid to do the job ... It's not money so much. It's the whole issue of dedication and commitment. (Congregation D)

Many of the people paid to do work in Congregations A and D received an honorarium and were not paid 'the rate for the job'. The rationale in both was that it was the payment principle rather than the amount that was important in securing commitment and good quality work. However, in both congregations, there were also employees who *were* paid the 'going rate' for the work they did. Some of the full-time employees in Congregation D were unhappy about what they saw as the blurring of the boundaries between volunteers and employees in this way:

> The synagogue is unprofessional in its ethos. People who are paid should be paid the right rate and volunteers should be recognized. The synagogue tends to merge things ... there are two cultures in the same organization. (Employee, Congregation D)

Another interviewee in Congregation D was very concerned about the cumulative impact of paying people – irrespective of the rate – on the 'voluntary ethos' of the congregation. He talked with disapproval of other synagogues which had created 'bureaucracies' over which lay leaders had little control. He thought that as the congregation spent more and more on paid staff, less and less work was actually done.

Member-employees

In both Congregations A and D, interviewees saw major advantages in having paid employees who were also active members of their employing congregation. One advantage was cost effectiveness.

> I don't mind putting in more hours than I am paid for ... this is my calling – just like a priest. (Employee, Congregation A)

> I am paid at a very low rate and they're getting much more ... I do not see myself as an employee ... it's an honorarium. (Employee, Congregation A)

> I worked 80 hours a week in the first few months ... (Employee, Congregation D)

> Nearly all our paid staff are also members of the community. I see this as a strength as people will do a great deal more than they are paid for out of a feeling for the community. (Lay Leader, Congregation D)

> I don't really work it [hours] out as I would if it wasn't my own community. (Employee, Congregation D)

There were other advantages for congregations in employing their own members. The Social Welfare Worker in Congregation A described how he was able to provide a tailored, accessible advice service to congregants because he knew them personally; he could approach people in church and ask them how they were getting on and people could approach him after services:

> I stand out on the pavement behind the priests so that people can find me. (Social Welfare Worker, Congregation A)

He also suggested that because he was himself a long-standing member of the congregation, he would provide a point of continuity as priests came and went:

> I represent continuity and permanence. I feel a connection to the church. I'll always be in contact … I feel that this is part of me whereas they are serving a period here … I've been here longer than any of them. (Social Welfare Worker, Congregation A)

Despite these perceived advantages, numerous difficulties were thought to surround the dual role of member *and* employee. It was difficult, for example, to issue instructions to such role holders or to control their work in any way. This was especially the case where employees had been members of their congregations prior to becoming employees and were widely known within their congregation.

> I see the lay employees as less accountable than the priests. We've chiselled away at the priests, but paradoxically we cannot get at [lay employees]. (Congregation A)

In the case of Congregation D, there were numerous cross-ties of family and friendship between individual employees, lay leaders and rabbis. The resultant difficulties of management and control led some interviewees to suggest that the member-employee role was unacceptable and that efforts should be made to have clear lines of authority and accountability for lay staff:

> There are a number of very difficult relationships, partly because most of the employees are also members … I do not rule out firing member employees. (Congregation D)

Member-employees could themselves find their position problematic. They were in an ambiguous position relative to other lay members who were, in a sense, their employers. An employee of Congregation D listed a range of difficulties consequent upon being a congregational employee including: not feeling able to attend worship services or social activities because people used the opportunity to raise work matters; a reluctance amongst lay leaders to 'manage' him; and feeling unable to ignore tasks that needed doing.

> My personal life and my work cannot be separated ... I can't just say 'to hell with it'. (Employee, Congregation D)

Organizational Integration

A number of interviewees suggested that the roles of lay employees were not fully integrated into the organizational structures of their congregations; that there was a lack of clarity about where the roles 'fitted' in relation to other congregational roles; where the boundaries of the roles were; what the role expectations were; and to whom employees were accountable.

> There is no clarification of who is my line manager ... I don't feel I have authority. (Employee, Congregation D)

Lay people in Congregation A had difficulty in 'positioning' employees who took on tasks which were formerly performed by priests (for example catechetics and social care). Were they one of the priests or one of the laity? Some parishioners saw such employees as poised between the two groups. Thus they felt able to make complaints or to argue with the lay pastoral assistant in a way which they could not do with the priests, yet they were expecting that she would convey their views to the priests:

> [Pastoral Assistant] is in the firing line of challenge. (Priest, Congregation A)

> [Pastoral Assistant] is a stepping stone to the priests. (Lay Member, Congregation A)

The Pastoral Assistant herself suggested that congregants generally thought in terms of two categories – priests and laity – and that, after initial confusion at the time of her appointment, parishioners saw her as part of the priestly world; even though this was not how she saw herself and it was not the intention of the priests who appointed her:

> There is a sort of line where parishioners are in the world and not just thinking about the church and their religion; and then there's a group of people who are living away from the world [priests] ... I was appointed to be *in* the world and *of* the world but people treat me as though I am one of the religious – they put me across the line. (Pastoral Assistant, Congregation A)

Some lay employees in both Congregations A and D were resentful about assumptions that they would demonstrate a higher commitment to the implementation of their roles than would be expected in a non-congregational context:

> I don't get much social life ... I've given my life to it. It was taken for granted that I would be available when people need me – evenings and weekends. (Congregation A)

> There's an expectation to do more and more. (Congregation D)

In Congregation D, some staff felt that they were not being treated 'as a professional'. This was reflected in a desire for more 'clarity' about matters such as reporting lines, job descriptions, and role boundaries. It was thought that opportunities for supervision, assessment and career progression were also missed.

> Paid jobs have to be clearly delineated and handled in a professional manner. There has to be proper assessment of work done and appropriate behaviour on both sides. (Employee, Congregation D)

> I and the other professional staff are not treated as employees are, or should be, in the big wide world. I feel strongly about this ... there is no evaluation of the way I do my job. (Employee, Congregation D)

CONCLUSIONS – LAY PEOPLE IN THE CONGREGATIONAL SETTING

Although there has been virtually no research interest up to now in the role of lay people in a congregational context (except in relation to the role of ministers), the data presented in this chapter suggest that this is a topic which deserves serious attention from students of organization. The findings indicate that it is not just ministers who have work problems in today's congregations; nor is the picture of ministers faced by demanding and intractable lay people a total perspective. The findings here and in Chapter 5 indicate that lay people too – both employees and volunteers – face a range of problems in implementing their roles and in working out their relationships with each other and with ministers. Moreover, lay people can play a key role in initiating and sustaining congregational activities.

Different Lay Roles

The findings also point to the need to distinguish between the many different roles held by lay people in congregations. From an organizational perspective, 'the laity' are not one collective body. A distinction can be made between paid employees, volunteers, and those who are not involved in congregational work.

Employees may range from full-time paid professionals to those paid an honorarium for occasional work. With respect to the group of people who do work on a voluntary basis in congregations, a distinction can be made between senior volunteers or lay leaders and 'ordinary' volunteers. The case studies demonstrate that these are distinctions made by people within congregations themselves. They also suggest that the issues perceived as surrounding the roles of lay people vary according to which of these groups are being discussed.

Thus the key issues for those who are senior volunteers arise from the heavy responsibilities they carry and the way in which they can be torn between their commitment to their congregation on the one hand, and their loyalty to their families, friends and outside employment on the other hand. Only if these senior volunteers are willing to allow their congregational work to dominate their non-work life, can they cope with the demands without burning out. This seemed to be a point well recognized in Congregation B whose members mostly *did* see the church as the priority in their lives.

For congregations as organizations, the key problems surrounding senior volunteers arise in controlling or managing them and in recruiting them in the face of the evident weight of responsibilities entailed. With regard to other volunteers, however, the main challenges for congregations are in discovering what people can contribute; in motivating them to become involved and to stay involved; and in matching people to tasks. Each of the case congregations had its own ways of recruiting and retaining volunteers but the role of the minister emerged as crucial in all of them. Ministers had well-developed skills in 'discerning' the potential of lay people.

The difficulties congregations face with respect to volunteers mirror those faced by secular agencies; difficulties of recruitment, retention, motivation and management (Pearce, 1993; Thomas and Finch, 1990). But congregations face additional difficulties; for example, the fact that the continuity of a crucial activity may be dependant on the enthusiasm and personal circumstances of just one or two committed people. On the other hand, congregations have the advantage of being able to call on congregants' religious commitment to motivate them to volunteer.

As only two of the case congregations had any full-time paid lay staff, only limited data has been presented on lay employees but it is sufficient to indicate that lay employees in congregations can face a range of competing expectations: that they are especially close to ministers; that they will take over tasks formerly done by volunteers; that they will be available for work matters even when attending congregation events as members; and that they do not need to be 'managed' or assessed. It seems, too, that problems arise in integrating lay employees into congregational organizational structures which primarily comprise lay volunteers and ministerial 'employees'. The implementation of clergy and lay volunteer roles – individually and in interaction – can be fraught with difficulties. The introduction of a third category of organizational actor – the lay employee – intensifies the problems. There seem to be powerful drives to treat lay employees as 'honorary ministers' or 'honorary volunteers', rather than to conceptualize them as a third, distinct, kind of organizational actor.

Cross-congregational Lessons

Although the issues surrounding the roles of lay people varied between the four congregations, when taken together the data in this chapter suggest some lessons that might be useful for other congregations. For example, Congregation C showed how those who are reluctant to volunteer can be involved through participating in rotas. Such rotas can be used to lower the frequency of a time commitment or the degree of responsibility which a volunteer needs to accept. The cases also demonstrate how people can be drawn into volunteering in an incremental fashion, beginning with doing a small bounded task or acting as an occasional 'helper' to an existing volunteer. By taking especial care over 'discerning' individual abilities and potential, congregations were often able to involve and retain the commitment of people who otherwise would not have volunteered their time at all.

At the same time, the data point clearly to the limits of voluntarism in a congregational context. Although many people may be willing to stretch themselves to their limits and to accept instructions because they see their congregational work as essentially furthering religious objectives, congregations cannot afford to ignore the fact that many people are motivated to volunteer because of the opportunities provided for autonomy, self-development and social exchange. There are, therefore, limits on the extent to which congregational volunteers can be controlled, monitored or 'managed'.

7

Taking Things Gradually?
Change, Growth and Organizational Structures

INTRODUCTION

When earlier findings on the organization of congregations were drawn together in Chapter 2, four major themes were distinguished. Two of those themes – organizational goals and the roles of ministers – have now been re-examined drawing on the case studies. This chapter returns to the two other themes identified earlier; organizational change and denominational structures. It also comments on some other issues, broadly to do with organizational structure, raised in the case study interviews. Like the issues surrounding the roles of lay people, congregational structures have been little mentioned by previous researchers.

ORGANIZATIONAL CHANGE

Earlier writers noted the impact of religious values on the scope for organizational change in congregations. The case studies confirmed that organizational change – both its anticipation and its implementation – was problematic in congregations. However, factors additional to religious principles seemed to be important and the extent of difficulties varied according to the type of change being considered; for example, changes in personnel, membership or physical fabric.

Changes in Personnel

The pastor of Congregation B and the rabbi of Congregation D had both been in their posts for many years and neither the period before their arrival nor the prospect of them leaving their congregations were contemplated by interviewees. However, in accordance with the customs and rules of their respective denominations, Congregations A and C had had frequent changes of clergy. In Congregation A, priests were moved regularly; a policy intended to prevent the accumulation of personal power. A senior priest had moved about a year before the case study and there was another change of clerical personnel during the study period. When research access to Congregation C was obtained, a new vicar had been in post for about 6 months. The previous vicar had been moved to another parish and the congregation had been without its own vicar for 18 months. Thus, in both Congregations A and C, issues surrounding change of clergy were at the forefront in many interviews.

Some were concerned about continuity; about the way in which activities or practices established by one priest could be abandoned or radically changed with the arrival of a new incumbent.

> Prophets don't carry people with them ... the decisions are not internalized ... then there is a problem when you leave about continuity. (Priest, Congregation A)

> [Employee] dislikes anything that moves away from the way [previous Priest] did things. (Lay Leader, Congregation A)

> Sick visiting ... doesn't really happen now ... that faded out in [previous Vicar]'s time. (Lay Leader, Congregation C)

Others pointed out how internal interest groups could take the opportunity occasioned by a change of incumbent to demand reconsideration of past decisions with which they disagreed, often opening old wounds.

> The parish is going through a transition at the moment ... the old guard re-establishing themselves. (Congregation A)

In both Congregations A and C, changes introduced by new clergy were seen as problematic. Whilst one group within the congregation might be pleased by new ideas and new ways of doing things, others could be alienated. In Congregation C, for example, those who favoured a 'businesslike' approach to meetings were delighted by changes introduced by the new vicar:

[Church meetings] go on and on with no decisions being reached … Things are better now that we have [new Vicar]. He chairs meetings firmly. (Lay Leader, Congregation C)

But those who enjoyed the old informality in Congregation C were unhappy. They were intending to withdraw from the Church Council at the following election, and were withdrawing from participation in social activities and voluntary work too. They were sceptical about the latest changes:

The changes introduced by the new vicar are excessive … He is just trying to stamp his own authority on things. (Lay Leader, Congregation C)

Changes of lay leaders or key lay employees were also seen as problematic in all the congregations. Resignations could threaten the survival of projects and activities, especially if, until then, they had been driven by just one or two people's enthusiasm.

Many activities feel flimsy. They depend on one or two people and the Council is not behind them. (Congregation D)

In fact, change of any kind in personnel could be seen as threatening by both lay people and ministers; either because it challenged their perception of the way things ought to be run in their congregation, or because it questioned what they saw as their prerogatives:

[When I was appointed, the priests] felt completely threatened. There was also lay fear … . They had been trained against accepting lay workers and women. (Pastoral Assistant, Congregation A)

There was no definite form [for healing services] but we all loved it because it was natural and we all said what we thought. [Previous Vicar] went around and laid hands on people. [New Vicar] did not like the service so now we have a different service. (Lay Member, Congregation C)

[The first time the chairman changed] I had a tremendous shock. I discovered my work was affected by who the chairman was.

Just how enormous this was had never been explained to me when I was in training. The change of chair changes the work of the rabbi. (Rabbi, Congregation D)

As with so many other issues raised in the case congregations, Congregation B seemed to be able largely to avoid the worst impacts of changes in personnel by having a well developed system for recruiting and training successors to existing leaders. On the other hand, it also lost the organizational benefits which can derive from new personnel bringing in new ideas; the emphasis was on doing things in the same way, irrespective of who was in post, and on one generation following on from the previous one by 'apprenticeship'.

[In planning activities] I draw on my own experience in the youth section because I grew up with it. (Youth Leader, Congregation B)

I learned how to do it from being taught myself. (Sunday School Teacher, Congregation B)

Changes in Membership

For Congregations B, C, and D, change in the characteristics of their membership was a major concern. Founder generations were ageing or dropping out of active participation and leadership succession was a problem.

I would like to see the young people [15–30 years] take more initiative ... We started the church when we were middle aged. (Congregation B)

We have lost many of the mature people who were doing work in the church – through moving away or emigration ... now we have young and newer [newly converted] people who are in training. This puts a burden on us. (Congregation B)

We need to do more work with the younger generation of families – the 20–40 age group – so that some will come in to leadership such as wardening ... The older generation is starting to stand aside but the new blood has not yet emerged. (Congregation C)

There's a missing generation of people setting up their careers and their families ... They never go to services and certainly don't go on to the committees. The older people don't know them so they don't approach them and they do not get drawn in. (Congregation D)

Demographic change in a congregation's catchment area or catchment group, whilst beyond control, could pose major challenges. Congregation A had adapted to the waves of immigrants into its area by making a decision to be positively welcoming to all ethnic and racial groups. However, the decision caused many existing congregants to leave and also necessitated wide-ranging adaptations in liturgy and social activities:

... [various immigrant groups] came in and they have been brought in and encouraged to participate and to involve themselves in their own and other groups ... When the parish first moved in that direction, a lot of people resented what they saw as the threat to community and left for other parishes. (Congregation A)

Congregation C had not been able to adapt to local demographic change:

[Congregation's] make up is a classic trap. There are very few whole families. There are a lot of very old people and a lot of young families ... We are missing middle aged people with older children ... We need a sense of recovery of family wholeness. This is urgent but I don't know how to tackle it. (Congregation C)

Congregation D was also having difficulties:

We have a growing number of single parents. Access to the absent parent is usually at weekends and this affects synagogue and religion school attendance ... We have not yet recognized the diversity of the family group. (Congregation D)

In Congregations C and D, the stage had been reached in which the desirability of membership growth was beginning to be questioned. Membership numbers were increasing but the resources added by the new members were not sufficient to sustain the necessary expansion of infrastructure:

Growth [in membership] could pose a physical problem. The church is already filled to capacity on a normal Sunday ... Major capital expenditure on the building will pose a problem. (Congregation C)

We lack money so we look to increase the membership to increase the income. But more members just lead to further pressures on the facilities. (Congregation D)

At the time of the study, Congregation D had organized a series of workshops to discuss the implications of increases in membership and to consider whether, in fact, they could curtail growth; by referring applicants to other synagogues, by developing area subgroups, or by being instrumental in starting a new congregation. Problems identified by interviewees as arising from membership growth included: difficulties in 'maintaining spirituality' in services; 'relentless pressure' on the rabbi; difficulties in recruiting lay leaders because of the responsibilities entailed; lack of physical space; difficulties in managing paid staff; and maintaining standards of child education. They feared further growth and yet could see no alternative:

There is a fear we will get too big and impersonal. But if we limit our size we will stagnate. (Lay Leader, Congregation D)

Can we crack having a large organization which is not bureaucratic? (Lay Leader, Congregation D)

Can you control the size of a religious organization? (Lay Member, Congregation D)

Changes in Buildings

Change to physical fabric could also be a source of discontent in the case congregations. In Congregation A, changes to the internal layout of the church had been delayed, in large part to avoid antagonizing congregants:

The church is out of date with theology. The font and the altar are now places of public ritual and should be positioned accordingly. But the problem has not been tackled ... You need a consensus before you do things. (Priest, Congregation A)

Those physical changes to Congregation A's building which *had* been made recently – to lighting and to the entrance doors – had been a cause of arguments between priests, who initiated the changes, and lay people who wanted the church to retain its familiar appearance. The arguments were partly a reflection of the struggle for power between priests and laity which were referred to in Chapter 5. However, they seemed also to stem from differing attitudes to the implementation of change – whether it should be imposed or only implemented once there was widespread support.

> There has been a lot of controversy about the lights ... [Priest] never explained the imagery or the historical links with the parish and the church. The people were not involved in the decision ... physical aspects of the church are very important to them. (Congregation A)

Issues about changes to physical fabric were also live in Congregation C. At the time of the study, a major source of hurt and anger in Congregation C was a decision by the (new) vicar and the warden to change the layout of chairs within the church. Whereas *they* saw this as a technicality; a means to facilitate movement and enhance dignity in services, regular church attenders were distressed that the church looked different when they came to worship. Moreover, the new layout had involved moving some chairs out of the church altogether; chairs which had been donated in memory of loved ones. What appeared initially to be a small practical change reopened splits within the congregation between the older and younger members, and between those who welcomed the new vicar and those who still missed his predecessor:

> ... instead of constructive suggestions and criticism, it becomes moans and groans and requests to put things back as they were ... They don't like change, especially the old people. (Congregation C)

Implementing Change

Several interviewees were concerned about the broad question of how best to promote change in their congregations:

[Congregation A] is waiting to be filled with ideas. Poorer people are always searching for something ... This accounts for the energy amongst the people and it is up to the church to respond and serve it. (Lay Leader, Congregation A)

They [previous leaders of the Social Committee] were stuck in a pattern of events that were old-fashioned and which worked well when they first started them – Strawberry Teas and Harvest Suppers ... We should show people that the church is not old fashioned and that it's something nice to come along to. (Lay Leader, Congregation C)

It's important for people to work with others who come from different backgrounds so that things in the synagogue don't become stale. (Lay Leader, Congregation D)

At the same time, the forces opposed to change posed dilemmas. There were traditionalists within congregations who were generally opposed to changes of any kind and who caused dissension. Some opposition, as anticipated in earlier literature, was grounded in concern about theological interpretation and religious practice:

Many of the older people have not come to terms with lay people doing so much more [in services]. (Lay Member, Congregation A)

I don't like lay people giving out communion. I wouldn't think I was good enough to do it and I don't understand the mentality of those who do it. (Lay Leader, Congregation C)

New people changed things in ways I didn't like ... The people with whom I have most sympathy are those who have had a traditional background. Those who have not experienced Judaism as youngsters and who have discovered it, or rediscovered it ... are the people who dominate because they are the ones with the missionary zeal. (Lay Leader, Congregation D)

But much opposition seemed to be grounded in nostalgia for more informal times; a protest against growth and its implications:

We used to have a system of street wardens that worked very well for a while in keeping people in touch ... [Then] it became formal and people were asked to fill in forms ... it was good when we knew what was going on. (Lay Member, Congregation C)

In Congregations A and C, where opposition to change was a major issue, priests and lay leaders were generally sympathetic to the traditionalist viewpoint. They thought that it is one of the functions of a religious congregation to provide a refuge from the difficulties of everyday life and a shield against a fast-changing society. They saw it as understandable that some people were reluctant to be challenged by changes in the congregational setting:

[Congregation A] is a refuge from the harshness of [inner city area]... People need a haven first. *Then* they can go out and change things. (Priest, Congregation A)

The big attraction of the Church of England is that there is total format continuity ... People don't want their routines disturbed. (Lay Leader, Congregation C)

In fact, ministers and lay leaders in all four of the congregations generally favoured a gradual approach to change. Some had learned lessons from previous attempts to impose change quickly.

I want to take things gradually ... I have to find out what makes [area] tick ... I want to integrate in to the community and build on what is there. (Priest, Congregation A)

You've not to be too powered. You can destroy a team like that. (Lay Leader, Congregation B)

You can soon clear your congregation if you try to change things too quickly ... He [new vicar] knows not to rock the boat ... he's only making changes slowly. (Lay Leader, Congregation C)

Thus interviewees argued for change through incrementalism and consensus-building; to allow people to adjust and internalize new ideas and to avoid alienating important groupings within the congregation:

The Team is making changes too quickly. People do not have time to get their feelings behind the decisions. (Priest, Congregation A)

Change happens at [Congregation C] by introducing things as an experiment ... [Congregation C] is very good at experiments which become permanent. (Lay Leader, Congregation C)

You have to take people with you. You can't run things like an autocratic business. (Congregation D)

The way in which major decisions were made in Congregation B, described in religious terms in interviews and reflecting findings in black-led congregations in the United States (Franklin, 1994), can also be seen as a means of slowly building consensus for change:

If [Pastor] sees a need, he asks the church officers to go down to the church for 2 or 3 days and nights of fasting to hear the spirit of God ... No food or drink is taken ... There is a prayer room with a shower attached, so nobody needs to leave the place ... After the period of fasting, we pray and reach a consensus about what should be done. (Lay Leader, Congregation B)

When there was an ambivalent or hostile attitude to a particular proposed change, the significant role of ministers as 'change agents' was highlighted. They not only generated new ideas but created a climate in which change could be seen as exciting rather than threatening:

The priests here are pushing out new frontiers ... they encourage new ideas. (Employee, Congregation A)

We do not make plans. We wait for [Pastor] to tell us what is God's will. (Lay Leader, Congregation B)

[New Vicar] has a lot of good ideas ... He's turned the church round both on services and on physical amenities. He's always willing to try things. (Lay Leader, Congregation C)

The Rabbi has a lot of good ideas. He starts a lot of things ... He's a great one for starting small groups to work on things. (Lay Leader, Congregation D)

The effectiveness of ministers as 'change agents' was partly accounted for by the fact that they were the key people involved in spanning the boundaries between congregations and other organizations which themselves were facilitators of change. Foremost amongst such organizations were the denominational institutions with which each congregation was linked.

DENOMINATIONAL INSTITUTIONS

Participation

Interviewees had a number of concerns about congregational participation in denominational activities. Several raised questions about those who attended denominational meetings; who they represented and what they contributed. Some Congregation A interviewees, for example, were resentful that key diocesan meetings were for priests only and that lay employees were excluded. They felt that opportunities were missed to broaden diocesan perspectives; and that, conversely, key actors in their own congregation were denied direct access to important diocesan decision-making. Access to denominational meetings by lay people was an issue too in Congregation C:

> I am not happy about the lack of mechanisms for ordinary people to make their voices heard. The [Church Council] and the other parish and deanery committees are not open and the minutes are not public ... If you want to get your voice heard, you have to rely on representatives who may, or may not, reflect your wishes. (Lay Member, Congregation C)

Similar views were expressed in Congregation D:

> I have never been to the Annual Conference [of the denomination]. The clique go. (Lay Member, Congregation D)

At the same time as there was concern about lay access to denominational structures, there was also concern – amongst ministers and some lay leaders – about the general reluctance of lay people to participate in denominational meetings; whether decision-making, worship or social.

> We don't meet as a parish as often as [Vicar] would like. But people's time is limited. (Lay Member, Congregation C)

The community takes [denomination] for granted. They don't see how important it is. (Lay Leader, Congregation D)

An interviewee in Congregation D thought that the congregation itself was losing valuable learning opportunities by not sending representatives to meetings of denominational congregations:

We should do more on networking between synagogues ... Nobody goes to the meetings ... It's about making the community of congregations useful to each other. If one congregation runs a successful event, they can share the formula with another one. (Lay Leader, Congregation D)

One possible explanation for this reluctance to participate in denominational activities was given in Chapter 4; congregation members' own needs and interests absorb so many resources that extra-congregational perspectives are eclipsed. Certainly, individuals who are active volunteers for their own congregation find it difficult to also serve their denominations. Those interviewees who had been, or were, involved in denominational institutions as well as their congregations described the stress:

For the last two years I have been [senior lay post in congregation]. I also provide support for the [branch congregation in another town]. I spend all day Sunday there and occasional weekday evenings ... On Sundays there are also visits to old people's homes, hospital visits and prayer meetings. I do most of the secretarial work [for the branch church] at home during the week. (Lay Leader, Congregation B)

I was Deanery Synod Representative *and* Parish Warden. [As a consequence] I was on every major committee. I was at meetings every night and I also had to have regular meetings with the Rector. (Lay Leader, Congregation C)

At the same time as I was [senior lay post in congregation], I was on the [denomination] Education Committee. I hardly ever saw my family. (Lay Leader, Congregation D)

The pressure on the time of volunteers was not the only difficulty. Many lay people did not think that denominational institutions were valuable for their congregation. As in the congregations studied by Warner in the United States (1994), their focus was on the congregation itself, irrespective of the formal polity. Only ministers and a handful of senior lay leaders thought that denominations could provide benefits:

> The Diocese was very useful over the lease of the hall. They gave good administrative back-up and their legal department dealt with things. (Lay Leader, Congregation A)

> As somebody new to the job, having colleagues ... is very comforting ... brings in wider expertise. (Vicar, Congregation C)

> I've become more aware of the work of [denomination] since I've been [lay leader post]. We need to work on overcoming the feeling of 'them and us'. (Congregation D)

And denominational meetings could be intimidating. A lay interviewee in Congregation C described a sense of alienation from the denominational structure beyond his own congregation:

> I was once on the PCC [Parish Council covering three churches]. It was far above me. I feel OK on the [Church Council] but I thought the PCC were too intelligent. I felt out of it. I didn't feel comfortable. (Lay Member, Congregation C)

A similar sense of not belonging was described by a member of Congregation D when she went as a representative to a denominational meeting:

> It felt quite political between different synagogues ... I felt people had narrow views and were not open to change. There was no welcome for a new face. (Lay Member, Congregation D)

Resource Distribution

Interview data indicated that denominational links can, in fact, give congregations access to a range of important resources; not only financial support but also expertise, administrative support, moral support and new ideas.

I bring in new ideas that I learn from playing in other churches and from courses in the Diocese ... ideas about liturgy, not just music. (Music Director, Congregation A)

We widen our experience ... you've always got help to fall back on. (Warden, Congregation C)

I know the teachers find it [denomination education department] an incredible resource and get a lot from it. (Lay Leader, Congregation D)

But even those interviewees who appreciated the resources of the denomination were very conscious of competition for resources between their own congregation and other congregations and institutions within the same denomination. Thus, interviewees in Congregation A expressed concern about the levy they paid to the diocese; the fact that it was related to numbers attending rather than to ability of congregants to pay was resented because the parish was so poor. Similarly, in Congregation C, interviewees suggested that the congregation was disadvantaged in relation to the other two churches in the parish grouping.

There has been competition and rivalry between the three churches over resources ... it feels as though [Congregation C] is the poor man of the parish. (Congregation C)

They were also sceptical about the amount of work generated by the parish and its utility:

There are far too many committees ... It's terribly bureaucratic ... they all churn out papers and minutes and they all have to go to everybody else in the parish ... It's not worth all the paper-work. (Congregation C)

Being itself a denominational headquarters, Congregation B was in a different position from the other three congregations studied. Yet it too experienced difficulties around competition for resources. Interviewees were proud of the way that the 'miracle' of their own development inspired other people to set up branch churches but the ongoing needs of the branches for financial and spiritual support and encouragement placed strains on their own volunteer and financial resources. Examples were given of congregational activities and projects that had withered because available resources had had to be directed towards the development of new branches.

In general, there was a high level of concern amongst interviewees about maintaining a fair balance of resource distribution between their congregations and their denominations. The link was seen as one which, ideally, should be reciprocal:

> It is important to be aware that there are resources beyond these four walls and we all belong to each other ... there is a two-way responsibility. (Vicar, Congregation C)

> [Denomination Education Department] is basically an opportunity to exchange ideas and resources between congregations. I draw out from it and contribute to it. (Religion School Head Teacher, Congregation D)

But many interviewees thought that the balance was tipped away from their congregations; that their congregations did not get a fair exchange for the resources they contributed.

> The diocese feels remote. They deal with the formalities well [eg marriage registrations, arranging leases] ... [but] they are just bureaucrats; they don't give us anything. (Congregation A)

> The building is unsatisfactory – mostly because it was built too cheaply. If the diocese had been more far-sighted at the beginning, we would have a proper church. (Congregation C)

> I can't see much return for the money we give ... I would like to feel a sense of gain from belonging to [denomination]. (Congregation D)

The early history of Congregation B illustrates how important the sense of fairness in resource distribution can be for congregational links with denominations. When Congregation B started, it was linked with a Pentecostal church in London. But they soon decided to operate independently:

> We heard that they were saying that we were one of their branches and that we were under their control ... They were

oppressive and were asking for money and trying to penalise us and we did not find it helpful to be with them ... so we broke away. (Congregation B)

Promotion and Prevention of Change

The fact that congregations were a part of a wider denominational framework could both encourage change and act as a brake on change. In Congregations A and C, both of which were part of centralized, episcopal denominational structures, examples were given of the way in which the implementation of congregational goals could be impeded by denominational officials. Congregation C had had to change the way in which it conducted informal 'healing' services to bring them in to line with approved Anglican practice. And Congregation A was engaged in a long-standing dispute with its diocese because it was flouting diocesan guidelines and recruiting girls as altar servers.[1] It was excluded from participating in various Catholic events and was risking alienating the Curia in Rome. In both congregations a great deal of resentment was expressed about the constraints by denominations in respect of policies which the congregation felt were right. A priest in Congregation A described how his conscience told him that recruitment of girl altar servers was not wrong and that, indeed,

> Somebody has to take a stand before change can take place. (Priest, Congregation A)

As well as putting brakes on change, denominations could also drive forward change. This too could be a source of problems if there was pressure to change quickly or if change required new resources to be found. As indicated in the previous part of this chapter, interviewees generally thought that change was best implemented in congregations gradually and through consensus-building. But denominations could be impatient:

> Fresh reforms in the liturgy, including non-gendered language, are on the way ... I hope the changes will be brought in gradually and that the changes will be softened by being anticipated. This would be in line with the English tradition of moderation. (Priest, Congregation A)

In any case, as indicated in Chapter 4, if congregations could not find somebody prepared to take a lead in implementing a change required by their denomination, they tended to quietly ignore it. The essentially voluntary nature of congregation participation meant that jobs not taken up by a minister or paid employee were only done if a volunteer could be found to take the job on.

ORGANIZATIONAL STRUCTURE

In all four of the congregations numerous examples were given of problems broadly to do with 'organizational structure'.[2] Some such issues have been referred to already in this and preceding chapters including relationships between clergy and lay leaders; relationships between lay people and lay employees; the authority of lay employees relative to clergy and laity; congregational links to denominational institutions; and adapting structures in response to internal and external pressures. This final part of Chapter 7 focuses on issues of organizational structure not so far addressed; those surrounding the work of councils, committees and other internal 'working groups', and those surrounding the interactions between those groups.

Councils, Committees and Other Working Groups

The purpose of the various 'working groups' within congregations was thought to be unclear by some interviewees.

The Parish Council should provide a forum for the people but it does not work well. It seems to have an endless brief with people raising everything there. (Congregation A)

Most of the people do not understand how the church works. You have to be on the [Church Council] to begin to understand. (Congregation C)

When I was [an employee of the congregation] I never knew where decisions were being taken or who to go to when a decision was needed. (Congregation D)

The Education and Youth Forum works in a frustrating way ... different people have different perceptions of what it should be doing. (Congregation D)

Where the functions of working groups were not widely understood, questions were also raised about the locus of congregational
decision-making. The involvement of informal, unofficial groupings in the making of key decisions in congregations was noted
with varying degrees of concern:

> I am not clear where the larger decisions are actually made and
> how they are made – especially those on wider, people problems
> ... I think the more important decisions are taken elsewhere. (Lay
> Member of the Parish Council, Congregation A)

> I tended to feel left out when they planned things and then just
> told me ... I was the last to be told. (Lay Leader, Congregation A)

> A lot has been decided before it comes to the Council. The
> Council gives the final yes or no. (Member of Church Council,
> Congregation C)

> The Council has less power than appears on paper. Most people
> agree with the wardens and the vicar ... Most people don't know
> enough about it to question things ... The Vicar is there all the
> time and there are some other people who have the time to be
> around the church a lot. (Member of Church Council,
> Congregation C)

> Sometimes the Council just rubber-stamps decisions taken else-
> where. And these are not just decisions taken by formal sub-com-
> mittees. Often the decisions are a long way along by the time
> they reach Council. [The Chairman] will say, 'I've had a chat
> with x and y and we think that... .' and as a Council member you
> feel you can't say anything against it. (Council Member,
> Congregation D)

Questions were also raised about the efficiency and effectiveness of
decision-making by committees:

> Too many different opinions [in the Parish Council] can lead to
> delays in implementing things. (Member of the Parish Council,
> Congregation A)

> People [on the Church Council] dither about making decisions.
> ... They cannot distinguish between chat and decisions.
> (Congregation C)

The Education committee is not qualified to look at the quality of education and they are intimidated by the paid staff. (Congregation D)

Committees are not efficient and business-like ... Meetings are often time wasting. They don't start on time and things go on to very late – after 11 pm. People won't make decisions quickly. (Lay Member, Congregation D)

Some interviewees suggested how existing groupings could be modified to respond to perceived difficulties. The desirability of increased formality was a frequent theme:

The Parish Council should go back to the people and there should be a two way process of discussion [between priests and laity] ... The Parish Council structure should be more formalized and more open. (Congregation A)

I feel I am being forced to make an intimate relationship with [other members of the committee] ... but I want to keep a distance. (Lay Member, Congregation D)

The composition of committees and the way in which individuals interacted within them also emerged as an important issue. In Congregation A, which had a managing Team comprising priests and lay employees, the need for priests and laity to cooperate closely raised issues about relative authorities and decision-making. Priests were uneasy:

The Team meeting represents a number of ambiguities. One of these is the mixture of lay workers and ordained priests. The pyramid is being watered down by allowing non-priests in. (Priest, Congregation A)

Some lay employees who were officially part of the Team had responded by not attending or by not participating in meetings:

They [other members of the Team] each have their own roles and I have mine ... I don't have their knowledge about the fineries of religion. I just keep quiet in meetings. (Employee, Congregation A)

They say they have a 'team' ministry but I'm not sure it is. I don't go to Team meetings ... I don't feel part of them. (Employee, Congregation A)

In Congregations C and D there were suggestions that groupings were 'incestuous'; that the same people were continually 'recycled' and that personal ties between individuals were barriers to efficient working.

I would like there to be less in-fighting ... There are historical animosities. Sometimes this inhibits decision-making. (Congregation C)

We need more people ... we are using the same people all the time ... Council elections are like a Cabinet reshuffle. (Congregation C)

A number of the old guard are still on Council and have been off and on since the beginning. (Congregation D)

Everything is incestuous. There are a lot of family interrelationships ... there are other significant close friendships. (Congregation D)

Links and Communications

Just as there were problems surrounding the relative authority of individual roles in congregations, there were also difficulties surrounding the relative authority of, and the links between, the various internal working groups.

In Congregation C, for example, there were a number of groups and committees which met on church premises but whose link with the church was unclear; for example, an Art Group met regularly in the Church Hall and paid a nominal fee to do so but most of those attending were not otherwise associated with the church. Under normal circumstances this kind of informality was not problematic, but from time to time there had been difficulties over accountability for the activities of such groups.

There was a problem with the Play Group. It was being led by people who were not members of the church ... There were complaints ... PPA [headquarters organization of play groups] and the vicar got involved. Eventually the leader left and took most of the staff with her. After that we drew up a proper constitution ... which specifies that the officers [of the Play Group] have to be approved by the [Church Council]. (Play Group Leader, Congregation C)

In Congregation D, questions were raised about the link between the Council and the various congregational committees. In practice, the committees were seen not to be accountable to the Council:

Sometimes, the Council does not have full awareness of what decisions are being taken. The relationship between committees and Council can be loose. (Congregation D)

A lot of things happen here *despite* the Council. (Congregation D)

Individual committees and groups seem to be able to do things without consulting Council. The link is lost ... there is a danger of things going off on a new policy if not caught quickly enough. (Congregation D)

The problem of getting cooperation between different interest groups within congregations was also mentioned by a number of interviewees.

I hope that [Vicar] will get round to pulling things together in a more coordinated way ... If a team is well organized and has a central pivot, the wheel runs smoothly. The vicar or the warden has to act as a pivot. (Lay Leader, Congregation C)

A lot of the issues are to do with personality and different interests. (Lay Member, Congregation D)

When cooperation was not achieved, resources were wasted in competition and squabbling:

Each group in the church [which uses the hall for meetings] pays for their own facilities and has space in the kitchen. This is another example of something which should be centrally organized but each section has its own cupboard of loot. ... It's symptomatic that nobody sees anything globally. (Congregation C)

There is tremendous wastage – of finances and personnel. ... there is no ultimate responsibility. There's too many bosses so lots of people duplicate things and nobody is finally responsible. (Congregation D)

More seriously from the point of view of congregational organization, the reluctance of groups to communicate and cooperate could lead to failure to consider issues in a broader context:

The Parish Council is problematic ... It comprises representatives of the various groups within the parish ... most people only come if 'their' project is on the agenda ... there is a lack of overview and no opportunities for participation by people who have a general commitment to the church. (Priest, Congregation A)

Although they differed in size, all four of the case congregations relied heavily on informal face to face meetings and telephone calls between individuals for coordination and information sharing. In Congregations A, B and C there was an assumption that key people would be present in the church building at some stage each week; they could therefore pick up mail and news-sheets and conduct informal business. In Congregation D, where regular attendance for public worship by lay people was not taken for granted, telephone calls and social meetings were a substitute for casual face to face meetings.

Whilst these essentially informal methods were functional in maintaining a 'community spirit' in the congregations, it could also give rise to problems. People could inadvertently be excluded from sharing important pieces of information. In Congregation C, a unilateral decision by the vicar to change the time of the Sunday morning Family Service had resulted in curtailing the time available for coffee afterwards. A lay member explained that this in effect hindered the informal network of care in the congregation which relied on hearing about sickness and other problems in this forum. In Congregation A, a member of the Parish Council who did not always worship on Sundays at the congregation's church missed out on information about meeting arrangements:

> Meetings [of the Parish Council] take place on an *ad hoc* basis and are often changed or cancelled at the last minute. I have turned up twice for meetings and then found they had been changed. (Member of the Parish Council, Congregation A)

Some interviewees suggested that a degree of informality, 'give and take' and muddle was an intrinsic feature of congregational work. The challenge was to learn to work *with* it:

> Generally, we all work together – like people do when they are part of the same household. (Congregation B)

> [Congregation C] needs a strong, proactive clergyman ... the incumbent has to be sensitive, steady and tolerant of muddle. (Congregation C)

> There has to be an element of good will and chaos ... There are no clear lines. Everything is all over the place. (Lay Leader, Congregation D)

CONCLUSIONS – ORGANIZATIONAL CHANGE AND ORGANIZATIONAL STRUCTURES

This chapter has re-examined two themes in the earlier literature; organizational change and links with denominational structures. It has also looked at issues which were barely mentioned by previous researchers but which emerged as important to the case interviewees; the work of internal committees and groups.

Organizational Change

Interviewees' views on organizational change varied widely. Some were concerned about barriers to change and how to achieve change by building consensus, whereas others were concerned about what they saw as the negative implications of change in the congregational context and were more concerned about how to *prevent* change. In two of the congregations these differing approaches were clearly identified with different groupings within the congregation. Ministers and senior lay leaders were generally left to build consensus for change incrementally and sensitively.

Some of the objections to change, as anticipated by the literature, were rooted in religious principles but most explanations were more to do with fears of formalization and congregants' wish for stability in their congregational lives. In a generally turbulent secular environment, congregations offered security. In opposing change, people were generally motivated by their perception of their congregation as a place of continuity, informal relationships and 'belonging'. Those who supported change were driven both by religious principles and by secular values about efficiency, being 'up-to-date' and the necessity of responding to a shifting environment.

Congregations were often struggling with changes which were imposed from outside or were the result of external circumstances beyond their control. But whatever adaptations they sought to make, they risked alienating key individuals and groups. As discussed in Chapter 4, reconciling competing viewpoints is a major challenge in congregations, especially in Christian ones where open conflict is frowned upon. As in other 'schismatic' organizations, the 'interdependence and functional unity of the system as a whole is to be seen as a precarious and managed unity, the preservation of which calls for continuous management of competing streams and tensions which often seek to move the system towards incompatible ends' (Morgan, 1981, p. 29).

Denominational Links

Amongst the external forces for and against change in congregations is their denominational structures. As anticipated by earlier writers, individuals within congregations often felt ambivalent, or even disillusioned, about the links with other institutions within their denomination and with denominational structures themselves. However, only in Congregation A was there any evidence of the tendency noted in the literature for clergy to be pulled between loyalty to their congregation and loyalty to their denomination. There was also no explicit reference in interviews to the discrepancies between official and actual power relationships, nor to possible loss of congregational autonomy.

Using a 'resource dependency' perspective,[3] the concern in congregations to maintain a reciprocal, balanced, relationship with denominations may be seen as a reflection of a power struggle in which congregations were seeking to minimize their dependency whilst procuring needed resources. When members of congregations felt that the exchange of resources between them and their denomination was tilted away from the congregation, they became resentful.

Organizational Structure

One of the advantages of the semi-structured interview method used for the case studies was that it allowed perspectives to emerge which were not foreseen by the researcher but which were important to interviewees. The final part of this chapter looked at the issues which arose in congregations in relation to the working of councils, committees and other internal working groups. Questions were raised about their purposes and their effectiveness. Issues also arose around the links *between* these groups and around the authority of groups in relation to individual role holders.

Taking together interviewees' perceptions of the issues in their congregations in the area of organizational structure, it is apparent that organizational structure is a matter that greatly concerns those who run congregations on a day-to-day basis – even though it has been barely mentioned by researchers up to now. The case studies suggest that not only role relationships and denominational links, but also the work of committees and other working groups can raise important issues in congregations. In addition, the tendency to combine formal internal structures with informal methods of communication and informal social relationships, can give rise to organizational anomalies which trouble members of congregations. It may be that, as indicated by the case of Congregation B, those running 'strict' congregations face fewer issues around organizational structure. But congregations which run according to more liberal religious principles, like case Congregations A, C and D, deserve more attention from researchers of organization.

Common Issues

This chapter provides further evidence of congregations experiencing common organizational problems. Leadership succession, building consensus behind change and implementing change without alienating internal groups and individual interests, were frequently-cited problems, or potential problems, in the case congregations. The data also suggest that where congregations experienced similar internal or environmental pressures, they also tended to experience similar difficulties in making organizational responses to those changes.

8

Serving a Useful Purpose?
Dilemmas of Caring

INTRODUCTION

One of drives behind this study was the expanding role of congregations in welfare provision in Britain and the need, therefore, to understand congregations as organizations. The case studies demonstrated the numerous ways in which congregations were contributing to social welfare. They also indicated the nature of the organizational challenges faced by congregations as they expanded their caring activities.

WELFARE ACTIVITIES IN CONGREGATIONS

Six forms of congregational welfare provision are distinguished in this part of the chapter: welfare projects, indirect welfare, informal care, informal care in an organized framework, mutual aid, and social integration.

Welfare Projects

Three of the four congregations had set up projects to provide welfare services on a regular basis. Congregation A ran a benefits advice service and did a weekly soup-run for homeless people. They had also established a housing association to provide hostels for homeless people. Congregation B ran a day centre for elderly people and short-stay accommodation for homeless people. Congregation D ran weekly lunches on their own premises for homeless people.

With the exception of Congregation A's advice service, which was run by a member of the congregation who was paid part-time, all the projects were run on a voluntary basis by lay people.

153

Projects were lay initiatives driven, at least in the first place, by the inspiration of just one or two key people. Ministers were supportive but were not prime movers. Once established, however, projects came to be acknowledged as integral to congregations by ministers and lay leaders alike. Indeed, in most cases, the question of the continuity of the project had been specifically addressed and a commitment had been made to its long-term future.

> Originally, we just gave [homeless] people a roof for a night or two. But now we have had grants from the Council to refurbish the houses and we can put people in to flats for longer periods. (Care Committee Chair, Congregation B)

> When the lunches [for homeless people] first started, we kept things fairly strictly controlled with rotas. We knew that once we started we would have to carry on with them. (Lunch Organizer, Congregation D)

Mostly the recipients of the welfare projects were not members of the congregations. However, this was not always the case and some projects, such as Congregation B's day centre and Congregation A's advice service, had originally started as facilities for congregation members but had quickly expanded their scope.

The projects were enjoyed by those providing the services. Much of their popularity with congregants lay in the fact that they provided a variety of opportunities for contributions:

> The good thing about it [the soup-run] is that you can contribute in your own way; you can make sandwiches rather than go on the actual run. (Lay Interviewee, Congregation A)

> What we were doing pervaded the whole community. People bring in things – clothes, money, food. The kindergarten children make sandwiches and cakes ... One man always gives me five or ten pounds every time he sees me. (Lunch Organizer, Congregation D)

Indirect Welfare Work

In addition to projects in which direct services were provided, congregations contributed to the welfare of both members and non-members in a variety of less direct ways. For example, people in need of services which the congregation itself could not provide were referred on to outside specialist agencies. Mostly this was done by ministers in the course of their pastoral work but informal referrals were also made by lay people. Another form of indirect welfare was through funding provided for outside welfare agencies; religious and secular. Sometimes this funding was considered to be part of day-to-day congregational expenditure and was met from regular income but it could also derive from specific fund-raising activities.

> The choir gives concerts in aid of good causes such as famine relief. The proceeds are given to charities. (Choir Member, Congregation B)

Congregations also assisted the welfare endeavours of outside voluntary agencies by sending representatives to sit on their boards or by contributing to coordinated local welfare efforts. Thus, Congregation B participated in a local volunteering agency which linked people in need with volunteers and Congregation C served as a local distribution centre for European Union food surpluses.

All of the congregations also took a longer term view of their caring obligations. Some, as noted in earlier literature (Finneron, 1993; Midgley, 1990), engaged in lobbying and pressure group activities, either alone or in conjunction with other churches or voluntary agencies. However, the Lunch Organizer in Congregation D, reflecting findings by Hornsby-Smith and his colleagues (1995), sounded a cautionary note about putting congregational effort in to lobbying:

> We know we should campaign to get things changed but the day to day reality is individuals who would be dead without our direct and immediate help. When you know the potential casualties, it's harder to turn your back and just do campaign work. (Lunch Organizer, Congregation D)

Informal Care

In addition to their efforts to respond, directly and indirectly, to the needs of those outside their membership, congregations also provided a wide range of help for their own members. Examples of practical or emotional support from one congregant to another included helping a family to move house, doing shopping and cooking for somebody who was sick, visiting the bereaved and babysitting for a single parent. Much of this might be described as 'informal care'; care 'provided on the basis of affective and particularistic ties which link particular individuals' (Bulmer, 1987, p. 17). However, it differed from informal help given between family, friends or neighbours in that the people involved did not necessarily know each other well, or at all, prior to the helping taking place. Also, both the helpers and the helped understood the care to be given on behalf of the congregation, rather than solely as a one to one relationship. The congregations provided an organizational framework within which help from one person to another in time of need was taken for granted, irrespective of prior acquaintance or friendship.

Informal care was further encouraged by the fact that ministers and employees were able to act as 'care catalysts'; to identify people in need of care and to then spread information to potential helpers and carers.

> I hear about people's needs through other members of the parish Team or parishioners tell me about problems that people are having. (Social Care worker, Congregation A)

> I know almost everybody because nearly everybody has kids who go through the school ... I hear things and can create links between people. (Religion School Head Teacher, Congregation D)

> I have an overview because I am constantly moving around the synagogue. (Rabbi, Congregation D).

This informal networking process was reinforced by religious norms which not only encouraged individuals to seek help in congregations but also to take initiatives and to do things for others in an unobtrusive manner. This latter approach was described by one interviewee as 'quiet care' and by several as being similar to what happens within families.

> If anybody comes in upset, they will not go away without somebody comforting them. The caring is prominent but not overdone. (Lay interviewee, Congregation C)

The minute you don't see someone in church ... it's your duty to pay a visit. You're not asked, you just go ... It's not organized, saying 'you go today and I'll go tomorrow'. It's like in a family. You just go. (Lay interviewee, Congregation B)

We are caring. When people have problems, we look after them – if they want to be looked after. (Lay Leader, Congregation D)

Informal Care in an Organized Framework

Whereas much of the informal care provided in congregations was unorganized and dependent on individual initiatives and sense of obligation, the case studies also provided examples of informal care which took place *within* a more organized, supporting, framework. It seemed, in fact, to straddle a boundary between the informal care described in the previous section, and the consciously organized welfare projects described earlier. Congregations, like the successful neighbourhood groups studied by Abrams and his colleagues, were able to provide 'formal frameworks for the cultivation of informality' (Abrams et al., 1981, p. 117).

Thus, Congregation B had a highly organized prison visiting service provided by congregants who committed themselves to making weekly visits and who took responsibility for finding a replacement for themselves if they were unable to attend. From the point of view of the prison chaplains and the prisoners, this was a regular service which could be relied upon. Yet, once within the prison, it was left to individual visitors to decide for themselves what they actually did; how they conducted themselves in face to face discussions and what, if any, group activities they organized. Visitors were providing a religiously-based befriending service:

When we go in to the prisons, we tell people how God can give you peace and hope ... What we basically do is to share our own personal experiences. (Member of Prison Visiting Group, Congregation B)

A further example of the way in which congregations consciously organized to sponsor or support informal care was provided by the systems established within congregations to support new adherents.

When people come in to the church and they accept Jesus Christ I follow it up. We offer to go and visit them and we encourage them to come to things in the Church ... Later, we do watch care; we keep an eye on people and try and support them as necessary. (Lay Counsellor, Congregation B)

Members of the Conversion Support Group adopt people while they are going through conversion. It gives them a point of reference. You phone them up from time to time ... when the festivals are coming up you discuss about customs and food. (Member of the Conversion Support Group, Congregation D)

Congregations also acted as 'mediating structures', creating circumstances in which 'informal and formal care can be brought together to flourish effectively' (Bulmer, 1987, p. 202). Thus, Congregation D had a 'social care network' in which formal and informal elements were explicitly mixed together. The network was intended to support the rabbi in his pastoral role and to provide 'befriending and psychological support' from one member of the congregation to another. Despite these informal-sounding terms, it was in practice highly formalized and professionalized in many ways. There was a selection procedure for becoming a 'visitor' which was overseen by a member of the congregation who was a qualified social worker and who also provided 'training'. Visitors worked 'on a confidential basis' and had a professional 'supervisor'.

Mutual aid

Mutual aid activities were also sustained within congregations. In Congregation A, for example, a group of older people started to meet informally on church premises once a week. They not only supported each other in a variety of practical and emotional ways, but they also began to visit others beyond the group:

There is a group which meets every week and they are older people, but they themselves go out and visit housebound people – like ministers to like. (Congregation A)

The same congregation also had a group for divorced and separated people; people who have generally been stigmatized in Catholic churches. A participant in the group described it in terms of the classic benefits of a self-help group (Gartner and Riessman, 1977):

> The people who run it have been there and you can share with people who've gone through it. (Lay Member, Congregation A)

Congregation C had a small group of people who were attempting to help each other in a different, more obviously 'religious' way, through having 'healing services' from time to time. The services, although advertised for all, attracted a small group of lay 'regulars' who planned and executed the services themselves:

> It's very moving and satisfying. It serves the need and fills a gap ... It's drawing in people who wouldn't normally go to church. (Lay member, Congregation C)

Thus, many of the people who do the caring in congregations are themselves also recipients of congregational care. Sometimes this is a simultaneous exchange in which somebody experiencing a problem is helped by being drawn in to caring for others. However, the case studies also suggested that 'serial reciprocity' was common; that is, people were helped in their own need and then helped others 'when their problems have largely passed or they have come to terms with living them' (Richardson and Goodman, 1983, p. 42). Their own motivation to care was driven by their gratitude for the care that they themselves had received.

> Some people actively want to put something back in to the community because they are grateful for help they received. (Vicar, Congregation C)

Social Integration

Another way in which people experiencing problems were helped was by being drawn in to religious, educational, social, welfare or administrative activities within the congregation. Sometimes this was done through 'befriending' action in which congregational members committed themselves explicitly to keeping in contact with one another. In other cases, ministers, paid staff or lay leaders made repeated invitations to people they regarded as needing support. Interviewees described being 'sucked in' to more and more activities until they suddenly realized that they were 'accepted'. A widow in Congregation C who had not been a church attender prior to her husband's death described how she had been drawn in to participating in church activities as a result of repeated visits and invitations. She had, she said:

> ... found a great deal of comfort from the clergy and the lay people through being associated with the church. (Lay Member, Congregation C)

Similarly, a single mother in Congregation A – which is situated in an inner city area described by one interviewee as having 'no natural sense of community' – told how priests and lay members of the church 'rallied round' when she was left alone with two young children. As a result of repeated invitations to participate in church activities, all her leisure hours were filled and she had a large group of friends:

> The church has turned my life around. (Lay Member, Congregation A)

A lay leader of Congregation C also talked about the way in which his church drew in people who were not integrated in to the wider society but who were made to feel at home.

> [Congregation C] is accessible to people who would otherwise be turned off. There are some mentally handicapped people who are happy here and are accepted. (Lay Leader, Congregation C)

Religion and Congregational Care

Thus, six different ways of caring in congregations are discernible from the case material. Many interviewees were motivated to do caring work within their congregations by the opportunities it offered for self-fulfilment, self-development and trying new things. Knowing their efforts were appreciated was also important.

> For me personally it is a great satisfaction knowing that you've helped someone. I get a lot from helping people. Most people come back and say thank you. (Welfare Worker, Congregation A)

People come back and tell us how much they have been helped through being on the list [of those named in healing prayers]. (Lay Member, Congregation C)

But religious values were a key factor too. In fact, as explained in Chapter 3, it was clear that interviewees regarded social care as an essential goal of a religious congregation.

You have to look outward to take up responsibility for injustice in society – everybody needs to establish the kingdom on earth. (Congregation A)

When you are born again you become a new creature in whom the Holy Ghost is indwelling ... Then, instead of you going to people for help, you become a person who other people come to for help. (Congregation B)

There is a Jewish responsibility to work for *tikkun olam* [Hebrew – repairing the world]. This is *not* because I will be rewarded in heaven, but because it is the right thing to do. (Congregation D)

The religiously-inspired motivation towards caring activity seemed to apply to men as well as women. In contrast with the situation which often prevails in secular welfare agencies, direct provision of care was not generally seen as a predominantly female responsibility in the congregations. Even in Congregations B and C, in which women were in a clear majority in both membership and participation, lay men were involved in a range of caring activities including the more informal forms of care. The 'taken for granted' nature of this male participation in care work in congregations may reflect the fact that 'pastoral care' is an expected and accepted aspect of the role of ministers – itself a traditionally male role.

The care activities themselves were affected to varying degrees by the fact that they were provided under the auspices of a religiously based institution. Sometimes 'religious' and 'welfare' purposes were intermingled and indistinguishable as in the prison visiting service provided by Congregation B or the healing services run at Congregation C. Similarly there was a 'prayer link' organized in Congregation C:

The idea is that a group of people commit themselves to prayer for a set period of one and a half hours each day and concentrate on praying for named people who are very ill or who have a serious problem ... [The effect is that] a person is held in prayer by somebody throughout a twelve hour period of the day ... People come back and tell us how much they have been helped through being on the list. (Prayer Link Coordinator, Congregation A)[1]

More often there was a religious element in the care provided which was an *additional* feature of welfare work. Thus, in Congregation B, a woman described how she had been doing the weekly shop for a housebound person for 12 years, noting in passing that:

I pray with her sometimes when I see that she's not looking too well. (Lay Member, Congregation B)

Also in Congregation B, the day centre for elderly people showed gospel videos for the main form of entertainment. At the least, the fact that welfare services were mostly provided on congregation premises and that ministers were regular visitors, or themselves involved, meant that those in receipt of care would always be aware of the special religious features of congregation-based care activity.

ISSUES IN CONGREGATIONAL CARE

Setting Priorities

In all four of the congregations, pride in the 'caring' qualities of the congregation coexisted with a number of concerns about the organization of care and its implications. One major theme in interviews was the difficulty of setting priorities in relation to welfare work; choosing between different care activities and balancing care activities against other necessary congregational activities.

The sick and elderly can dominate the time of a parish team if you let it. (Priest, Congregation A)

Such organizational challenges may also be faced by other welfare-providing agencies but special features may make them especially intractable in congregations. For example, care activities in congregations constitute just one aspect of a much broader 'mission'. Welfare is one amongst many goals (Webb, 1974) and often the people most active in welfare work are also engaged in other competing aspects of congregational life. Also, as mentioned in earlier literature on the goals of congregations, the question arises of how to balance the needs of members against those of non-members.

> At one time the Community Services group was serving both the needs of synagogue members and those of the surrounding community. I felt the broader community focus went too far. We needed to look at our own needs ... I thought that we had a growing number of elderly people, for example, and that we should think about their needs. (Lay Leader, Congregation D)

Although the needs of members and the needs of non-members were rarely seen as so directly in competition with each other,[2] many interviewees were concerned about their congregation's apparent inability to handle adequately the needs of congregants *and* people living locally who were not members or participants in the congregation:

> The church needs to tackle how they are present in the area in serving the community – beyond getting people to come in and be religious ... we need a more clearly defined understanding of serving the community. (Congregation C)

Setting Boundaries

In the light of religious injunctions to 'care', it can be difficult for congregations not only to set priorities, but also 'to manage the institution's boundaries' and to avoid 'responding to all society's casualties' (Carr, 1985, p. 44). A lay member of Congregation A, who had professional knowledge about welfare benefits, put a notice in the congregational newsletter offering to help people.

> I got phone calls at all hours of the day and night – four or five a week – from people who were destitute or who needed general advice about benefits. (Social Care Worker, Congregation A)

Ministers, perhaps inadvertently, can play a part in over-burdening lay carers:

> [A previous vicar] expected people to give their all to the church. (Lay Leader, Congregation C)

> There are problems about over-committing lay people. Once you say 'yes' to anything, you get pulled in more and more ... The Rabbi flatters people into doing things and people enjoy working with him. But people don't ask themselves whether they *can* do it. (Lay Leader, Congregation D)

On the other hand, ministers were themselves particularly exposed to the wide range of competing demands for care, and the sheer number of demands:

> Priests are terribly overworked. There are always a number of balls in the air at once. In addition to the parish basics – visits, sacramental preparation and collaborative ministry – there are too many good causes that can overwhelm you. (Priest, Congregation A)

As they are 'on the spot', religious functionaries find it hard to turn their back on needy people who present themselves:

> The church has become an informal extension of the DSS ... we feed 15–20 homeless men each day ... we also get a number of one-off requests. Mostly we don't give out money but we get a lot of abuse from people whose requests for help are rejected. (Priest, Congregation A)

The problem of *not* responding to need, especially in the light of religious injunctions to care, can also be experienced by congregations as a whole. Even when they know that they are being manipulated or exploited, they find it difficult to turn away requests for help:

> Sometimes people take advantage of us. They say they are destitute but really they just want somewhere to stay and eat for a couple of nights ... What can you do? You have to do your best for your fellow man. (Lay interviewee, Congregation B)

At the same time, awareness of unmet needs in their surrounding communities was a constant source of concern for both ministers and lay people. Practically every person interviewed offered a personal list of things that they thought their congregation should be doing, or should be doing to a greater extent.

> We need to work on letting in the marginalized; for example, travellers, homeless people, single-parents and those who have had abortions. (Lay Leader, Congregation A)

> I would like to see us persuading the Council to do more things for ethnic minorities in the area. (Lay Leader, Congregation B)

> We should speak out more on political things ... we could be saying things to the local authority about what they could be doing to help the unemployed. (Lay Leader, Congregation C)

Securing Commitment and Continuity

In general, the *informal* care activities in congregations had their own internal dynamism and did not seem to be dependent for their survival on any particular individual, or on the support of paid staff. Interviewees described 'networks' and loose groupings which seemed to be well-rooted in congregational tradition. However, several interviewees were concerned about the apparent fragility of some of the more formal welfare projects. For example:

> The main problem with the soup-run is getting drivers ... If I walked away, it might collapse. I've put the momentum behind it and I keep it going. (Soup-run Organizer, Congregation A)

> It's very hard to get people empowered ... More and more mothers are working and they cannot make a regular commitment ... I've been scraping round this week to try to find somebody to run the Mother and Toddlers group. (Lay Leader, Congregation C)

A former chairman of Congregation D described how his own awareness of the problems of continuity had led him to veto a project to run a hostel for discharged patients from the local mental hospital:

I said 'no way unless you find the money and enough people who will undertake to run it' ... There were a lot of people with ideas but there was a history of leaving things in the lurch. (Lay Leader, Congregation D)

The fragility of welfare projects in congregations may be explained in part by the way in which successful projects can place major burdens of time and responsibility on volunteers. The lunches for the homeless at Congregation D, for example, had thrown up a range of practical problems such as doing large weekly shopping trips, and dealing with petty theft on synagogue premises. There had also been violent incidents which had involved volunteers having to clean up blood. In such cases, the continuity of projects is dependent on the extent of volunteer commitment and determination:

I accept final responsibility. I try to deal with things which happen as 'incidents' rather than as big issues. (Lunch Organizer, Congregation D)

Coping with Growth and Change

In addition to the implications for volunteer commitment, successful welfare projects can give rise to a number of other difficulties for congregations. Several interviewees described how they had had to adapt to the implications of growth. An informal group in Congregation A had formed a small housing association with a view to providing temporary accommodation for homeless people. Eventually they were 'taken on' by one of the largest housing associations which enabled them to apply for a Housing Corporation grant. They then found they had to change their original plans to provide temporary accommodation as money was only available for permanent accommodation and for 'special needs' housing. They felt they had been pushed into a very different arena from their original, modest, vision.

Some welfare projects eventually outgrew the capacity of congregations to sustain them. Interviewees regretted that growth, which in itself was welcome, also entailed relinquishing valued forms of mutual care:

We used to have a system of street wardens that worked very well for a while in keeping people in touch. Then people dropped out and there was new building so that it became too much to keep in touch. (Lay Leader, Congregation C)

Paradoxically, the ultimate 'success' – of having a project adopted by an outside funder in the governmental or voluntary sector – was often regarded as a mixed blessing by congregations. Whilst they were glad to be relieved of constant anxiety about finding financial and human resources, they also resented their loss of control and were anxious about being pulled in to a more formal caring world. Thus, the day centre for the elderly run by Congregation B had just been taken over by the local Social Services Department at the time of the study. Concern was expressed about the fact that the church would no longer be free to choose who attended:

When we were running the Day Centre in the church we could let anybody in. Now it is much more formal ... I'm not sure if the Centre is still ours. We are not happy at the idea that somebody should take over as the big boss ... but we are delighted that a big burden has been lifted from us. (Day Centre Organizer, Congregation B)

Similarly, the local authority in the area of Congregation D had recently agreed to provide a building in which activities for the homeless, including lunches, could be carried out. The Organizer of the lunches said,

I will be less involved in running the Day Centre. I don't want to get involved in a formal committee – even if it's not bureaucratic. (Lunches Organizer, Congregation D)

Again, Congregation C's Play Group was battling with the implications of its recent affiliation to the Pre-School Play Groups Association. The affiliation brought essential contacts and expertise in to the group but also created pressures to professionalization and formality. Additionally, and as with the Day Centre in Congregation B, questions were raised about the extent to which the Play Group was still a *congregational* project.

We'll be getting into a different ball game ... Because we are a church organization, we pay more for the Hall and we pay less to the play leaders. This is out of loyalty to the church. And we pay all the staff the same ... PPA wants us to give staff contracts of employment and to deduct tax. (Lay Leader, Congregation C)

CONCLUSIONS – CONTRIBUTING TO WELFARE

The four case congregations discussed in this chapter were selected without prior knowledge about their welfare role; but each was found to be engaged in numerous caring activities ranging from informal care to, in the case of three congregations, significant welfare projects. Nor was the welfare contribution of congregations confined to the pastoral care work of ministers. Lay people, usually working on a voluntary basis, provided care not only for other members of their congregation, but also for non-members.

The data confirm that congregations can be important constituents of the mixed economy of welfare. Their members are recipients of a range of supporting and caring activities and contributions are also made to the welfare of people in the community beyond the congregation itself. Is there scope, then, for expanding the welfare role of religious congregations?

It does seem that members of congregations are likely to be interested in principle in caring for others – for both religious and self-development reasons. It also appears that a congregation can provide an organizational framework within which those in need and those willing to help can be put in touch with each other, and in which care initiatives can be developed and supported. Ministers, lay employees and key congregational members put people in need in touch with others in the normal course of their work and overlapping friendship networks can act as further conduits of information about who is in need of care and who is available to provide care. Also, as pointed out in Chapter 4, congregations provide an atmosphere in which people with new ideas can pursue them and experiment. Thus congregations may have much to contribute as innovators in responding to social problems.

At the same time, however, the findings about the organizational issues that surround the provision of welfare in congregations suggest that congregations may be able to support some forms of caring more successfully than others. Members of congregations sustain with relative ease 'quiet care'; the less 'organized' types of welfare such as mutual aid, social integration and various kinds of informal care. This is the 'religious caring and giving' which

Wuthnow (1990) has noted as occurring 'through the informal relationships nurtured within the local congregation'.

In the case of the more formal welfare projects, however, the studies suggested a number of limitations, or potential limitations. For example, they have to compete for resources with a range of other important congregational activities; their continuity may be dependent on the enthusiasm and personal circumstances of just one or two committed people; and untrained, unsupported volunteers may be faced with complex social problems.

It also seems that much of the attraction of these projects for volunteer congregants is their autonomy. Where projects are subject to the intervention of outside sponsors, the commitment and enthusiasm of volunteers may melt away. Even though such sponsorship reflects project success and offers the possibility of expansion with less responsibility, it may also take from volunteers what they most value; the ability to control the project and run it according to their own preferences.

Part III
Congregations in Perspective

9

An Organizational Perspective on Congregations

INTRODUCTION

The closing part of this book reconsiders congregations in the light of the starting purposes of the study. This chapter looks at congregations as organizations and the final one considers them in the context of broader policies and expectations.

A prime purpose of this project was to respond to the organizational issues and problems faced by those who work in and with congregations – specifically churches and synagogues. This has been done in a number of ways. First, the disparate earlier literature about the organization of churches and synagogues was drawn together; thus providing an initial building block for a new body of specialist knowledge and a starting agenda for an empirical study. Then, the data from four case studies was used to sketch out key organizational features of congregations and their environments in order to better understand their nature and operations. Part II provided a detailed analysis of the challenges faced by those who worked in the four congregations; an analysis which drew attention to both the similarities and differences in the issues which arose in the congregations and possible explanations for them.

The current chapter brings together the main findings from the earlier literature and the case studies and discusses the similarities and differences between congregations revealed by the empirical data. Models are proposed in order to provide broader explanations for the organizational issues congregations face and a basis for discussion and change within them.[1]

WHAT CONGREGATIONS HAVE IN COMMON

The hypothesis that churches and synagogues share organizational features and issues underlies this study. The descriptive data from

173

the case congregations suggest that English congregations in the 1990s *do* have a number of organizational features in common – irrespective of factors such as their religion, denomination, strictness of guiding theology, history, funding, membership, staffing, size and geographical location. Such common organizational features may include similar broad purposes; a key role for religious functionaries in activities; members attracted by opportunities for social integration and self-expression; and a responsive approach to local, cultural and organizational environments.

When the organizational challenges faced by congregations are analysed, the similarities between the case congregations are even more striking. All four of the congregations, for example, found setting and implementing congregational goals problematic in the face of members' demands to have their individual needs met. All were also obliged to make pragmatic adaptations of their goals in response to pressures from their local communities and the secular environment; all had to give higher priority to organizational maintenance than longer term visions; and all were struggling with a sense of failure engendered by official, but inherently unachievable, religiously based purposes.

All four of the congregations also struggled with issues of organizational change. Change of any kind was unwelcome for many internal groups and individuals. Ministers and senior lay people had to build consensus behind change and create an environment in which change was seen as an opportunity rather than a threat. With respect to links with other organizations within their own denomination, the four congregations were all concerned to find ways of ensuring an equitable balance of resource exchange.

The four congregations also experienced similar difficulties in relation to their formal welfare projects. Such projects competed for human and financial resources with other congregational activities and their continuity was often dependent on the enthusiasm and personal circumstances of just one or two committed lay people. There was also the 'problem' of success; the more successful projects became, the more likely they were to become subject to the control of outside funders or agencies; a move which, in turn, could destroy the motivation of the volunteers sustaining them.

In addition to these many challenges which were faced by all four of the congregations, there were a number of other issues which were raised by interviewees in three of the four congregations; with Congregation B, the Pentecostal church, apparently able to largely avoid the problems faced in Congregations A, C and D. The latter three congregations had internal interest groups which competed for available resources and caused ill-feeling if their wishes were not complied with; internal groups were often only 'loosely coupled' to the committees which officially controlled them; and decision-making by formally appointed groups was often pre-empted by informal networks and interest groups.

Congregations A, C and D also reported similar problems surrounding the roles of ministers and lay people and the relationship between them. Ministers found it difficult to balance the numerous demands placed on them by their congregants and by their own professional and religious ideals. Difficulties in the relationship between lay people and ministers were widespread, with evidence of power struggles and questions raised about relative authority. Senior volunteers in the three congregations were hard to recruit and retain and once in post they were often overloaded. Enormous amounts of time and tact had to be expended on recruiting and motivating less senior volunteers.

EXPLAINING ORGANIZATIONAL ISSUES

Why was Congregation B apparently able to avoid so many of the problems faced by the other three case congregations? Interview data suggested that the key explanatory factor was the strict religious values which were consciously used as a guide to all matters to do with running the congregation, as well as to individual lifestyles. These values were widely shared by all members of the congregation and constantly reinforced through worship and bible study. Key elements in the religious principles guiding behaviour in Congregation B were total respect for the authority of the pastor as the interpreter of God's will and therefore as a key decision-maker; an assumption that decisions could be reached by consensus and that, once reached, decisions would not be questioned; an understanding that voluntary donation of time and money was an honour; and an assumption that church commitments were a way of life with high priority relative to other possible 'free time' activities.

In addition to the impact of their strict religious values, there were other possible factors in the relatively problem-free situation of Congregation B. For example, the system of 'apprenticeship' to key voluntary posts meant that people were eased into the more onerous positions and that there was little danger of important activities being abandoned for lack of people able or willing to do them. Second, the congregation was small – barely a hundred members – and most congregants were physically present at the church premises at least once a week. Thus, communication could be done on a face-to-face basis and more formal communication systems of committees and meetings were less essential to the smooth running of the congregation. Opportunities for misunderstandings and delays were minimized as problems could be quickly dealt with before they escalated. It was also possible for informal monitoring and guidance to be provided in an unobtrusive fashion by the pastor and senior lay leaders. Third, cultural factors – including gender, age and ethnic origin – must be taken in to account. The overwhelming majority of Congregation B's members were women, middle-aged or older, and of Afro-Caribbean origin; these characteristics could have helped to ensure both that the (male) pastor's decisions were accepted and that high standards of work discipline were maintained.[2]

That religious factors can contribute directly to the organizational challenges faced, or not faced, by congregations is confirmed to some extent by found differences between Congregation D and the other three case congregations. For example, as predicted by earlier literature, it did seem that the three Christian congregations had strong norms against open conflict and debate which were not in evidence in the Jewish congregation where interviewees talked openly about 'rows'. Again, in Congregation D there was more uncertainty than in the other three congregations about the right of the minister to have the final word in decision-making. There was, as in the other congregations, a reluctance to challenge him publicly and explicitly, but there was far less evidence that lay people thought he had the ultimate right to be 'the boss'. Perhaps this reflected traditional Jewish ideas of the rabbi as a teacher, rather than a priest with special powers and authority in relation to lay people. But, as in Congregation B, there may have been additional, non-religious factors at play; for example, Jewish cultural norms of disputatiousness (Roshwald, 1978), and the large size of the congregation which meant that there were practical limitations on what the rabbi could accomplish.

Religion was a possible explanation for other issues raised in the case congregations. For example, some of the feelings of disappointment about goals not achieved were traceable to strongly-held religious values about helping the needy, educating young people, or bringing in new people into a congregation's traditions. And some of the tensions between ministers and lay people were apparently to do with ministers seeing themselves as embodiments of religious, and therefore unchallengeable, congregational goals; as well as to do with ministerial difficulties in implementing theologies of lay empowerment which had raised lay people's expectations. Problems in congregations could also prove especially difficult to resolve if groups or individuals justified their cause (such as a wish to start a project or a desire for nothing to change) with an argument grounded in religious principles.

Thus, religion was clearly an important element in the organizational issues faced by the case congregations – as would be anticipated from the very fact that congregations are self-proclaimed 'religious' or 'faith-based' organizations. What is perhaps more noteworthy is the extent to which religion did *not* emerge as a contributory variable, or at least not the main one, in so many of the organizational issues raised in the congregations.

THE ASSOCIATION MODEL

If the 'religion factor' on its own is not sufficient to account for the practical problems faced by those who work in and with churches and synagogues, can any better understanding of congregations as organizations be developed from the case data? Theories about the organization of voluntary membership associations can be helpful here.[3]

What are Voluntary Associations?

Voluntary associations are groupings which offer 'the chance to come together with others to create or participate for collective benefit' (Bishop and Hoggett, 1986, p. 3). They are characterized 'by their common purpose of defending and promoting functionally defined interests' (Streek and Schmitter, 1991, p. 231) or 'in terms of participation, shared objects and resources, mutuality, and fairness' (Lohmann, 1992, p. vii). They generally have a name, a governing body of some kind, articulated goals or purposes, and people who are 'members' (Billis, 1993a). Associations do not 'depend on paid-staff for the principle accomplishment of organizational tasks' but are 'essentially run by volunteers' (Smith, 1994, p. 1 and p. 4). This concept of a voluntary association can be applied to self-help groups, professional associations, trade associations, trade unions, neighbourhood associations, leisure groupings and community action groups.

Research-based literature on organizational aspects of associations is not plentiful but there is sufficient to indicate that they typically have a number of features. First, if their members do not receive the material, social or psychological benefits they expect or if they are discomforted in some way by their associational participation, they will leave (Ahrne, 1996; Oropesa, 1995). This essentially voluntary nature of participation in associations means that high priority must be given to responding to individuals' demands and needs to ensure that they remain members. It also means that leaders of associations 'have at their disposal only weak instruments for convincing other members to follow their suggestions or orders' (Milofsky, 1988, p. 191). If work allocated to an association member is not carried out, or is not carried out as expected, there are a limited range of sanctions available. Volunteer members resist coercion and can be controlled only through 'normative' power (Etzioni, 1961).

A second noted feature of associations is that members seek from them 'expressive' social and personal benefits such as friendship, mutual support and exchange of news. Thus, they tend not to be interested in formal procedures and deadlines and they are not especially task-oriented in their approach to associational activities. In meetings they may expect the *process* of discussion and decision-making to carry intrinsic rewards (Mason, 1995; Milofsky, 1988); an expectation that can be at odds with 'businesslike' procedures and speedy decision-making. Since associations also have a tendency to factionalism because of competing internal interests and values (Hoggett, 1994), the difficulties in decision-making can be compounded as time and energy is channelled into consensus-building.

Another feature of associations is that the role and status of staff, where they are employed, can be ambiguous. Is their role to assist and support the members who retain prime responsibility for carrying out the association's work or is it to do mainstream operational work which would otherwise be done by volunteer members? Members of associations in which staff do operational work may feel that they are being pulled into different organizational territory, into the 'bureaucratic' world in which work outputs are generated by paid staff (Billis, 1993a). The accompanying trends to professionalization and formalization may alienate those members who value informality, friendliness and member-focused activities (Chapin and Tsouderos, 1956). As associations grow, it can become increasingly difficult for members to carry out all the work that seemingly needs to be done, yet the employment of staff can raise more problems than it solves.

In short, a key organizational feature of associations is their essentially voluntary nature. Members come and go as they wish, they value social interaction, and whatever work is done is mostly done without pay. Growth of associations can give rise to pressures towards formalization and professionalization which conflict with drives to remain small, informal and member-focused (Klausen, 1995; Knoke and Prensky, 1984).

Congregations as Voluntary Associations

Juxtaposing this sketch of the organizational features of voluntary membership associations with the case data, numerous similar themes are apparent. Irrespective of the formal statements of theologians, denominational headquarters and ministers of religion, it seems that *in practice* many lay members of congregations generally behave as they would in any other kind of voluntary association. They do not feel obliged to join in the first place, they feel free to participate or not as it suits them, and they assume that they should be able to contribute in whatever way, to whatever extent, and for whatever time period, they wish. They do not generally expect to be told what to do and how to do it in 'their' organization and they expect their relationships with other members of the association to be informal and fulfilling. Their attitudes to any paid staff, including ministers of religion, may be ambivalent and they may be uncertain about the role of such staff in the congregational context. Their focus is the congregation itself and they are not much interested in links with outside organizations, other than those which can provide needed resources.

It is not suggested that members of congregations *consciously* treat their participation in this way. The argument is simply that people 'routinely employ theories about social order' (Silverman, 1993, p. 29) and carry with them 'images of organization' (Morgan, 1986). In the case of contemporary congregations, the 'theory' or 'image' that many people apply to their participation is that of a voluntary membership association.

These insights about how lay people view their participation in congregations provide a broad explanation for many of the issues and problems found in the case congregations. For example, the association model offers an explanation for the tensions between lay people and both ministers of religion and paid lay staff. The religious principles which ministers learn in their training make universal claims to authority and allegiance and generally assume that the activities which take place in and around congregations are the centre of people's lives.[4] Their training also encourages ministers to see themselves as prime interpreters of a congregation's mission. In the case of lay paid staff, many of them draw their organizational models from the professional and bureaucratic worlds in which people have set hours and conditions of work, are managed and monitored, and have clear role boundaries. Such images of organization are very different from that of a voluntary association. If ministers, paid staff and lay people are holding different and incompatible organizational assumptions about their congregations, clashes over roles, role relationships and relative authorities are highly likely to occur and to be difficult to resolve.

In fact it is noteworthy that in Congregation B, where lay people generally *did* share the minister's ideas about the universal claims of their religion and about the congregation as a way of life, the tensions in the relationship between the two which were found in the other three congregations were minimized. Also noteworthy is the way in which lay employees in Congregations A and D were often treated by lay volunteers as though they too were volunteers and thus part of their associational world.

The associational model also accounts for why some senior lay leaders in congregations were so impatient with what they saw as slow decision-making, gossip during committee meetings, non-adherence to 'authentic' behaviour, and 'unreliable' volunteers. Perhaps these were people who, like some paid staff and ministers, did not share the dominant model of the congregation as an association. If they were drawing their own organizational images of congregations from the world of business or professional employment, then they would indeed see much congregational activity as 'chaotic', 'unprofessional', 'amateur' or 'inefficient'. On the other hand, for the majority of their fellow congregants who placed a high value on associational features such as informality, friendship, social interaction, open discussion of problems, and opportunities for self-development, such criticisms would be seen as totally inappropriate.

The idea that the associational 'world' has different organizational features from the more formal world of 'bureaucracies' in which paid staff do the main operational work (Billis, 1993a), helps to explain not only differing viewpoints about appropriate behaviour within congregations but also resistance to change. In the case congregations, many of the objections to changes in personnel, membership and physical fabric were underpinned by fears that such changes were moves towards formality and adherence to prescribed procedures. There were also fears that the interests of individuals and internal groups were threatened. Whereas opposition to change was seen as short-sighted and selfish by those in congregations who had longer-term visions of drawing in more people and responding to more and wider needs, it is quite consistent with an associational idea of the congregation as a place where individual members all know each other, where personal needs can be met, where 'business' is conducted in a relaxed and informal manner and usually face-to-face, and where helping efforts are directed mainly towards other members.

The focus on 'mutual benefit' rather than 'commonweal' forms of helping behaviour which is characteristic of associations, explains as well why the congregations studied found it difficult to sustain formal welfare projects and services but sustained with relative ease the more informal and 'unorganized' forms of care. In the context of a voluntary membership association, informal and even 'semi-organized' forms of caring can be taken for granted; as can the idea of keeping an eye open for people who might need help. On the other hand, the idea of an ongoing regular commitment or the giving of care to 'strangers' beyond the circle of members is outside of the associational world model and closer to a bureaucratic model of a welfare agency in which services are provided by staff to third parties (Billis, 1993a; Harris, 1994). When congregations are seen as voluntary associations, the organizational fragility of their welfare projects is explained, as is the concern about successful projects being adopted by outside funders and agencies.

It is also understandable that members of congregations who see themselves as participating in a voluntary association and who are aware of the heavy dependence of their congregation on voluntary

donations of time and money, should feel uneasy about attempts
to limit the freedom of their congregation to set its own goals.
Thus they may be generally uninterested in, or even resentful
towards, denominational structures which prescribe and monitor
adherence to goals – ranging from broad religious purposes to
adult education aims. They may also feel antagonistic towards
their ministers whose very role reflects the 'fixed' aspect of congregational goals; the aspect which cannot be changed even if
members want to do so.

In sum, the model of associations is useful in helping to explain
organizational features and issues raised in both the earlier literature and in the case congregations. Once congregations are seen as
voluntary associations, explanations are provided for why so many
people, mostly lay people, behave the way they do in the congregational context; why they have the expectations they have; and why
they make the assumptions they make. The occurrence of clashes
and unresolvable disputes between individuals and internal groups
is also understandable – there are alternative organizational models
which can be held within the same congregation, without any of
the different assumptions ever being made explicit.

A MODEL OF CONTEMPORARY ENGLISH CONGREGATIONS

Beyond the Voluntary Association Model

The purpose of this chapter is not to make judgements about what
kind of organizations congregations *should be*. The suggestion is
only that the voluntary association model appears to be the one
guiding the behaviour and expectations of many people who are
members of contemporary congregations and who work within
them. Not only lay people, but ministers as well, seem to operate, at
least in part, according to an associational model. Examples were
given in the case studies of ministers tolerating long, chatty meetings and socializing after services of worship; supporting essentially social events; and sensitively 'discerning' the capacities of
individuals and supporting them in volunteering.

The association model has considerable explanatory power in
relation to congregational organizational issues. It also accords with
what is known of the recent history of churches and synagogues.
Whatever they may have been in the past, contemporary English

congregations are, in effect, one of a number of organizations – religious and secular – which compete for members and for voluntary contributions of time and money.

At the same time, the voluntary association model is not *sufficient* to account for more than *some* of the study findings. In the first place, religious factors are also important in explaining why organizational problems arise in the way they do in congregations. Second, it seems clear that the associational model is not universally employed by people working in congregations; and that some people, including ministers and senior volunteers, seem to employ other models instead of, or in addition to, the voluntary association one. Indeed, the clash between a voluntary association assumption and other organizational assumptions was at the root of many of the organizational issues uncovered in the case studies.

The challenge, then, is to build on the basic voluntary association model to develop a more comprehensive theoretical explanation of congregational organizational issues. Here the empirical data generated by the case studies suggest two features of contemporary English congregations which need to be taken into account; the special role of ministers of religion and the special nature of goals. Both features are linked to the fact that congregations are 'religious' or 'faith-based' organizations.

Special Role of Ministers

The position of *any* paid employee in an associational context is ambiguous and a potential source of confusion and dispute. So even if they are just seen as paid employees, ministers of religion represent a deviation from the norm of an 'association' unless they are in a clearly subordinate role to lay volunteers. But, in fact, ministers are not just paid employees like any other nor are they comfortable with the notion of congregants seeing them as a 'hired hand' (Hutton and Reed, 1975; Neusner, 1972). As the case studies illustrated, they generally see themselves, and are seen to be, in a very different category from either lay paid staff or lay members of congregations – for two main reasons.

First, ministers are seen by themselves and by lay people as having an authority that is different in quality and derivation from that attributed to secular organizational roles. Using Christian theological language, the authority they have is rooted in divine inspiration.[5] Using Weberian terminology (1964), ministers of religion acting in their congregational context carry 'charismatic' or 'traditional' authority, or some combination of the two. Ministers perceive themselves, and are perceived, as being part of a different authority structure from the 'rational legal' one which lay people generally apply to their work relationships.[6] Moreover, the authority which ministers are seen as having includes the 'right' to direct and control lay people and to interpret the overall purposes and values of the congregation – a viewpoint supported and confirmed by ministers' training, their peers and by denominational institutions.

The second source of ministers' distinctiveness in a congregational context is the status they occupy as boundary-spanners between the individual congregation and its organizational environment, most particularly any denominational institutions. The congregational minister faces in two directions; towards his or her congregation and towards other organizations and individuals who share the same denominational allegiance (Scherer, 1972). The extent to which a congregation's minister is subject to direction and oversight by a denominational headquarters varies, as the case studies illustrate, according to the theology of the denomination and the resources of the individual congregation. But the general principle is that ministers see themselves, to a much greater degree than even senior lay volunteers, as closely linked into a wider denominational world of which the congregation is just a part. For lay people, on the other hand, the dominant concept remains what Warner (1993, p. 1066) has termed 'de facto congregationalism' in which congregations are 'affectively significant associations under local and lay control' and in which responding to the local environment is more important than responding to denominational demands.

Congregations can be seen, then, as having two different systems of authority; the traditional or charismatic one which attaches to ministers of religion in their congregational context, and the rational-legal one which is more familiar in secular voluntary organizations. Since the two systems run in parallel,[7] ongoing disputes between clergy and laity about who has authority over whom are endemic. And the problems are not open to resolution. At the upper echelons of a conventional hierarchical organization there is usually a single role to which all other roles are ultimately accountable. The person occupying the peak role can adjudicate in the case of disputes lower down the organizational tree – even where, for example, professionals and administrators work within separate, parallel authority structures lower down in the organization. In congregations, however, clergy and lay people are more likely to be left in a perpetual power struggle, with no final point of conflict resolution available within the congregation itself.

Special Nature of Congregational Goals

A second organizational feature of congregations which distinguishes them from secular voluntary associations is that they have comparatively little control over defining their own goals. The usual expectation in a membership association is one of exchange; individuals voluntarily donate their time and money to sustain an organization and, in return, they have substantial influence over the purposes and goals of the organization (Knoke and Prensky, 1984). In congregations, as the case studies demonstrated, there is heavy, often exclusive, dependence on the resources of members. Yet the extent to which congregation members can influence goals is limited by the fact that religious principles, by their very nature, are relatively fixed: not open to debate or negotiation. Indeed, there is frequently an assumption underpinning religious organizations that membership, and commitment to fixed goals, is in some way a matter of obligation rather than choice (Thompson, 1970).

To varying degrees, members of congregations are free to debate and decide lower-level means and ends (such as role definitions and operating priorities). But compared with most secular voluntary associations, there is a low ceiling in congregations above which goals move up into the category described by Scott (1987, p. 47) as 'ultimate'.[8] Such goals cannot be challenged because to do so 'calls into question the premises around which the entire enterprise is structured'. Members of congregations must operate below that ceiling and both ministers and denominational structures try to ensure that they do. This is not necessarily seen as problematic by congregants; as the case studies showed, the unchanging elements in congregational life are often highly valued in the context of an otherwise rapidly changing social environment. But those who *are* unhappy about the 'ultimate' goals of their congregation must either give up their membership or remain silent, since goals and structures based on theological principles cannot generally be changed (Cantrell et al., 1983).

Not only can members of congregations not *reject* or question higher level goals, they also become obligated in joining a congregation to positively *accept* higher level goals, even if they themselves would rather give priority to other matters or activities. Thus, churches and synagogues feel obliged to implement 'commonweal' goals as well as 'mutual benefit' ones, irrespective of limited resources and the fact that they may not have an appropriate organizational infrastructure, because both goals fall into the category of 'ultimate' goals in the Judaeo-Christian tradition. And new ideas or requests for resources which are backed up by claims to religious inspiration may have to be given higher priority than might be the case using 'rational' planning criteria.

An Organizational Theory of Congregations

These two key characteristics of congregations – the special authority of ministers and the low ceiling of ultimate goals – can now be used to modify the basic model of voluntary associations such that the modified model provides a more comprehensive explanation of the challenges faced by congregations.

Congregations can be seen as 'special case voluntary associations' in which the actions of members are limited and prescribed in at least two important respects and in ways which would not normally apply in a secular voluntary association. The challenge for ministers, lay staff and lay volunteers then, is one of operating the basic voluntary association model in a way that *also* takes into account the two special organizational features of congregations. The application of the voluntary association model without taking into account the other two features as well can give rise to problems in a congregational context. Conversely, failure to take into account the widely held assumptions about the congregation as a voluntary association can also be a source of difficulties.

An alternative way of thinking about congregations is to view them as organizations which uniquely combine three key elements:
1. associational features (such as a tendency to informality and dependence on voluntary resources of time and money);
2. ministerial roles (which span the boundary between the congregation and denominational institutions and are seen to have traditional and/or charismatic authority); and
3. ultimate goals (that is goals which are non-negotiable) pitched at a low ceiling.

All three of the elements are intrinsic to congregations and interact with each other. For example, ministers can play a key role in empowering lay people in the work they do in their voluntary associational capacity. Conversely, ministers cannot perform the 'prophetic' aspects of their own roles unless the formally-stated ultimate goals of the congregation are accepted by its members. No congregation will survive very long unless it is able both to meet the needs of members *and* to be a credible 'witness' to proclaimed religious goals.

The challenge for a congregation, then, is one of negotiating and maintaining the balance between the three elements in a way appropriate to its own features such as religion, denominational polity, size, type of membership, funding, history and geographical location. Many of the organizational problems which arise in congregations can be seen as reflecting the need to resolve tensions between the elements.

A model of a congregation as a 'special case voluntary association' or as a 'triple element organization' is not a *description* of any particular congregation. Nor is it a prescription of how congregations *ought* to be.[9] It is offered as an explanatory theory; a way of understanding the organizational issues that arise in contemporary English congregations. Each congregation, as the case studies demonstrate, differs from others. But there seem to be sufficient commonalities to suggest that the model may be useful across religions and denominations and that congregations may be able to learn from one another's organizational experiences.

CONCLUSIONS

This chapter has drawn together the main findings from the case studies and earlier literature and discussed the organizational similarities and differences between congregations. The hypothesis that churches and synagogues have in common organizational features and problems is in part upheld. Religion is an important factor in accounting for both the similarities and the differences between congregations.

The idea of congregations as voluntary associations was introduced and found to be helpful in explaining a range of problems encountered by those who work in congregations. Building on this insight, a 'modified voluntary association' model of congregations was proposed which takes into account two special features of congregations with respect to clergy and organizational goals.

Models and theories provide not only descriptions and explanations of problems but also points of comparison and focus for debate. Previous work by the author and colleagues (Billis, 1984 and 1993a; Harris, 1993 and 1994) suggests that models of the kind proposed here can be useful in teasing out the assumptions and aspirations of different organizational actors and easing the process of consensus-building, priority-setting and organizational change.

The following, final, chapter moves away from a close focus on congregations themselves and views them in the context of their environment and the public policy expectations that they face.

10

A Public Policy Perspective on Congregations

INTRODUCTION

This book has focused on congregations and on their work and organization specifically. The previous chapter of this closing Part drew together the findings from empirical studies of individual congregations and proposed a theory of congregational organization. This final chapter steps back from the close-up focus on congregations in order to see them in their organizational context and to make some contributions to current policy debates. First, the many and complex ways in which the case congregations were found to be embedded into their organizational environments is discussed. Then the contribution that religious congregations are making, and can make, to the 'mixed economy of care' and to 'civil society' is considered. The chapter closes with some thoughts about future directions for the study of religious congregations.

CONGREGATIONS IN THEIR ENVIRONMENTS

Open systems theory and institutional analysts emphasize that organizations cannot be understood in isolation from their environments; they affect, and are affected by, their geographical, organizational, cultural and public policy contexts. Chapter 3 outlined some of the key players in the environments of the case congregations (denominational institutions, other religious organizations, local secular voluntary agencies and governmental agencies) and subsequent chapters referred to a range of external influences on them, including pressures to build credibility and legitimacy in their immediate neighbourhoods. Here the web of links between individual congregations and the wider world is re-examined briefly in order to build a fuller picture of where local congregations, as organizations, fit into broader societal activity.

Environmental Influences

Congregations are influenced by their environments but are not passive in relation to such influences. This was particularly evident in the case congregations in relation to their goals. In addition to religious expression and education goals, all four of the congregations had welfare, continuity and social integration goals which were, to some extent at least, a response to their specific social and cultural environments. Using a 'population ecology' perspective (Hannan and Freeman, 1977), the responsiveness of congregations to their environments can be seen as a 'niche-building' exercise; by meeting needs unmet by other local organizations, congregations were creating a special, even unique, place for themselves within their surrounding localities and catchment areas. In so doing, they were helping to ensure their own organizational survival.

Yet it would be simplistic to regard this niche-building as a cynical act of 'goal displacement' (Merton, 1949) by congregations; for the drives towards organizational survival could not be said to have *displaced* religious and educational goals. On the contrary, interviewees generally regarded the implementation of welfare, continuity and social integration goals as implicit in the religious principles officially adhered to in their congregations. Indeed, many interviewees referred to the implementation of these goals in overtly religious language such as 'saving souls for Jesus' (Congregation B), 'being Christ-like' (Congregation A) or 'repair of the world' (Congregation D). Thus, although the congregations were indeed responding and adapting to their environments, they were attempting to do so in a fashion consistent with their own religious values.

In fact, as theories of resource dependency would predict (for example, Pfeffer and Salancik, 1978), all four of the case congregations attempted in various ways actively to *manipulate* their environments in order to ensure implementation of their goals. For example, congregations accepted that they were obliged to maintain formal links with a range of other organizations but beyond those formal obligations, each congregation forged its closest links with organizations which had the most resources to offer them. Congregation B maintained close links with local Christian churches which were historically a source of moral and financial support and which were also potential sources of new members. Congregation C's main organizational environment comprised the congregations and groupings within its own parish through which it was able to plug gaps in its own provision (for example, adult study and clergy to cover for absences) and on whom it could rely for a financial cushion. Congregation A maintained close involvement in the selection of pupils for the local Catholic schools and had given one of the priests special responsibility for liaison with the nearest school because 'If the schools did not exist, attendance and commitment [at the church] would be much lower'.

Contrary to neo-institutional theory (di Maggio and Powell, 1991) which emphasizes the non-rational behaviour of organizations, congregations appeared here to be behaving very rationally; with a view to maximizing organizational benefits to themselves. This was so even when rational behaviour involved turning away from, or giving minimal attention to, organizations with which they were *officially* expected to maintain close links; neighbouring congregations of the same denomination or the denominational hierarchy, for example.

Despite such evidence of the ability of congregations to manipulate and make an impact on their environments, there were also many examples of intractable problems in congregations which reflected environmental factors, including demographic change and the state of the economy, over which they had no control. For example, Congregation B faced a steadily rising average age of membership because of social changes in the Afro-Caribbean population; younger people born in Britain were less interested in pentecostal religion than their immigrant parents. Again, Congregation A faced problems because it happened to be situated in an area of rapid population turnover; a situation which not only gave rise to administrative problems in keeping track of local Catholic residents, but also placed limits on the extent to which lay people could be relied on to carry long term commitments. Congregation D was experiencing major problems in relation to its funding and leadership, both of which problems were regarded as a direct consequence of the economic recession. Those who had lost their jobs were less able to contribute to the congregation financially and were often turning to the congregation for psychological support. At the same time, those still in work were having to give it their full attention, at the expense of their voluntary commitments of time to the synagogue.

In short, the case congregations were influenced by their environments and they also consciously, and often successfully, tried to control those environments. But there were aspects of their environments over which they had little or no control. The findings about the nature of congregations' interaction with their organizational environments have implications for public policy debates about the role of congregations in social welfare and civil society.

THE ROLE OF CONGREGATIONS IN SOCIAL WELFARE

The prospect of an expanded role for congregations in social welfare provision was cited in Chapter 1 as one of the reasons for embarking on this project. Since the 1980s, there have been public policy expectations in the UK that churches and synagogues, like other non-governmental agencies, will take a more prominent role in mainstream social welfare provision and become an integral part of a pluralist welfare-delivery system. How realistic are these expectations on congregations in the light of the study findings?

A Variety of Contributions

The case data confirm findings in the United States (for example Wineburg, 1992) that congregations can make important contributions, in a variety of ways, not only to the welfare of their own members, but also to that of the wider community. Indeed, they suggest that Judaeo-Christian principles generally discourage congregants from making firm distinctions between their 'own' and 'others' in the face of social problems and individual distress. The four case congregations were engaged in numerous welfare activities ranging from informal care to, in the case of three congregations, significant welfare projects requiring regular commitments of voluntary time and substantial financial contributions from the congregation itself. And the welfare activities included not only the pastoral work of clergy but also the care efforts of lay people – men as well as women.

The case data reflect findings in both Europe and North America that members of religious congregations may be predisposed to participate in 'caring' and 'neighbourly' activities (Barker et al., 1992; Cnaan et al., 1993; Hodgkinson et al., 1993). They also show how congregations can provide organizational frameworks within which those in need and those able to give help can be linked up and within which care initiatives can be developed and supported. Clergy, lay employees and lay leaders put people in touch with one another in the normal course of their work. Overlapping friendship networks act as further conduits of information about who is in need of care and who is available to provide it. In fact, much of the welfare work of the four case congregations seemed to exemplify the principles of successful neighbourhood care identified by Abrams and his colleagues (1981, p. 113): 'informality, reciprocity and locality'. And unlike many of the neighbourhoods studied by the Abrams team, congregations seem to have organizational characteristics which enable them to overcome, or avoid, the 'absolutely crucial problem ... of matching care to need – and of doing so in ways that permit the growth of friendly, mutually supportive relationships...' (ibid).

Practical Limitations

The findings about the organizational issues that surround the provision of welfare in congregations (discussed in Chapter 8), also suggest that congregations may be able to support some forms of caring more successfully than others. Members of congregations sustain with relative ease the less 'organized' types of welfare such as mutual aid, social integration and various kinds of informal care. In fact, as Abrams pointed out, common membership of a church is a factor which 'legitimate[s] intrusion' into the life of another person known to be in need of help (in Bulmer, 1986, p. 114). In the case of more formal welfare projects, however, it seems that social policy-makers should be cautious about their expectations on congregations. Congregational welfare projects have to compete for resources with a range of other highly valued congregational activities. Their continuity may be dependent on the enthusiasm and personal circumstances of just one or two committed people.

The data also indicate that much of the attraction of welfare projects for the volunteers who run them is the opportunity they provide for self-development and autonomous decision-making. Where projects are subject to the intervention of outside sponsors, the commitment and enthusiasm of volunteers may melt away. Even though such sponsorship reflects project success and offers the possibility of expansion with less responsibility, it may also take from volunteers what they most value; the ability to control the project and run it according to their own preferences.

An Expanded Role in Welfare?

In such circumstances, there is not much potential for congregations to expand their provision of formal or large-scale welfare services whose continuity can be relied on and which conform with professional standards. Congregations are already contributing in 'quiet' ways to social welfare, especially through the emotional and practical support they provide to members who might otherwise have to seek help from other agencies. But there is little scope for congregations to increase their contribution to the mixed economy of welfare by taking on more formal welfare projects. The initial enthusiasm and demand from members may be present but the organizational capacity to sustain such projects is unlikely to be found in congregations.

From a public policy perspective, it is perhaps more useful to see congregations as 'nurseries' for more formal welfare projects; hospitable environments in which new ideas and appropriate organizational structures can be nurtured in response to social needs at the local community level. Through their own sole efforts or through their involvement in coordinated local initiatives, congregations can provide policy-makers with examples which can be adopted and adapted for wider use. But if projects are to be sustained in the longer term and if they are to meet the needs of substantial numbers of people, they will require income, expertise and regulation of a kind which most congregations in England are unlikely to be able to supply without substantial external support. In some cases denominational institutions may provide necessary help, as happened, for example, with the Church Urban Fund which supported local initiatives by Anglican churches. But a more likely scenario is the 'floating off' of the original projects to become independent charities, or their absorption into the welfare provision of national voluntary agencies or local governmental agencies.

A public policy perspective which sees congregations as sustainers of informal care but as no more than initiators or nurturers of more formal projects, would be in tune with two further findings from the case congregations. First, there is an ever-present danger in congregations of well-disposed people (volunteers, lay staff and clergy alike) over-extending themselves. Religious principles about caring and the peer pressure of a membership association can induce people to make ambitious commitments which they cannot fulfil or which they fulfil to the detriment of their health, their families or their outside employment. Second, as indicated in Chapter 8, the welfare provided in a congregational context reflects in a range of ways the religious values underpinning congregational activity. Often 'religious' and 'welfare' activities are intermingled and indistinguishable, with prayer being a central or additional feature of care. These special religious aspects of congregational welfare may well not conform with secular models of social welfare provision. A social policy which pressurizes congregations to minimize religious aspects or which positively encourages over-commitment would be highly questionable.

CONGREGATIONS IN CIVIL SOCIETY AND THE VOLUNTARY SECTOR

There has been renewed global interest recently in the public space which is the sphere of neither the state nor individuals and households. Disillusion with 'big government' and 'nation states', a concern about the implications of individualism, and the puzzle of how to build new societies in the countries of Eastern and Central Europe and the South – all of these have focused attention on ways in which people can do things for themselves and for others through collective action which is not dominated or coerced by the state.

As discussed in Chapter 1, this public space is referred to in a number of ways by commentators rooted in a variety of disciplinary, theoretical and philosophical perspectives. The terms 'civil society', 'the voluntary sector' and 'the third sector' are often used. But all of these are contentious concepts and questions about their definition and their normative connotations have been the subject of numerous articles and books (see for example, Seligman, 1992 and Walzer, 1995 on civil society; Kendall and Knapp, 1996 and Van Til, 1988 on the voluntary sector; and Evers, 1993 on the links between the concepts of civil society and the third sector).

The purpose of this section is not to revisit these definitional and normative debates, important though they are, but to focus instead on what may be expected of congregations as one of the constituents of that public space which is the sphere of neither the state nor individuals. To facilitate discussion, the terms 'civil society', the 'third sector' and the 'voluntary sector' are used here to refer to that public space and are used interchangeably.[1]

Congregations in the Public Space

The civil society public space is occupied by a range of discourses, activities, movements, groupings and organizations – of which congregations are one example. Congregations are at the boundary of the private and public spheres of activity; through them religion moves from the private sphere of individual devotion and household practices into the public arena of collective worship and social activities, and back again (Berger and Neuhaus, 1996; Casanova, 1994).

In the UK, interest in civil society and the third sector has been expressed in both negative terms (concern to counter the disempowering tendencies of the 'nanny state' or the growth of marketization and consumerism) and positive terms (praise for volunteers from all parts of the political spectrum) (Bryant, 1995). As indicated earlier in this chapter, there have been numerous initiatives to transfer functions and responsibilities, including social welfare, from the public sector to the voluntary sector.

Those who advance the case for building and maintaining civil societies and third sectors suggest a range of benefits that can accrue from the activities of their constituent groupings and organizations: promoting social change, informing public policy, nurturing citizenship skills, providing mediating structures between individuals and the state, providing fora for debate, fostering voluntarism, promoting social cohesion and trust, and responding to social problems (Etzioni, 1992; Putnam et al., 1993). Suggested possible benefits for individuals who participate in civil society and the third sector include self-development, self-fulfilment, being cared for and being integrated into broader groupings (Kumar, 1993; Lohmann, 1992; Mason, 1995).

What, then, do the findings suggest about the current and potential contribution of congregations to civil societies and voluntary sectors? Research in the US has suggested that membership of religious congregations encourages individual involvement in both political processes and voluntary organizations (Bellah et al., 1985; Hall, 1996; Hodgkinson et al., 1993; Stackhouse, 1990; Verba et al., 1995). What contributions can English congregations make?

The Contribution of Congregations

One of the most striking findings from the case studies was the proficiency with which congregations generally perform 'social integration' functions; creating links between individuals and also providing routes into other institutions and networks beyond congregations themselves (Durkheim, 1965; Mason, 1995). For those who feel rootless, marginalized or alone in the area in which they live, or for those experiencing a personal crisis, congregations provide a physical place for gathering – meeting face-to-face – with other local residents. Through participation in specific activities in congregations, many of them extending well beyond strictly 'worship' activities, acquaintanceships, friendships and mutual aid between individuals and households are nurtured (Jerrome, 1989).

Congregations can provide a framework in which people can meet others of similar background, viewpoint and experience and similarities are not confined to opinions on religious matters. Congregations can bring together people from similar ethnic groups, countries and classes, people who have a common interest in particular 'leisure-time' pursuits, and people who have shared experiences of a particular personal or social problem. Even more striking in the context of a discussion of social integration, is the potential capacity of congregations to bring together people from *different* backgrounds – people from different ethnic and occupational backgrounds and from different age groups who would not otherwise have had the opportunity to get to know each other or to participate in shared activities.

The relationships nurtured within congregations, in turn, help people to develop their personal and social identity. In the context of a congregation people can experience a sense of belonging, of being valued, of being protected and of being 'at home'; a feeling that has been likened by Warner (1994, p. 66) to being 'a member of a large family in a huge living room'. This feature of congregations makes them particularly important in the era of 'high modernity' in which individuals may be searching for new ways of establishing the kinds of trusting relationships which are essential for their sense of the security but which are no longer necessarily provided by families and neighbourhoods (Giddens, 1990).

Congregations are also crucibles within which individual self-development and self-fulfilment can take place. They provide opportunities to learn organizational and communication skills, to try out ideas, to take responsibilities, to have new experiences and to interpret current issues. As Dempsey (1989, p. 11) has noted, congregations 'can provide the social context in which self-realization, the experience of bondedness of close relationships and a sense of belonging can occur.'

In addition to the intrinsic benefits they offer in drawing people into their own internal activities and networks, congregations also provide a means through which people are linked to other organizations and events beyond the congregation, in the local area and in the wider national environment.[2] Thus, through their congregations, members hear about local activities and issues, they attend outside meetings and events as representatives of their congregations, they participate in activities organized by other organizations but held on the congregation's premises, and they may hear a range of interpretations of the events occurring in the broader religious and secular worlds.

In short, a prime contribution of congregations to contemporary UK society derives from their twin features of being locally based and being *de facto* voluntary associations. As such, they can respond flexibly and sensitively to local needs and provide a response to the marginalization of minority groups and individual feelings of rootlessness. They can provide a refuge for individuals and *simultaneously* enable them to integrate into the society beyond the congregations themselves. In general, congregations can counterbalance contemporary trends towards social fragmentation; a situation in which 'People participate segmentally, that is, on the basis of special interests and occasions rather than as whole persons, and they do so in groups that are themselves only weakly bound into the rest of society' (Selznick, 1994, p. 5).

At the same time as they facilitate self-development and provide expressive rewards to their members, congregations also generate 'social capital' (Coleman, 1988; Putnam et al., 1993). In effect, congregations can teach people the benefits, obligations, norms and skills of collective action; learning which becomes a resource for the public good because it encourages and enables people to work together on problems and tasks. The case congregations provided numerous examples of people being socialized into group decision-making processes, learning the implications of voluntarism, being helped to develop leadership competence, being encouraged to speak in public, and learning the realities of achieving organizational change. Through their welfare projects congregations also raised members' awareness of broader social problems (homelessness, for example). All these experiences are applicable and transferable to other contexts. And as people develop confidence in their own abilities, they are more likely to be willing to engage in collective activities beyond their immediate congregational context.

It seems, then, that English congregations may indeed provide many of the benefits anticipated by earlier writers on civil society including the development of citizenship skills, fostering of voluntarism, promoting social cohesion and responding to social problems. However, the case studies provided little evidence that congregations are directly involved in promoting social change, informing public policy or acting in a 'prophetic' role. Such work *was* mentioned by several interviewees but usually in the context of a concern that it was always crowded out by the imperative to respond to immediate needs of members and local communities. At least in the English context it is probably more indirectly – through denominational institutions and denominational religious leaders – that congregations make their impacts on public policy. Reports on the inner city published by the Church of England and books by the Chief Rabbi, for example, have generally attracted the attention of both the mass media and politicians (Archbishop of Canterbury, 1985; Sacks, 1995)

The Expectations on Congregations

It seems clear that religious congregations can make important contributions to the maintenance of civil society, especially through facilitating social integration, self-identity, self-realization and interest in wider civic engagement. The facilitating role is essentially a product of their local roots and of the framework that they provide for voluntary 'gathering' or 'association'. However, as indicated in Chapter 9, congregations are appropriately seen as 'special case' voluntary associations; they have two key organizational features which are additional to their associational nature – the role of ministers and the low ceiling of their fixed (religious) goals. What are the implications of these special features for the debate about the role of congregations in civil society?

In the first place, expectations that congregations will play an important role in integrating people into their local communities need to be tempered by an awareness that senior lay leaders,

ministers of religion and denominational institutions do not necessarily see social integration as a prime purpose of congregations.
This is especially the case with Christian congregations; trends to
encourage 'fellowship' in churches through, for example, lay pastoral visiting and refreshments after services, have not met with
universal approval amongst religious leaders (Greenwood, 1988;
Warner, 1994). If participation in social welfare service-delivery or
participation in local civic activities become too dominant in the
constellation of a congregation's activities, congregational leaders
are likely to raise questions about whether 'core' religious purposes
are being eclipsed (Gilkey, 1994; Jeavons, 1994).

Second, and in so far as associational activities *are* tolerated or
even encouraged, it is within a contextual assumption that a congregation, by reason of its religious purposes, is not subject to the
directions and pressures of the state or the market. Any attempt by
politicians or business-people to instruct congregations in their
duties are likely, therefore, to be counter-productive; a lesson
which is being painfully learned in Eastern Europe where churches
are playing a key role in the building of civil societies but are also
fighting to retain their autonomy from governments (Liborakina,
1996).

Interviewee responses in the case congregations were underpinned by assumptions about a facilitating, and non-exploitative
governmental approach to religious congregations. What congregations want from governmental organizations is a loose and supportive, political and legal framework which allows them to pursue
their own purposes and to contribute to the well-being of their own
members and their local communities to the extent, and in the
manner, they feel able (Carter, 1994; Roozen, 1984).[3] They do not
want to be overwhelmed with externally imposed rules or responsibilities, such as an expectation that they will take responsibility for
responding to major social problems or that they will 'tone down'
the religious principles underlying their work (Berger and
Neuhaus, 1996). They may choose to do some of these things but
they are resentful of assumptions that they *will* do so.

Like many other constituent organizations of civil society and the
voluntary sector, religious congregations contribute well to the
public good when they are left to pursue their own chosen goals
in an autonomous space. But because their contributions are often
attractive to politicians and policy-makers, the latter can be
tempted to intervene in goal-setting by congregations; to encour-

age them, for example, to branch out into new public-benefit activities. There may also be a temptation to encourage congregations to play down their more distinctive purposes such as religious worship or to move away from an associational way of doing things and conform to more bureaucratic and professional norms.

The public policy temptations need to be resisted both by congregations themselves and by those who value distinct voluntary sectors and civil societies. In fact congregations might need to be more proactive in advocacy than they presently are, in order to ensure that their views on their own roles are heard and accepted. For attempts to co-opt congregations to the governmental agenda could threaten the special combination of features which make them so valuable at present, both to their members and to their surrounding localities. It must not be forgotten that congregations are basically volunteer-run organizations; and that volunteers whose autonomy is threatened tend to vote with their feet.

LOOKING AHEAD

Preceding chapters have focused closely on the work and organization of congregations and the challenges faced by those who run them. This final chapter has widened the perspective to look at the ways in which congregations are embedded into their environments and the link between congregational activities and public policy expectations – what Barrett and Fudge (1981) have referred to as the 'policy-action relationship'.

Drawing on empirical data about congregational organization, observations have been offered about the contributions congregations are making, and can make, to the 'mixed economy of welfare' and to 'civil society'. It seems clear that public and social policy analysts should give more attention to religious congregations. They are significant players in that public space which is outside of the state and the market. At the same time, congregations have limitations as instruments of public policy which derive from their distinctive organizational features.

This book has made an initial attempt to tease out those distinctive features and to explain the organizational challenges faced by lay people and ministers who work in congregations. Congregations of different denominations and even different religions clearly have much in common. Yet they also differ organizationally in important respects, not all of which are accounted for by their differing religious orientations. I have proposed some explanations for the various findings but there is scope for wider and deeper investigation of the topic now that the foundations have been laid.

The four cases at the heart of this book produced rich data and allowed for the building of theoretical insights but more such case studies are now needed to facilitate the testing and further development of congregational organizational theory. Again, there are limitations on the depth of understanding that can be achieved about a congregation by a researcher who is a religious outsider, and future studies by a religiously-mixed research team could expect to uncover a deeper understanding of the organizational issues facing individual congregations and how they are perceived.

Another possible focus for future research is the organizational environment of religious congregations. In this project it was only possible to make initial and relatively simplistic analyses of elements in the environment of congregations but a more specific examination of the 'fields', 'networks' and 'constituencies' of which congregations are a part would help to throw more light both on the organizational issues faced by congregations and on their public policy roles.

Finally, it must be said that this book confined itself to the local congregations of Christianity and Judaism. The question immediately arises of how far its findings are applicable to the congregations of other religions.

So there is much work still to be done on congregational organization. All the same, I hope this book will prove useful. It has much to say to policy-makers and to students of the voluntary sector. But, above all, I hope it will provide insights, support and inspiration for those who work in local congregations and who are curious about the challenges they face as they try to organize God's work.

Appendix:
Research Approach and
Fieldwork

RESEARCH APPROACH

Social Administration

This study is embedded in the interdisciplinary tradition of *social admin-istration*. It attempts to 'shed light on particular institutions or systems' (Titmuss, 1986 p. 58); 'to identify and clarify problems' (Donnison, 1973, p. 36); and to develop 'usable theory' or 'ideas that make sense and can be utilized by those whose business it is to cope with the complexity and chaos' (Billis, 1993a, p. 2). While focusing on institutions, it also keeps in mind the organizational and public policy environment within which they operate.

Institutional Analysis

The study is theoretically driven by institutional and neo-institutional approaches to organizational analysis. (A summary of the institutional school is found in Perrow, 1986, Chapter 5, and of neo-institutional thought in di Maggio and Powell, 1991. Selznick, 1994, Chapter 9, provides a discussion of institutional theory.) Elements in institutional and neo-institutional approaches which have informed the approach to this study include:

— analysis of the whole organization;
— use of case studies for research;
— respect for the meanings and explanations given by organizational actors themselves;
— interest in historical roots of current situations;
— assumption that there are links between organizational structures and functions;
— interest in unplanned change and unanticipated consequences of change;
— interest in power and power relationships;
— interest in informal processes and functions and taken-for-granted practices underlying formal structures;
— acceptance that there are constraints on rational organizational behaviour;
— interest in values, goals and policy;
— interest in organizational problems;

— emphasis on the way in which organizations both affect and are affected by their environments; and
— interest in commonalities between organizations.

Case Studies with a Qualitative Methodology

The decision to conduct case studies reflected the research objectives and focus including:

— working within the framework of institutional theory (see above);
— building knowledge in a relatively unexplored area;
— generating descriptive and analytical material;
— identifying generic elements across organizations; and
— building explanatory theory through the elaboration of emergent patterns and themes (Bryman, 1989).

The decision to combine a qualitative approach with the case study method reflected the theoretical and practical aims of the study. These suggested the need:

— to be sensitive to the impact of religious values on those who work or participate in congregations;
— to give weight to interviewees' own perspectives and understandings;
— to have an approach acceptable to those who work in congregations;
— to take into account the special problems of research access arising from the outsider status of a researcher who is not the same religion or denomination as the congregation being studied and may not be the same gender or race as interviewees (Rhodes, 1994);
— to uncover organizational perspectives and insights additional to those available in the limited existing literature and not anticipated by the researcher (Van Maanen, 1979); and
— to generate usable, explanatory theory grounded in practical experience (Glaser and Strauss, 1967; Turner, 1983).

In sum, the proposed study seemed to conform with the criteria for combining case studies with a qualitative approach, described by Powell and Friedkin (1987, p. 183): 'The methodology ... is typically used in research when the issues under investigation are complex, multi-faceted, nonrepetitive, and highly contextual, making more formal analysis impossible. ... The ideal case study offers plausible explanations and develops a detailed picture of the complexity of the issues that are involved in the case. The rich contextual material that is presented may also enable the reader to develop alternative explanations ...'

Theory Building

The departure point for this study was anecdotal evidence of problems faced by those working in and with congregations and a wish to provide explanations for those problems. A starting agenda for the empirical investigation was provided by themes in earlier academic and 'practitioner' literature (Chapters 1 and 2).

The analytic strategy for handling the case study evidence involved both 'pattern matching' and 'explanation building' (Yin, 1994). In so far as there was earlier relevant material, the empirically found patterns were compared with them. The findings from the four cases were also compared with each other. Theoretically-based explanations were sought for differences from earlier literature and for differences between cases. Topic-by-topic explanations (Chapters 4–8) were brought together in Chapter 9 to develop broader explanations of the organizational issues found in the case congregations.

This process of theory development reflects the 'iterative mode of explanation-building' in which 'the case study evidence is examined, theoretical positions are revised, and the evidence is examined once again from a new perspective' (Yin, 1994, p. 111). The development of explanatory models in the social and public administration traditions is discussed in Chapter 15 of Billis, 1984.

FIELDWORK

Securing Interviews

In each of the congregations 'a key informant' was identified to maintain liaison with the researcher and to help her secure a list of possible interviewees. Key informants were asked to suggest at least one potential interviewee in each of the following categories:

— minister of religion
— lay paid staff (if applicable)
— congregation teacher
— lay celebrant or religiously specialist lay person
— lay leader or lay officer
— other senior or regular volunteer
— lay elder no longer actively involved
— boundary spanner between the congregation and its environment
— outsider familiar with the congregation

A total of 12 interviews were sought in each congregation with the group of interviewees being varied as to length of time involved with the congregation; gender; employment status; and age. In Congregation A, which was the only congregation which was ethnically mixed, interviewees were also varied as to their ethnic backgrounds.

In Congregation A, potential interviewees were approached via the priest who was the key informant but in the other three congregations, the researcher was able to write directly to identified people.

The Interviews

A total of 49 interviews were finally conducted; 13 in Congregation D and 12 in each of the other three congregations. In general, the total interviews achieved in each congregation reflected a range of characteristics and roles. For Congregation B, it was possible to interview only two men and there were no under-30s in the interviewee list; but this reflected the gender and age balance within the congregation itself. The interviews achieved in Congregations C and D reflected not only a wide range of characteristics but also a range of known viewpoints within the congregations.

In Congregations A, C and D, there were no substantial difficulties in securing interviews. Although twelve interviews were eventually achieved in Congregation B, a number of difficulties were experienced in finding individuals willing to be interviewed; despite the openness and warmth with which the researcher was received at meetings and worship in the congregation. This experience reflects Lee's contention (1993, p. 133) that, even when 'physical access' is readily granted to a researcher, subsequent 'social access' can still be problematic.

The interviews themselves in Congregation B were also different. Several interviewees were reluctant to talk about anything other than their personal religious experiences and several wanted to use the interview time for evangelizing (Warner, 1988). The fact that the researcher was white and not a 'born-again' Christian was clearly a barrier; as was the fact that social research itself is not valued in the Pentecostal tradition which 'devalue[s] worldly knowledge in favour of divine revelation' (Lee, 1993, p. 6). There were two further factors which seemed to contribute to the difficulties. One, which only emerged during the course of the interviews themselves, was the tradition in the congregation of giving maximum authority to the pastor; many interviewees were uncomfortable about making statements about the congregation and frequently referred the researcher to the pastor. In addition, because of the fundamentalist beliefs espoused by the congregation, they tended to regard *all* aspects of congregational life – including organizational matters – as part of their 'sacred ministry' and not something to be shared with an outsider.

Study Report

Access to congregations and to individuals within them was secured against an undertaking of confidentiality and anonymity. In view of this and the fact that the researcher wished to avoid creating unnecessary distress or dissension within the case congregations, a number of precautions have been taken in presenting the data. First, only minimal information is given about characteristics of the four congregations. Second, some 'rules of thumb' are used for identifying the source of quotations and viewpoints.

— All are attributed to the relevant congregation.
— An indication is given of the role or status of the interviewee where it is relevant for the significance of what was said and/or where factual and apparently non-contentious matters were under discussion.
— Role or status is given as far as possible in general rather than specific terms; for example, 'Lay Leader' is used to refer to senior lay officers, other senior volunteers and lay elders.
— Statements which contain strong criticisms and/or which are readily identifiable, are not attributed to speakers.
— Small changes have been made occasionally to help disguise the source of quotations.
— Potentially controversial quotations, including personal criticisms, have been omitted altogether.

Notes

CHAPTER 1

1. This use of the term 'congregation' follows Hopewell (1987) who refers to groups of people who 'regularly gather for what they feel to be religious purposes' (p. 5). See Glossary.
2. The terms 'minister' and 'minister of religion' are used throughout this book to refer collectively to the religious functionaries of Christian and Jewish congregations. The term 'clergy' is used to refer to Christian religious leaders. See Glossary.
3. There *is* a body of knowledge known as 'ecclesiology' which deals with the theology of church structures. In contrast, the purpose of this book is to provide a contribution to *social scientific* knowledge.
4. The inclusion of religious institutions within the ambit of academic fields which have traditionally focused on governmental institutions is not a major conceptual leap. Tiller (1983 p. 52) reminds us that the very roots of current public service are religious: 'Ministry is service to individuals or to a community. In this country the tradition of public service was formerly expressed by the description of government departments as ministries and the government itself as an administration.'
5. For the definition of this and other specific terms see Glossary.
6. Contemporary social theory points to the problematic nature of the concept of 'authenticity'. The concept imputes authority to whatever it is applied to and in so doing it ignores the constructed and synthetic nature of 'history' and the role of power (see, for example, Foucault and Gordon, 1980). In using the concept in this section, I am merely reflecting the literature on churches and synagogues.
7. The North American literature includes some examinations of individual congregations and local groups of congregations conducted by consultants and academics. The disciplinary base of these 'congregational studies' and the reasons for doing them vary (Carroll et al., 1986; Dudley et al., 1991; Roozen et al., 1984; Wind and Lewis, 1994). Scherer (1980, p. 369) points out that congregational studies generally have been more interested in a congregation's relation to its 'environing community' than in its organizational features.

CHAPTER 2

1. The terminology differs from both common usage and the usage adopted in this study (see 'church' and 'denomination' in Glossary). It should also be noted that the typology was developed for use in relation to *Christian* groupings and institutions (Hill, 1973). Liebman

(1983, p. 323) argues that the typology cannot be applied to contemporary synagogues since it 'assumes a closed society in which the religious order is confronted only by the secular order and the individual needs of its members'.

2. The translation of *Gesellschaft* as 'association', is potentially confusing to English-speaking readers. Although the intention of the original theory was to make a conceptual distinction between informal, affective forms on the one hand, and rational, structured organizational forms on the other hand, the word 'association' is usually linked in English with ideas about people coming together freely in to groups to do things for each other – as in the term 'voluntary associations'.

3. This paragraph refers to *Christian* theological perspectives on the organization of *churches*. There is no comparable literature on synagogues because, unlike churches, synagogues are not construed in Judaism as inherently 'sacred' or 'God-constructed'. They traditionally fulfil sociological functions as places of prayer, study and meeting.

4. This is not an exhaustive overview of theoretical and analytical approaches. Herman's 1984 analysis of a Canadian Anglican congregation, for example, uses a form of *social network analysis. Role and task analysis* is used by Sklare (1955) in his study of US synagogues and by Ranson and his colleagues (1977) in their study of the work of clergy in the UK.

5. The term 'organizational goal' is used here in a broad sense to refer to 'purposes' or 'ends' – both those provided by official statements and ideologies and those which motivate participants in churches and synagogues. See also Chapters 3 and 4.

6. See Glossary.

7. In this section and throughout this book the term 'role' is used to refer to 'a set of expectations of behaviour in a given social situation' (SSORU, 1974, p. 266), and the term 'functions' refers to duties 'prescribed for a particular position within an organisation' (p. 257) such as 'casework' or 'community organisation'. They are ongoing and open-ended 'in contrast to 'tasks' which imply some specific objective and time limit' (p. 257).

CHAPTER 3

1. Details of the research approach and fieldwork are provided in the Appendix.

2. The information given here refers to the period January 1992–June 1993 when the bulk of the research data was obtained. It does not necessarily apply at the time of publication of this book.

3. Quote from congregation interview.

4. Extract from the service sheet for the 25th Anniversary Celebration Eucharist of Congregation C, May 1993.

5. The deacons and deaconesses were people who were ordained for special service by the congregation but who worked in secular

employment. The pastor explained in interview that the organizational structure of the congregation is biblically inspired. He referred to Acts, Chapter 6 which describes 'deacons' who care for the material side of ministry.

6. The term 'goal' is used here in a broad sense to refer to 'purposes' or 'ends' – both those provided by official statements and ideologies and those which motivate participants in churches and synagogues (see also Chapter 4). Data derive from congregational publicity material; answers to questions about the aims of specific congregational activities; and interviewees' hopes for the future of their congregations. Pilot interviews indicated that it would not be appropriate to ask direct questions in interviews about goals or purposes of congregations since they could be misconstrued as a questioning of the individual's religious commitment or the congregation's legitimacy.

7. Extract from 30th Anniversary Service Booklet of Congregation B.

8. 'Members' of congregations are defined here by social identification rather than by official statements, as those people who regard themselves as regular participants in the activities of a congregation and are regarded by others as such. See Glossary.

CHAPTER 4

1. Useful discussions about the concept of an 'organizational goal' are found in Etzioni (1961), Perrow (1970) and SSORU (1974).

2. There was no evidence in earlier studies or the case study of Congregation D that this point applies to non-Christian congregations. In fact, interviewees in Congregation D recounted examples of public 'rows' amongst lay leaders and between lay leaders and the rabbi.

3. The terms are from Hirschman (1970).

4. Etzioni (1970, p. 2) identified this as a problem common to all kinds of organizations: 'the instrumental processes of adaptation to the environment and of goal implementation have to be balanced by the expressive processes of social and normative integration.'

CHAPTER 5

1. As in previous chapters, the terms 'religious functionary' and 'minister' are used here to refer generically to religious leaders (see Glossary). The term 'role' is used to refer to 'a set of expectations of behaviour in a given social situation' (SSORU, 1974 p. 266).

2. These distinctions are derived from the work of Weber (1964). Their use by other writers on congregational organization was referred to in Chapter 2.

CHAPTER 6

1. The emphasis in earlier social science research on the role of religious functionaries and the lack of attention to the roles of lay people, may be explained by the tendency of social scientists until recently to focus on men's experiences. Stanley and Wise (1993, p. 27) point out that '... although women are frequently massively present within whatever is studied, we but rarely appear in the end products of this. This may be because women are simply not 'seen' by researchers, are ignored by them or else our experiences are distorted by them.'

2. The term 'volunteer' is used in this book to refer to a lay person who makes a commitment to do work on an unpaid basis in, or on behalf of, his or her congregation. See Glossary.

CHAPTER 7

1. Since the study, the Vatican has ruled that women and girls may be altar servers, although no bishop is obliged to permit it within his own diocese.

2. The term 'organizational structure' refers here to groupings of 'organizational roles'. This follows Scott (1987, p. 15) who defines 'social structures' as 'the patterned or regularized aspects of the relationships existing among participants in an organization'.

3. Scott (1987, p. 181) summarizes the resource dependence approach to organizational analysis as follows: 'Since no organization generates all the resources necessary for its goal attainment or survival, organizations are forced to enter into exchanges, becoming interdependent with other environmental groups ... Unequal exchange relations can generate power and dependency differences among organizations, which are therefore expected to enter into exchange relations cautiously and to pursue strategies that will enhance their own bargaining position.'

CHAPTER 8

1. Intercessory prayer has been reported in medical journals as having a positive impact on patient recovery (Byrd 1988).

2. See discussion in Chapter 4 about 'mutual benefit' and 'commonweal' goals.

CHAPTER 9

1. The methodology of using case studies to build explanatory theory is outlined in the Appendix.

2. This cultural explanation is speculative as it was not a point made explicitly by any interviewees.

3. The term 'association' is used in this chapter as in recent social science literature and not in the very specific sense in which it has been used to refer to churches in some literature, nor in the sense of *Gesellschaft* (Tonnies, 1955). See Chapter 2 for a discussion of these points.

4. This is despite the widely held view that 'most of the situations of modern social life are manifestly incompatible with religion as a pervasive influence upon day-to-day life' (Giddens, 1990, p. 109).

5. As discussed in earlier chapters, rabbis are not 'priests' (see Glossary). The discussion here is about perceptions rather than what is officially the case.

6. The discussion here is about how ministers see themselves and are seen in their congregational context. The formal polities of many denominations, especially episcopal ones such as Roman Catholicism and the Church of England, describe the relationship between a denominational hierarchy and congregational ministers in terms which may be seen as 'bureaucratic' and based on rational legal authority (Harrison, 1960; Luidens, 1982).

7. The suggestion here that there are 'dual' or 'parallel' authority structures in operation within congregations builds on an analysis by Chaves (1993) of Protestant denominations in the US. He conceptualizes them as 'dual structures ... constituted by two parallel organizational structures: a religious authority structure and an agency structure' (p. 8).

8. In this respect, faith-based organizations share features of some political groups, social movements and service-providing non-profit organizations. In congregations, however, the low ceiling of ultimate goals combines uneasily with associational expectations that members should have freedom to control goals at all levels, even ultimate goals.

9. This point needs emphasis. The organizational models provided here are intended to be explanatory and *not* prescriptive. The findings about how people perceive the work and organization of congregations may not match official or theological statements about what *ought to be* the case. Warner (1994) points out that some Christian theologians are especially uncomfortable with the idea that congregations may perform 'social integration' functions as well as 'religious' ones.

CHAPTER 10

1. In defining civil society and the voluntary sector in this broad way as the public space between the state and individuals and households, I am following Selznick (1994, p. 358) who argues that 'definitions in social theory should be weak, inclusive, and relatively uncontroversial' ... the point is not to eliminate controversy but to transfer it to a more appropriate place ...'.

2. Hall (1995, p. 15) notes that in a civil society membership of autonomous groups must be 'both voluntary and overlapping'.
3. This accords with most theories of civil society which assume 'the existence of rule-of-law conditions that effectively protect citizens from state arbitrariness' (Mouzelis, 1995, p. 225). States can be both a threat and a safeguard for civil societies.

Glossary

Church
In this study the term 'church' refers to an *organization*: a coming together at the local level of Christians for worship, instruction and other religious activities. **Clergy** may be appointed by or to the organization and there may, or may not, be other paid staff. A local church may, or may not, be based within a building. This working definition derives from common usage. Sociologists sometimes use the term 'church' to refer to one 'ideal type' of religious organization (see also see **Denomination**). And Christian theologians distinguish between local churches and the much broader 'Church' or *ekklesia* or 'assembly of God' which is the whole community of Christian believers.

Clergy
The term 'clergy' is used in this study to refer broadly to *Christian* religious functionaries including 'priests', 'vicars', 'curates', 'ministers', 'presbyters', 'rectors', 'preachers' and 'pastors'. (The different terms reflect differing theological interpretations of religious authority.) Some Christian denominations and groups do not have separate clergy roles; for example, the Society of Friends and House Churches. Of those that do, many, such as the Salvation Army, do not invest the clergy with special sacramental privileges. (See also **Priest** and **Religious Functionary**.)

Congregation
This study follows Hopewell's definition (1987, p. 5) of a congregation as a local organization in which people 'regularly gather for what they feel to be religious purposes' and as 'a group that possesses a special name and recognized members who assemble regularly to celebrate a more universally practised worship but who communicate with each other sufficiently to develop intrinsic patterns of conduct, outlook and story' (p. 12). The term 'congregation' refers in this book to 'institutionalized' structures – organizations with relatively stable sets of roles, status expectations and legitimating procedures (O'Dea, 1961; Scott, 1987). It excludes both religious social movements and informal groupings.

Denomination
The term 'denomination' is used here according to common usage; to refer to a grouping within a religion, for example 'Methodism', 'Congregationalism', 'Reform Judaism'. As with the term **Church**, sociologists have used the term 'denomination' in a special sense to refer to a specific ideal type of organization.

Emancipation
During the period 1770–1870, largely as a result of the impact of the French Revolution and the 'Enlightenment', 'Jewish communities [in

Europe] underwent a transformation that changed their legal status, their occupational distribution, their cultural habits, as well as their religious outlook and behavior ... Jews moved ... toward the standard common in their non-Jewish surroundings' (Katz, 1978, p. 1). The physical and metaphorical breaking down of the ghetto walls resulted in Jews combining secular learning with religious learning as they moved into the wider society.

Established Church
The Church of England, as the 'established church' in England, has a distinctive status as the official ecclesiastical authority which is enshrined in law. Parishes and deaneries cover the whole country so that every individual has, in principle, a link to an Anglican parish church.

Members
Members of congregations are defined in this book by social identification, as those people who regard themselves as regular participants in the activities of a congregation and are regarded by others as such. Roman Catholic churches do not have an official membership. In Anglican churches, the electoral roll is the official membership list but it does not necessarily reflect participation. In 'congregational' structures, where churches and synagogues are totally self-supporting, a 'member' is strictly speaking somebody who has paid the current year's subscription.

Minister: See Religious Functionary

Parish
Jackson (1974, p. 152) defines a parish as 'the basic unit whereby a church with universal claims makes provision for spiritual ministry to a population'. In England, the Anglican and Roman Catholic Churches are both organized on a parish basis. Each parish may have one or many individual **Congregations**.

Priest
A priest has special authority in religious ritual; 'an individual set aside for cultic functions especially prayer and sacrifice' (Dulles, 1978, p. 151). Priestly duties involve being 'a mediator ... between God and the people' (Fichter, 1954, p. 125). Christian **Clergy** may or may not be priests in this sense. Although **Rabbis** may carry out ceremonial and ritualistic tasks during acts of worship in synagogues, there is no longer a Jewish priesthood. With the destruction of the Second Temple by the Romans in AD 70 and the dispersal of the Jewish people, the functions of the priestly caste became redundant. The descendants of the priestly caste remain a distinctive group within Judaism with some special obligations and privileges but without the right to leadership.

Rabbi

A rabbi is a Jewish religious leader. He (rarely she) is *not* a **Priest**. 'The effective exercise of the rabbinic role rests essentially on the incumbent's superior knowledge and superior interpretive skill, not on his descent or personal magnetism' (Israel, 1966, p. 389). Only those who have taken a recognized course of study and preparation with existing rabbis are considered 'rabbis'. Other Jewish religious functionaries are referred to as 'ministers' (Goulston, 1968).

Religious Functionary

The term 'religious functionary' follows Ranson et al. (1977) and refers to religious leaders of all denominations and religions, including not only Christian **Clergy** but also, for example, **Rabbis**. The terms **Minister** and **Minister of Religion** are used similarly.

Second Vatican Council: See Vatican II

Synagogue

The term is used here to refer to an *organization*; specifically, a coming together, or bringing together at the local level of Jews for worship, education and other communal activities. One or more **Religious Functionaries** (called 'rabbi' or 'minister') may be appointed by or to the organization and there may, or may not, be other paid staff. A local synagogue may, or may not, be based within a building.

Vatican II

The second Vatican Council took place between 1962 and 1965 and was 'a historical watershed in the modern history of Roman Catholicism' (Kim, 1980, p. 84). It was 'intended to renew the life of the Church and to bring up to date its teaching, discipline and organization ... the Council gave an enormous impetus to changes of attitude in the RC Church ... These included the use of the vernacular in worship, a new liturgy, and a less authoritarian attitude, with the attendant tensions inherent in rapid change' (Livingstone (ed.) 1977, p. 534). Vatican II paved the way for a deeper appreciation of the role of lay people.

Volunteer

A volunteer is here a lay person who makes a commitment to do work on an unpaid basis in, or on behalf of, his or her congregation. This reflects terminology commonly used within congregations. It also reflects the findings of Thomas and Finch (1990) about the meanings and images of 'volunteering' held in Britain and the definition of a congregational volunteer used in a recent major study in the United States (Hodgkinson et al., 1993). The latter study found the use of 'volunteers' by congregations to be 'an almost universal practice' (p. 58), with volunteers working an average of eleven hours per month.

Bibliography

Abrams, Philip, Abrams, Sheila, Humphrey, Robin, and Snaith, Ray (1981) *Action for Care: A Review of Good Neighbour Schemes in England.* Berkhamsted: The Volunteer Centre.

Ahrne, Goran (1996) 'Civil Society and Civil Organizations' *Organization* 3(1), 109–20.

Archbishop of Canterbury's Commission on Urban Priority Areas (1985) *Faith in the City: A Call for Action by Church and Nation.* London: Church House Publishing.

Ashbrook, James (1966) 'The Relationship of Church Members to Church Organization', *Journal for the Scientific Study of Religion* 5, 397–419.

Baker, Adrienne (1993) *The Jewish Woman in Contemporary Society.* London: Macmillan.

Barker, David, Halman, Loek, and Vloet, Astrid (1992) *The European Values Study 1981–1990.* London: Gordon Cook Foundation.

Barnett, Leonard (1988) *This is Methodism.* London: Methodist Publishing House.

Barrett, Susan and Fudge, Colin (1981) 'Examining the Policy–Action Relationship' in Barrett, Susan; and Fudge, Colin (eds) *Policy in Action.* London and New York: Methuen.

Bartholomew, John Niles (1981) 'A Sociological View of Authority in Religious Organizations', *Review of Religious Research* 23(2), 118–32.

Beckford, James A. (1973) 'Religious Organization. A Trend Report and Bibliography', *Current Sociology* 21(2), 1–170.

Beckford, James A. (1975) 'Organisation, Ideology and Recruitment: The Structure of the Watch Tower Movement' *Sociological Review,* 23(4), 893–909.

Beckford, James A. (1985) 'Religious Organizations' in Hammond, Phillip (ed.) *The Sacred in a Secular Age: Towards Revision in the Scientific Study of Religion.* Los Angeles: University of California Press.

Bellah, Robert, Madsen, Richard, Sullivan, William, Swidler, Ann, and Tipton, Steven (1985) *Habits of the Heart: Individualism and Commitment in American Life.* Berkeley: University of California Press.

Benson, J. Kenneth, and Dorsett, James H. (1971) 'Toward a Theory of Religious Organizations', *Journal for the Scientific Study of Religion* 10, 138–51.

Berger, Peter (1967) *The Sacred Canopy: Elements of a Sociological Theory of Religion.* New York: Doubleday.

Berger, Peter and Luckmann, Thomas (1967) *The Social Construction of Reality.* London: Allen Lane.

Berger, Peter and Neuhaus, Richard (1996) *To Empower the People: From State to Civil Society* 2nd edn. Washington, DC: AEI Press.

Biddell, Jeff (1992) 'Religious Organizations', in Clotfelter, Charles (ed.) *Who Benefits from the Nonprofit Sector?* Chicago: University of Chicago Press.

Billis, David (1984) *Welfare Bureaucracies.* London: Gower.

Billis, David (1993a) *Organising Public and Voluntary Agencies*. London: Routledge.

Billis, David (1993b) *Sliding into Change: The Future of the Voluntary Sector in the Mixed Organisation of Welfare*, Working Paper 14. London: Centre for Voluntary Organisation, London School of Economics.

Billis, David and Harris, Margaret (1992), 'Taking the Strain of Change: U.K. Local Voluntary Agencies Enter the Post-Thatcher Period', *Nonprofit and Voluntary Sector Quarterly* 21(3), 211–26.

Bishop, Jeff and Hoggett, Paul (1986) *Organizing around Enthusiasms*. London: Comedia.

Bishops' Conference of England and Wales (1986) *Synod 87 – Summary of the Consultation: Called to Serve*. London: Catholic Media Office.

Blau, Peter and Scott, W. Richard (1963) *Formal Organizations: A Comparative Approach*. London: Routledge and Kegan Paul.

Blizzard, Samuel W. (1956) 'The Minister's Dilemma', *Christian Century* 73, 25 April, 508–10.

Bonham-Carter, Victor (1952) *The English Village*. Harmondsworth: Penguin Books.

Bowpitt, Graham (1989) 'The Church of England and Social Policy in the 1980s', in Brenton, Maria and Ungerson, Clare (eds) *Social Policy Review 1988–89*. London: Longman.

Brannon, Robert (1971) 'Organizational Vulnerability in Modern Religious Organizations', *Journal for the Scientific Study of Religion* 10(1), 27–32.

Brierly, Peter and Wraight, Heather (eds) (1995) *UK Christian Handbook 1996/97 Edition*. London: Christian Research.

Brinkman, B. R. (1988) 'Vicar with Power', *The Month*, June, 735–45.

Bryant, Christopher (1995) 'Transformation and Continuity in Contemporary Britain', in Bryant, Christopher and Mokrzycki, Edmund (eds) *Democracy, Civil Society and Pluralism in Comparative Perspective: Poland, Great Britain and the Netherlands*. Warsaw: IFIS Publishers.

Bryman, Alan (1989) *Research Methods and Organization Studies*. London: Unwin Hyman.

Bulmer, Martin (1986) *Neighbours: The Work of Philip Abrams*. Cambridge: Cambridge University Press.

Bulmer, Martin (1987) *The Social Basis of Community Care*. London: Allen & Unwin.

Byrd, Randolph (1988) 'Positive Therapeutic Effects of Intercessory Prayer in a Coronary Care Unit Population', *Southern Medical Journal* 81(7), 826–9.

Cameron, Helen (1994) 'Unnumbered but Not Unknown: Setting the Welfare Activities of the Local Church in a National (UK) Context', Paper presented to the *Annual Meeting of the Association of Researchers in Nonprofit and Voluntary Action*. Berkeley: ARNOVA.

Cantrell, Randolph, Krile, James, and Donohue, George (1983) 'Parish Autonomy: Measuring Denominational Differences', *Journal for the Scientific Study of Religion* 22(3), 276–87.

Card, Terence (1988) *Priesthood and Ministry in Crisis*. London: SCM Press.

Carlin, Jerome E. and Mendlovitz, Saul M. (1958) ' The American Rabbi: A Religious Specialist Responds to Loss of Authority', in Sklare, Marshall (ed.) *The Jews: Social Patterns of an American Group*, 377–414. Glencoe, Illinois: Free Press.

Carr, Wesley (1985) *The Priestlike Task*. London: SPCK.

Carroll, Jackson W. (1981) 'Some Issues in Clergy Authority', *Review of Religious Research* 23(2), 99–117.

Carroll, Jackson W. (1985) 'Policy Formation in Religious Systems' in Hammond, Phillip (ed.) *The Sacred in a Secular Age: Towards Revision in the Scientific Study of Religion*. University of California Press.

Carroll, Jackson, W. (1991) *As One with Authority: Reflective Leadership in Ministry*. Louisville: Westminster/John Knox Press.

Carroll, Jackson W., Dudley, Carl S. and McKinney, William (eds) (1986) *Handbook for Congregational Studies*. Nashville: Abingdon.

Carter, Stephen (1994) *The Culture of Disbelief: How American Law and Politics Trivialize Religious Devotion*. New York: Doubleday.

Casanova, Jose (1994) *Public Religions in the Modern World*. Chicago: University of Chicago Press.

Chapin, F. Stuart and Tsouderos, John (1956) 'The Formalization Process in Voluntary Associations', *Social Forces* 34, 342–4.

Chaves, Mark (1993) 'Intraorganizational Power and Internal Secularization in Protestant Denominations', *American Journal of Sociology* 99(1), 1–48.

Clark, Elizabeth (1989) *Commitment to Community? The Church's Role in Care in the Community*. Maidstone: Joint Care in the Community Project, Kent Ecumenical Council.

Cnaan, Ram (1995) *Social and Community Involvement of Philadelphia Religious Congregations Housed in Historic Religious Properties: Final Report*. Philadelphia: School of Social Work, University of Pennsylvania.

Cnaan, Ram, Katernakis, Amy and Wineburg, Robert (1993) 'Religious People, Religious Congregations, and Volunteerism in Human Services: Is there a link?' *Nonprofit and Voluntary Sector Quarterly* 22(1), 33–51.

Coate, Mary Anne (1989) *Clergy Stress: the Hidden Conflicts in Ministry*. London: SPCK.

Cohen, Michael and March, James (1974) *Leadership and Ambiguity: the American College President*. New York: McGraw-Hill.

Cohen, Steven M. (1983) *American Modernity and Jewish Identity*. London: Tavistock.

Coleman, James (1988) 'Social Capital in the Creation of Human Capital', *American Journal of Sociology* 94, Supplement S95–S120.

Crittenden, William, Crittenden, Vicky and Hunt, Tammy (1988) 'Planning and Stakeholder Satisfaction in Religious Organizations', *Journal of Voluntary Action Research* 17(2), 60–73.

Currie, Robert, Gilbert, Alan, and Horsley, Lee (1977) *Churches and Church-Going: Patterns of Church Growth in the British Isles since 1700*. Oxford: Clarendon Press.

Davie, Grace (1990) 'An Ordinary God': The Paradox of Religion in Contemporary Britain', *British Journal of Sociology* 41(3), 395–421.

Davies, J. (1982) 'Introduction', in Davies, J. (ed.) *Religious Organization and Religious Experience*. London: Academic Press.

Davies, Rupert E. (1988) *What Methodists Believe*. London: Epworth Press.

Demerath, N. J. and Hammond, Philip (1969) *Religion in Social Context, Tradition and Transition*. New York: Random House.

Demerath, N. J., Hall, Peter Dobkin and Williams, Rhys (eds) (forthcoming) *Sacred Companies: Organizational Aspects of Religion and Religious Aspects of Organizations*. Oxford: Oxford University Press.

Dempsey, Kenneth C. (1969) 'Conflict in Minister/Lay Relations in Martin, D. A. (ed.) *Sociological Yearbook of Religion in Britain* 2, 58–73.

di Maggio, Paul and Powell, Walter (1983) 'The Iron Cage Revisited: Institutional Isomorphism and Collective Rationality in Organizational Fields' *American Sociological Review* 48, 147–60.

di Maggio, Paul and Powell, Walter (1991) 'Introduction' in di Maggio, Paul and Powell, Walter (eds) (1991) *The New Institutionalism in Organizational Analysis*. Chicago: University of Chicago Press.

Donnison, David (1973) 'The Development of Social Administration', in Birrell, W. D., Hillyard, P. A. R., Murie, A. S., and Roche, D. J. D. (eds) *Social Administration: Readings in Applied Social Science*. Harmondsworth: Penguin.

Donnison, David, Chapman, Valerie, Meacher, Michael, Sears, Angela and Urwin, Keith (1975) *Social Policy and Administration Revisited*. London: George Allen & Unwin.

Doohan, Leonard (1984) *The Lay-Centered Church: Theology and Spirituality*. Minnesota: Winston Press.

Douglas, Mary (1990) 'The Devil Vanishes', *The Tablet*, 28.4.90, 513–14.

Drane, John (1986) *Introducing the New Testament*. Tring: Lion Publishing.

Dudley, Carl (ed.) (1983) *Building Effective Ministry: Theory and Practice in the Local Church*. New York: Harper & Row.

Dudley, Carl, Carroll, Jackson and Wind, James (eds) (1991) *Carriers of Faith: Lessons from Congregational Studies*. Louisville, Kentucky: Westminster/John Knox Press.

Dulles, Avery (1978) *Models of the Church: A Critical Assessment of the Church in all its Aspects*. Dublin: Gill and Macmillan.

Durkheim, Émile (1965) *The Elementary Forms of the Religious Life*. New York: Free Press.

Ecclestone, Giles (ed.) (1988) *The Parish Church?* Oxford: Mowbray.

Elazar, Daniel J. (1978) 'Covenant as the Basis of the Jewish Political Tradition', *Jewish Journal of Sociology* 20, June, 5–37.

Elazar, Daniel J. (1983) 'Decision-Making in the American Jewish Community', in Sklare, Marshall (ed.) *American Jews: A Reader*. New York: Behrman.

Etzioni, Amitai (1961) *A Comparative Analysis of Complex Organizations*. New York: Free Press.

Etzioni, Amitai (1970) 'Modern Theories of Organization' in Etzioni, Amitai (ed.) *A Sociological Reader on Complex Organizations*, 2nd edn. London: Holt, Rinehart & Winston.

Etzioni, Amitai (1992) *The Spirit of Community: Rights, Responsibilities and the Communitarian Agenda*. New York: Simon & Schuster.

Evers, Adalbert (1993) 'The Welfare Mix Approach: Understanding the Pluralism of Welfare Systems', in Evers, Adalbert and Svetlik, Ivan (eds) *Balancing Pluralism: New Welfare Mixes in Care for the Elderly*. Hampshire: Avebury.

Falbo, Toni, New, Lynn and Gaines, Margie (1987) 'Perceptions of Authority and the Power Strategies used by Clergy', *Journal for the Scientific Study of Religion* 26(4), 499–507.

Fichter, Joseph H. (1954) *Social Relationships in the Urban Parish*. Chicago: University of Chicago Press.

Finneron, Doreen (1993) *Faith in Community Development*, Manchester Monographs. Manchester: University of Manchester Centre for Adult and Higher Education.

Fletcher, Ben (1990) *Clergy under Stress: A Study of Homosexual and Heterosexual Clergy*. London: Mowbray.

Foucault, Michel and Gordon, Colin (1980) *Power-Knowledge: Selected Interviews and Other Writings 1972–1977*. Brighton: Harvester Wheatsheaf.

Franklin, Robert (1994) 'The Safest Place on Earth: The Culture of Black Congregations', in Wind, James and Lewis, James (eds), *American Congregations: Volume 2: New Perspectives in the Study of Congregation*. Chicago: University of Chicago Press.

Freedman, Leslie R. (1988) *The Dimensions and Management of Rabbinic Stress* Paper presented to Annual Meeting of the Academy for Jewish Religion, Atlantic City, January.

Freedman, Maurice (ed.) (1955) *A Minority in Britain: Social Studies of the Anglo-Jewish Community*. London: Valentine, Mitchell.

Fukuyama, Francis (1995) *Trust: The Social Virtues and the Creation of Prosperity*. London: Hamish Hamilton.

Gartner, Alan and Riessman, Frank (1977) *Self-Help in the Human Services*. San Francisco: Jossey Bass.

Gay, John D. (1971) *The Geography of Religion in England*. London: Duckworth.

Gerard, David (1985) 'Religious Attitudes and Values', in Abrams, Mark, Gerard, David, and Timms, Noel *Values and Social Change in Britain*. London: Macmillan.

Giddens, Anthony (1990) *The Consequences of Modernity*. Cambridge: Polity Press.

Gilkey, Langdon (1994) 'The Christian Congregation as a Religious Community', in Wind, James and Lewis, James (eds) *American Congregations: Volume 2: New Perspectives in the Study of Congregation*. Chicago: University of Chicago Press.

Glaser, Barney and Strauss, Anselm (1967) *The Discovery of Grounded Theory: Strategies for Qualitative Research*. London: Weidenfeld & Nicolson.

Glaser, Joseph B. (1986) 'The Authentic Reform Rabbi: A Personal View', *CCAR Yearbook XCVI*, 92–7.

Glennerster, Howard (1995) *British Social Policy since 1945*. Oxford: Blackwell.

Glinert, Lewis (1985) *Aspects of British Judaism*. London: SOAS, University of London.

Goldner, Frederick H., Ference, Thomas P. and Ritti, R. Richard (1973) 'Priests and laity: a profession in transition', *Sociological Review Monographs* 20, December, 119–37.

Goulston, Michael (1968) 'The Status of the Anglo-Jewish Rabbinate 1840–1914', *Jewish Journal of Sociology* 10, 55–82.

Greenwood, Robin (1988) *Reclaiming the Church*. London: Fount.

Hall, John (1995) 'In Search of Civil Society' in Hall, John (ed.) *Civil Society: Theory, History, Comparison*. Cambridge: Polity Press.

Hall, Peter Dobkin (1996) 'Founded on the Rock, Built upon Shifting Sands: Voluntary Associations, and Nonprofit Organizations in Public Life 1850–1990'. Paper presented to the *Silver Anniversary Conference of ARNOVA*. New York: Association for Research on Nonprofit Organizations and Voluntary Action.

Hamilton, Malcolm (1995) *The Sociology of Religion: Theoretical and Comparative Perspectives*. London: Routledge.

Hannan, Michael and Freeman, John (1977) 'The Population Ecology of Organizations', *American Journal of Sociology* 82, 929–64.

Hardon, John A. (1971) *American Judaism*. Chicago: Loyola University Press.

Harris, C. C. (1969) 'Reform in a Normative Organisation', *Sociological Review* 17(2), 167–85.

Harris, Margaret (1993) 'Exploring the Role of Boards Using Total Activities Analysis', *Nonprofit Management and Leadership* 3(3), 269–81.

Harris, Margaret (1994) 'The Power of Boards in Service Providing Agencies: Three Models', *Administration in Social Work* 18(2), 1–15.

Harris, Margaret (1995) 'The Organization of Religious Congregations: Tackling the Issues', *Nonprofit Management and Leadership* 5(3), 261–74.

Harrison, Paul M. (1959) *Authority and Power in the Free Church Tradition*. Princeton: Princeton University Press.

Harrison, Paul M. (1960) 'Weber's Categories of Authority and Voluntary Associations', *American Sociological Review* 25(2), 232–7.

Heilman, Samuel (1976) *Synagogue Life: A Study in Symbolic Interaction*. Chicago: University of Chicago Press.

Herman, Nancy (1984) 'Conflict in the Church: A Social Network Analysis of an Anglican Congregation', *Journal for the Scientific Study of Religion* 23(1), 60–74.

Hernes, Helge (1996) 'Post-Baptism Educational Activities in The Church of Norway'. Paper presented to the *Silver Anniversary Conference of ARNOVA*. New York: Association for Research on Nonprofit Organizations and Voluntary Action.

Hill, Edmund (1988) *Ministry and Authority in the Catholic Church*. London: Geoffrey Chapman.

Hill, Michael (1973) *A Sociology of Religion*. London: Heinemann.

Hinings, C. Robin and Foster, Bruce D. (1973) 'The Organisational Structure of Churches', *Sociology* 7(1), 93–106.

Hirschman, Albert (1970) *Exit, Voice, and Loyalty: Responses to Decline in Firms, Organizations and States*. Cambridge, Mass.: Harvard University Press.

Hirst, Paul (1994) *Associate Democracy: New Forms of Economic and Social Governance*. Cambridge: Polity Press.

Hodgkinson, Virginia, Weitzman, Murray, Kirsch, Arthur, Noga, Stephen and Gorski, Heather (1993) *From Belief to Commitment: The Community Service Activities and Finances of Religious Congregations in the United States*. Washington, DC: Independent Sector.

Hoggett, Paul (1994) *The Future of Civic Forms of Organization*. London: DEMOS.

Hollenweger, Walter (1976) *The Pentecostals*. London: SCM Press.

Hopewell, James (1987) *Congregation: Stories and Structures*. London: SCM Press.

Hornsby-Smith, Michael (1989) *The Changing Parish: A Study of Parishes, Priests, and Parishioners after Vatican II*. London: Routledge.

Hornsby-Smith, Michael, Fulton, John and Norris, Margaret (1995) *The Politics of Spirituality: A Study of a Renewal Process in an English Diocese*. Clarendon Press: Oxford.

Hougland, James and Wood, James (1982) 'Participation in Local Churches: An Exploration of its Impact on Satisfaction, Growth and Social Action', *Journal for the Scientific Study of Religion* 21(4), 338–53.

Hutton, Jean M. and Reed, Bruce R. (1975) *The Rural Deanery: Its Leadership, Tasks and Structure*. London: Grubb Institute.

Iannacone, Laurence (1990) 'Religious Practice: A Human Capital Approach', *Journal for the Scientific Study of Religion* 29, 297–314.

Isichei, Elizabeth (1967) 'From Sect to Denomination among English Quakers', in Wilson, Bryan (ed.) *Patterns of Sectarianism: Organisation and Ideology in Social and Religious Movements*. London: Heinemann.

Israel, Herman (1966) 'Some Influences of Hebraic Culture on Modern Social Organization', *American Journal of Sociology* 71, January, 384–94.

Jackson, M. J. (1974) *The Sociology of Religion: Theory and Practice*. London: Batsford.

Jeavons, Thomas (1992) 'When the Management is the Message: Relating Values to Management Practice in Nonprofit Organizations', *Journal of Nonprofit Management and Leadership* 2(4), 403–17.

Jeavons, Thomas (1994) *When the Bottom Line is Faithfulness: Management of Christian Service Organizations*. Bloomington and Indianapolis: Indiana University Press.

Jerrome, Dorothy (1989) 'Age Relations in an English Church' *The Sociological Review* 37(4), 761–84.

Katz, Irving I. and Schoen, Myron E. (1963) *Successful Synagogue Administration*. New York: Union of American Hebrew Congregations.

Katz, Jacob (1978) *Out of the Ghetto: The Social Background of Jewish Emancipation*. New York: Schocken.

Kendall, Jeremy and Knapp, Martin (1996) *The Voluntary Sector in the UK*. Manchester: Manchester University Press.

Kim, Gertrude (1980) 'Roman Catholic Organization Since Vatican II' in Scherer, Ross (ed.) *American Denominational Organization: A Sociological View*. Pasadena: William Carey.

Klausen, Kurt (1995) 'On the Malfunction of the Generic Approach in Small Voluntary Associations' *Nonprofit Management and Leadership* 5(3), 275–90.

Klausner, Samuel (1981) 'Four Sociologies of American Jewry: Methodological Notes', in Gittler, Joseph B. (ed.) *Jewish Life in the United States: Perspectives from the Social Sciences*. New York: New York University Press.

Knoke, David and Prensky, David 'What Relevance do Organization Theories have for Voluntary Associations?' (1984) *Social Science Quarterly* 65, 3–20.

Kumar, Krishan (1993) 'Civil Society: an Inquiry into the Usefulness of an Historical Term', *British Journal of Sociology* 44(3), 375–95.

Laughlin, Richard C. (1990) 'A Model of Financial Accountability and the Church of England', *Financial Accountability and Management* 6(2), 93–114.

Lauer, Robert H. (1973) 'Organisational Punishment: punitive relations in a voluntary association', *Human Relations* 26, 189–202.

Lee, Raymond (1993) *Doing Research on Sensitive Topics*. London: Sage.

Leege, David C. and Gremillion Joseph (eds) (1985) *Notre Dame Study of Catholic Parish Life* Report 2. Indiana: University of Notre Dame.

Lewis, Jane (1993) 'Developing the Mixed Economy of Care: Emerging Issues for Voluntary Organisations', *Journal of Social Policy*, 22(2), 173–92.

Liborakina, Marina (1996) 'Women's Voluntarism and Philanthropy in Pre-Revolutionary Russia: Building a Civil Society', *Voluntas* 7(4), 397–411.

Lieberman, Morris (1970) 'The Role and Functions of the Modern Rabbi', in *CCAR Yearbook*, 211–34. New York: CCAR.

Liebman, Charles S. (1983) 'Orthodoxy in American Jewish Life', in Sklare, Marshall (ed.) *American Jews: A Reader*. New York: Behrman.

Livingstone, Elizabeth A. (ed.) (1977) *The Concise Oxford Dictionary of the Christian Church*. Oxford: Oxford University Press.

Lohmann, Roger (1992) *The Commons: New Perspectives on Nonprofit Organizations and Voluntary Action*. San Francisco: Jossey Bass.

Luckmann, Thomas (1969) 'The Decline of Church-Oriented Religion', Robertson, Roland (ed.) *Sociology of Religion*. Harmondsworth: Penguin.

Luidens, Donald (1982) 'Bureaucratic Control in a Protestant Denomination', *Journal for the Scientific Study of Religion* 21(2), 163–75.

McCann, Joseph (1993) *Church and Organization: A Sociological and Theological Enquiry*. London: Associated University Presses.

McGuire, Meredith (1987) *Religion: The Social Context*, 2nd edn. California: Wadsworth Publishing.

Maccoby, Hyam (1989) *Judaism in the First Century*. London: Sheldon Press.

Marcus, Jacob, and Peck, Abraham J. (eds) (1985) *The American Rabbinate: A Century of Continuity and Change 1883–1983*. New York: Ktav Publishing.

Martin, David A. (1978a) *The Dilemma of Contemporary Religion*. Oxford: Basil Blackwell.

Martin, David A. (1978b) *A General Theory of Secularization*. Oxford: Basil Blackwell.

Martin, David A. (1980) *The Breaking of the Image: A Sociology of Christian Theory and Practice*. Oxford: Basil Blackwell.

Martin, David (1988) 'A Cross-Bench View of Associational Religion', in Ecclestone, Giles (ed.) *The Parish Church?* Oxford: Mowbray.

Martin, David (1996) *Reflections on Sociology and Theology*. Oxford: Oxford University Press.

Mason, David (1995) *Leading and Managing the Expressive Dimension: Harnessing the Hidden Power Source of the Nonprofit Sector*. San Francisco: Jossey Bass.

Mason, David and Harris, Margaret (1994) 'An Embarrassed Silence: Research on Religious Nonprofits'. Paper presented to the Annual Conference of the Association for Research on Nonprofit Organizations and Voluntary Action, Berkeley: ARNOVA.

Merton, Robert (1949) *Social Theory and Social Structure*. Glencoe, Illinois: The Free Press.

Meyer, John (1984) 'Organizations as Ideological Systems', in Sergiovanni, J. and Connally, J. E. (eds) *Leadership and Organizational Culture: New Perspectives on Administrative Theory and Practice*. Urbana, Illinois: University of Illinois Press.

Meyer, John and Rowan, Brian (1977) 'Institutionalized Organizations: Formal Structure as Myth and Ceremony', *American Journal of Sociology* 83, 340–63.

Midgley, James (1990), 'Religion, Politics and Social Policy: The Case of the New Christian Right', *Journal of Social Policy* 19(3), 397–403.

Miller, Maureen (1983) 'From Ancient to Modern Organization: The Church as Conduit and Creator' *Administration and Society* 15(3), 275–93.

Milofsky, Carl (1988) 'Structure and Process in Community Self-Help Organizations', in Milofsky, Carl (ed.) *Community Organizations: Studies in Resource Mobilization and Exchange*. Oxford: Oxford University Press.

Moberg, David O. (1962) *The Church as a Social Institution: The Sociology of American Religion*. Englewood Cliffs, NJ: Prentice Hall.

Morgan, Gareth (1981) 'The Schismatic Metaphor and its Implications for Organizational Analysis' *Organization Studies* 2(1), 23–44.

Morgan, Gareth (1986) *Images of Organization*. London: Sage.

Morley, Leslie (1996) *Recovering Confidence: The Call to Ordained Ministry in a Changing World: Report of the Recruitment Strategy Working Party*. London: Central Board of Finance of the Church of England.

Mouzelis, Nicos (1995) 'Modernity, Late Development and Civil Society', in Hall, John (ed.) *Civil Society: Theory, History, Comparison*. Cambridge: Polity Press.

Nelson, John (ed.) (1996) *Management and Ministry*. Norwich: Canterbury Press for Modem.

Nelson, Reed (1993) 'Authority, Organization, and Societal Context in Multinational Churches', *Administrative Science Quarterly* 38, 653–82.

Neusner, Jacob (1972) *American Judaism: Adventure in Modernity*. Englewood Cliffs, NJ: Prentice Hall.

Newman, Aubrey (1977) *The United Synagogue 1870–1970*. London: Routledge & Kegan Paul.

Niebuhr, Richard H. (1929) *The Social Sources of Denominationalism*. New York: Henry Holt.

O'Dea, Thomas (1963) 'Sociological Dilemmas: Five Paradoxes of Institutionalization', in Tiryakian, Edward A. (ed.) *Sociological Theory, Values and Socio-Cultural Change*. New York: Free Press.

Oropesa, Sal (1995) 'The Ironies of Human Resource Mobilization by Neighbourhood Associations', *Nonprofit and Voluntary Sector Quarterly* 24(3), 235–52.

Osborne, Stephen and Kaposvari, Aniko (1996) 'Toward a Civil Society? Exploring its Meanings in the Context of Post-Communist Hungary'.

Paper presented to the *Silver Anniversary Conference of ARNOVA*. New York: Association for Research on Nonprofit Organizations and Voluntary Action.

Paul, Leslie (1973) *A Church by Daylight*. London: Chapman.

Pearce, Jone (1993) *Volunteers: The Organizational Behavior of Unpaid Workers*. London: Routledge.

Pemberton, Alec (1990) 'Rescuing the Good Samaritan: An Exposition and Defence of the Samaritan Principle in the Welfare State', *Journal of Social Policy* 19(3), 281–98.

Perrow, Charles (1970) *Organizational Analysis*. London: Tavistock.

Perrow, Charles (1986) *Complex Organizations: A Critical Essay*, 3rd edn. New York: McGraw-Hill.

Pfeffer, Jeffrey and Salancik, Gerald (1978) *External Control of Organizations*. New York: Harper & Row.

Pinker, Robert (1993) 'Social Policy in the Post-Titmuss Era', in Page, Robert and Baldock, John (eds) *Social Policy Review 5*. Canterbury: Social Policy Association.

Poloma, Margaret (1989) *The Assemblies of God at the Crossroads: Charisma and Institutional Dilemmas*. Knoxville: University of Tennessee Press.

Powell, Walter and Friedkin, Rebecca (1987) 'Organizational Change in Nonprofit Organizations', in Powell, Walter (ed.) *The Nonprofit Sector: A Research Handbook*. New Haven: Yale University Press.

Pugh, Derek, Hickson, David, Hinings, Chris and Turner, Chris (1969) 'The Context of Organization Structures', *Administrative Science Quarterly* 14, 91–114.

Putnam, Robert, Leornardi, Robert and Nanetti, Raffaella (1993) *Making Democracy Work*. New Jersey: Princeton University Press.

Ranson, Stewart, Bryman, Alan and Hinings, Bob (1977) *Clergy, Ministers and Priests*. London: Routledge & Kegan Paul.

Reed, Bruce (1980) *The Persistence of Clericalism*. London: Grubb Institute.

Reinharz, Shulamit (1983) 'Experiential Analysis: A Contribution to Feminist Research', in Bowles, Gloria and Klein, Renate Duelli (eds) *Theories of Women's Studies*. London: Routledge & Kegan Paul.

Rhodes, Penny (1994) 'Race-of-Interviewer Effects: A Brief Comment' *Sociology* 28(2), 547–58.

Richardson, Ann and Goodman, Meg (1983) *Self-Help and Social Care*. London: Policy Studies Institute.

Romain, Jonathan (1985) *Anglo-Jewry in Evidence*. London: Michael Goulston Educational Foundation.

Roozen, David, McKinney, William and Carroll, Jackson (1984) *Varieties of Religious Presence*. New York: Pilgrims Press.

Roshwald, Mordecai (1978) 'Authority, Skepticism and Dissent in Judaism', *Jewish Sociological Studies*, Summer/Fall, 189–230.

RSGB (Reform Synagogues of Great Britain) (1986) *Report of the Rabbinic Manpower Working Party*. London: RSGB.

Rudge, Peter F. (1968) *Ministry and Management: The Study of Ecclesiastical Administration*. London: Tavistock.

Russell, Anthony (1980) *The Clerical Profession*. London: SPCK.

Sacks, Jonathan (1995) *Faith in the Future*. London: Darton, Longman & Todd.

Sandmel, Samuel S. (1973) 'The Rabbi and his Community', in Marmur, D. (ed.) *Essays on Reform Judaism in Britain*. London: Alden and Mowbray.

Scherer, Ross (1972) 'The Church as a Formal Voluntary Organization', in Smith, David Horton, Reddy, Richard and Baldwin, Burt (eds) *Voluntary Action Research: 1972*. Lexington, Mass: Lexington Books.

Scherer, Ross (1980) 'The Sociology of Denominational Organization', in Scherer, Ross (ed.) *American Denominational Organization: A Sociological View*. Pasadena: William Carey.

Schmool, Marlena and Cohen, Frances (1997) *British Synagogue Membership 1996*. London: Board of Deputies of British Jews.

Schwarz, Jacob D. (1957) *The Life and Letters of Montgomery Prunejuice*. New York: Union of American Hebrew Congregations.

Scott, W. Richard (1987) *Organizations: Rational, Natural and Open Systems*. Englewood Cliffs, NJ: Prentice Hall.

Seligman, Adam (1992) *The Idea of Civil Society*. New York: Free Press.

Selznick, Philip (1957) *Leadership in Administration*. New York: Harper & Row.

Selznick, Philip (1994) *The Moral Commonwealth: Social Theory and the Promise of Community*. Berkeley: University of California Press.

Sharot, Stephen (1975) 'The British and American Rabbinate: A Comparison of Authority Structures, Role Definitions and Role Conflicts', *Sociological Yearbook of Religion in Britain* 1975, 139–58.

Sigel, Louis J., Katz, Robert, and Polish, Daniel (1980) 'The Modern Rabbi' *CCAR Yearbook* 90, 119–43. New York: CCAR.

Silverman, David (1993) *Interpreting Qualitative Data: Methods for Analysing Talk, Text and Interaction*. London: Sage.

Sklare, Marshall (1955) *Conservative Judaism*. Glencoe, Illinois: Free Press.

Smith, David Horton (1983) 'Churches are Generally Ignored in Contemporary Voluntary Action Research: Causes and Consequences', *Review of Religious Research* 24(4), 295–305.

Smith, David Horton (1993) 'Public Benefit and Member Benefit Nonprofit Voluntary Groups', *Nonprofit and Voluntary Sector Quarterly* 22(1), 53–69.

Smith, David Horton (1994) 'The Rest of the Nonprofit Sector: The Nature, Magnitude, and Impact of Grassroots Associations in America' Paper presented to 1994 Annual Meeting of ARNOVA, Berkeley, California.

Solomon, Norman (1991) 'The Context of the Jewish Christian Dialogue', *Christian Jewish Relations* 24(1) and (2), 54–75.

SSORU (Social Services Organisation Research Unit) (1974) *Social Services Departments*. London: Heinemann.

Stackhouse, Max (1990) 'Religion and the Social Space for Voluntary Institutions', in Wuthnow, Robert, Hodgkinson, Virginia and Associates *Faith and Philanthropy in America*. San Francisco: Jossey Bass/Independent Sector.

Stanley, Liz and Wise, Sue (1993) *Breaking Out Again: Feminist Ontology and Epistemology*. London: Routledge.

Streeck, Wolfgang and Schmitter, Philippe (1991) 'Community, Market, State – and Associations? The Prospective Contribution of Interest Governance to Social Order', in Thompson, Grahame, Frances, Jennifer, Levacic, Rosalind and Mitchell, Jeremy (eds) *Markets, Hierarchies and Networks: The Coordination of Social Life*. London: Sage.

Takayama, K. Peter (1975) 'Formal Polity and Change of Structure: Denominational Assemblies', *Sociological Analysis* 36, 17–28.

Takayama, K. Peter and Cannon, Lynn Weber (1979) 'Formal Polity and Power Distribution in American Protestant Denominations', *Sociological Quarterly* 20, 321–32.

Thomas, Andrew and Finch, Hazel (1990) *On Volunteering: A Qualitative Research Study of Images, Motivations and Experiences*. Berkhamsted: Volunteer Centre UK.

Thompson, Kenneth A. (1970) *Bureaucracy and Church Reform: The Organisational Response of the Church of England to Social Change 1800–1965*. Oxford: Clarendon Press.

Thompson, Kenneth A. (1973) 'Religious Organisations: the Cultural Perspective', in Salaman, Graeme and Thompson, Kenneth A. (eds) *People and Organisations*. London: Longman.

Tiller, John A. (1983) *A Strategy for the Church's Ministry*. London: CIO.

Titmuss, Richard (edited by Abel-Smith, Brian and Titmuss, Kay) (1986) *Social Policy*. London: George Allen & Unwin.

Tonnies, Ferdinand (1955) *Community and Association (Gemeinschaft und Gesellschaft)*. London: Routledge & Kegan Paul.

Towler, Robert and Coxon, Anthony (1979) *The Fate of the Anglican Clergy*. London: Macmillan.

Troeltsch, Ernst (1931) *The Social Teachings of the Christian Churches*. New York: Macmillan.

Turnbull, Michael (1995) *Working as One Body: The Report of the Archbishops' Commission on the Organisation of the Church of England*. London: Church House Publishing.

Turner, Barry A. (1983) 'The Use of Grounded Theory for the Qualitative Analysis of Organisational Behaviour', *Journal of Management Studies*, 20(3), July, 333–49.

Turner, Victor (1969) *The Ritual Process: Structure and Anti-Structure*. London: Routledge & Kegan Paul.

Van Maanen, John (1979) 'Reclaiming Qualitative Methods for Organisational Research: A Preface', *Administrative Science Quarterly* 24, 520–6.

Van Til, Jon (1988) *Mapping the Third Sector*. New York: The Foundation Center.

Verba, Sidney, Schlozman, Kay Lehman and Brady, Henry (1995) *Voice and Equality: Civic Voluntarism in American Politics*. London: Harvard University Press.

Walzer, Michael (1995) 'The Concept of Civil Society' in Walzer, Michael (ed.) *Toward a Global Civil Society*. Providence, RI: Berghahn Books.

Warner, R. Stephen (1988) *New Wine in Old Wineskins: Evangelicals and Liberals in a Small Town Church*. Berkeley: University of California Press.

Warner, R. Stephen (1993) 'Work in Progess Toward a New Paradigm for the Sociological Study of Religion in the United States', *American Journal of Sociology* 98(5), 1044–93.

Warner, R. Stephen (1994) 'The Place of the Congregation in the Contemporary American Religious Configuration', in Wind, James and Lewis, James (eds) *American Congregations: Volume 2: New Perspectives in the Study of Congregation*. Chicago: University of Chicago Press.

Webb, Ronald J. (1974) 'Organizational Effectiveness and the Voluntary Organization', *Academy of Management Journal* 17, December, 663–77.

Weber, Max (1964) *The Theory of Social and Economic Organization*. Toronto: Free Press.

Williams, Melvin (1983) 'The Conflict of Corporate Church and Spiritual Community: An Ethnographic Analysis' in Dudley, C. S. (ed.) *Building Effective Ministry: Theory and Practice in the Local Church*. New York: Harper & Row.

Wilson, Bryan R. (1968) 'Religious Organization' in Sills, David (ed.) *The International Encyclopedia of the Social Sciences* 13, 428–37.

Wilson, Bryan R. (1969) 'Religion in a Secular Society' in Robertson, Roland (ed.) *Sociology of Religion: Selected Readings*. Harmondsworth, Penguin.

Wind, James and Lewis, James (eds) (1994) *American Congregations: Volume 2: New Perspectives in the Study of Congregation*. Chicago: University of Chicago Press.

Wineburg, Robert (1992), 'Local Human Services Provision by Religious Congregations', *Nonprofit and Voluntary Sector Quarterly* 21(2), 107–18.

Winter, Michael (1973) *Mission or Maintenance*. London: Darton, Longman & Todd.

Wuthnow, Robert (1990) 'Religion and the Voluntary Spirit in the United States: Mapping the Terrain', in Wuthnow, Robert, Hodgkinson, Virginia and Associates (eds) *Faith and Philanthropy in America*. San Francisco: Jossey Bass.

Yin, Robert (1994) *Case Study Research: Design and Methods*, 2nd edn. London: Sage.

Yinger, John Milton (1957) *Religion, Society and the Individual*. New York: Macmillan.

Young, Ken (1977) 'Values in the Policy Process', *Policy and Politics* 5, 1–22.

Zald, Mayer and McCarthy, John (1987) 'Religious Groups as Crucibles of Social Movements', in Zald, Mayer and McCarthy John (eds) *Social Movements in an Organizational Society*. New Jersey: Transaction.

Index